THE WONDER OF IT ALL

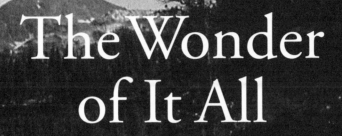

The Wonder of It All

100 STORIES FROM
THE NATIONAL PARK SERVICE

PREFACE BY JON JARVIS
FOREWORD BY DAYTON DUNCAN
EDITED BY YOSEMITE CONSERVANCY

YOSEMITE CONSERVANCY
Yosemite National Park

YOSEMITE
CONSERVANCY.

yosemiteconservancy.org

Library of Congress Control Number: 2015947645
Cover and book design by Nancy Austin
ISBN 978-1-930238-62-6
Printed in the United States of America by Worzalla.
Manufactured using recycled paper and soy inks.
All materials are from sustainable sources.

1 2 3 4 5 – 18 17 16 15

MIX
Paper from
responsible sources
FSC® C002589
www.fsc.org

CONTENTS

"The Yosemite, the Yellowstone, the Grand Canyon are national properties in which every citizen has a vested interest; they belong as much to the man of Massachusetts, of Michigan, of Florida, as they do to the people of California, of Wyoming, and of Arizona."

—STEPHEN MATHER, FOUNDING DIRECTOR OF THE NATIONAL PARK SERVICE, 1920

PREFACE

Standing before many large, tattooed Hawaiian men bearing shark-toothed war clubs, feeling rather vulnerable in the *lavalava* I was wearing (which is little more than a six-foot-long wedgie), I had the honor of being chanted into the circle for the annual *'ava* (*kava*) ceremony at Pu'ukoholā Heiau National Historic Site on the big island of Hawai'i. This is the place where King Kamehameha united the islands for the first time, and it is still the center for passionate discussions of Native Hawaiian sovereignty. After hours of singing, chanting, dances, and many coconut-shell cups of the mouth-numbing *kava* elixir, I was asked to speak before the traditionally dressed group. I said I was both honored and humbled by the responsibility to care for these sacred places, which are not only important for their history but also for their inspirational and cultural value. I said we of the National Park Service are the stewards of the place, but it is our partnership with Native Hawaiians that keeps the stories alive over the centuries. I said we commit to carrying this place and its story into perpetuity. At the end of the ceremony, a man came to me and thanked me; and to seal the deal in the Hawaiian way, we touched foreheads and shared our breath.

National Park Service employees and our many park friends are, at our core, storytellers through place. I have said many times that we must speak for three entities that have no voice: the people of the past, the children of the future, and nature itself. They deserve to be heard, for our actions affect how the past will be remembered, what the future generations will inherit, and how our planet will be treated. Our most powerful tool is story, told with passion and intelligence on the ground where the story emerged. We shoulder the task of understanding these stories from a scientific and scholarly foundation, and must present them, without bias, to a listening public, hoping they will go home with a better understanding and a deeper passion for the past, future, and our environment.

Like my colleagues in the National Park Service and the contributors to this book, we gather our own stories from moving experiences. It can be an encounter with a visitor, especially a child, whose curiosity and wonder are ignited by our skill at showing them the natural world. It can be the act of standing in a place of history, on the bloody fields of the Civil War, or at Thomas Jefferson's desk, feeling the chill of being in the spot that shaped our country's independence. It can be the edge of an arroyo, with the canyon wren trilling as the sun settles into the desert. It can be a mountain forest, where the only sound is the soft shush of falling snowflakes. These moments accumulate in us, they give us strength—they reinforce our resolve that these parks need us. And when we share these stories, they build our nation's commitment to the preservation of our national parks for the enjoyment of future generations.

This book is dedicated to inspiring stories from inspiring places—from the past, and for the next one hundred years and beyond. We invite you to find your park and create your own stories.

—Jon Jarvis

Jonathan B. Jarvis has worked for the National Park Service for thirty-eight years. He is its eighteenth director.

FOREWORD

One hundred years ago, when there were only about a dozen national parks (all of them in the west), an energetic and farsighted businessman named Stephen Mather launched a campaign to create a single agency to protect these treasures. He offered a range of reasons why they are essential to America.

Like his hero, John Muir, who called them "places to play in and pray in," Mather understood that parks can restore a person's health—mental health as well as physical health—by providing both recreation and inspiration. Mather then added a practical rationale for parks: by generating millions of tourism dollars, he said, they were also "an economic asset of incalculable value." More than that, he said, they served a deeper, patriotic purpose. He called parks "vast schoolrooms of Americanism," by which he meant that people who enjoyed their national parks would have greater pride in the nation that created them.

Mather's arguments won the day. On August 25, 1916, President Woodrow Wilson signed the law creating the National Park Service, and Mather was named its first director. As the National Park Service enters its second century, its dedicated members now stand as guardians of more than four hundred special places—vast and majestic landscapes, to be sure, but also small pieces of the mosaic of our shared history; canyons and geysers and environments that nurture threatened species, as well as sites that commemorate our proudest moments as a people and sites that serve as reminders of darker episodes that a truly great nation must never ignore or forget.

Cadres of park rangers now provide guided hikes and campfire lectures on the science and history of their individual parks, expanding Mather's vision of "vast schoolrooms of Americanism" into actual schoolrooms. The stories in this book demonstrate the passion they bring to the task—and they also demonstrate something more.

The real power behind the national park idea is always personal. It is something you *feel*. It is an experience you never forget. As part of the National Park Service's centennial, when it invites all Americans to "Find Your Park," it is also launching an ambitious program to get every fourth-grade student in the nation to some park, hoping that the youngsters we expose to any park today will become tomorrow's guardians of "America's best idea." We can't predict what their encounter will do for them. But I think we all know they will be better for it. I know this from personal experience; and since this is a book of stories, I will add my own.

In 1959, when I was a fourth grader in a little town in Iowa, I had my first encounter with national parks. Both of my parents worked—an unusual thing in those days—and until then, what vacations they had were more likely spent repainting our house or staying close to home. We couldn't afford long trips. But that summer, we borrowed my grandmother's car and some friends' camping equipment and headed west, because my mother wanted to broaden my sister's and my horizons. In preparation, she assigned me to look over maps and tourist brochures from the states we would visit to help plan where we would go. She said that national parks would be a major part of our trip: they were important, she believed, but they were also places we could afford.

We visited the Badlands of South Dakota and stopped to see those massive stone faces of four great presidents at Mount Rushmore; saw that geologically astonishing stone pillar in Wyoming called Devils Tower; and in Montana, toured the Little Bighorn Battlefield National Monument, where George Armstrong Custer and his 7th Cavalry met Sitting Bull and Crazy Horse in 1876. In Yellowstone, I saw my first geysers, my first truly majestic waterfalls, my first moose, my first bear. At Grand Teton National Park, we camped at Jenny Lake and looked across it to those spectacular mountain peaks, so close you thought you could reach out and touch them.

Because of national parks, those Badlands, that tower, that battlefield, those geysers, and that view at Grand Teton were essentially the same as they had been for generations before me; and if we nurture the national park idea, they will remain that way for generations yet unborn.

That trip was the greatest adventure of my young life, still vivid in my memory and my imagination as all those new vistas opened up for me. I can't say that I returned home already knowing that I would end up spending most of my adult life traveling the backroads of this great country, getting to know its varied landscapes and the history that has unfolded in our nation's own journey across it. But that is what I have ended up doing. Looking back, I think the seed for it was surely planted by my mother when she gave me those maps and those brochures; encouraged me, as a fourth grader, to study them; and then took me to see those places in person.

Up to the end of her life, my mother's eyes would get a little misty as she talked about that family adventure—about the time we all went to new places together and shared everything, from very long days in the car to magical mornings when the sun first hit the Tetons and they were reflected in the tranquil waters of Jenny Lake. That view, she would always say, was the most beautiful thing she had ever seen.

And so, forty years later, after I had become a parent, I took *my* family on a similar trip. I got to watch as *my* children saw their first geyser, their first moose, their first bears at Yellowstone. And at Grand Teton National Park, we stood on the shores of Jenny Lake and saw that same, unchanged, still exquisite and breathtaking scene.

My daughter shares the same name as my mother, Caroline Emily Duncan, and as I held her little hand as a father, I could also feel the touch of my mother's hand as a son, nearly half a century earlier. I could feel the passing of generations pulsing through our hands, the past and the present united in that transcendent moment in the presence of something bigger than any of us.

In my imagination, I could sense the future as well. I could imagine— I could *feel*—my daughter holding the small hand of one of her children some day at that same, still unchanged place, feeling the same thing. And I thought, this is as close to an encounter with eternity as I will ever get in this life.

That's what national parks really do. They connect us to something bigger than ourselves. They connect us to our shared history, to the land we inhabit, to nature itself. And they connect us to one another.

—Dayton Duncan

Dayton Duncan is a filmmaker and the author of twelve books, including *The National Parks: America's Best Idea* and *Seed of the Future: Yosemite and the Evolution of the National Park Idea*. He is also an honorary park ranger.

ACKNOWLEDGMENTS

Yosemite Conservancy thanks the two hundred and fifty individuals who responded to the call for remembrances that resulted in this book honoring the centennial of the National Park Service (NPS). The submissions were read by a team of volunteer reviewers who, without identification of authors, ranked and categorized each story to determine the one hundred stories selected. We are humbled by the response and the trust of *all* the writers who participated.

This book would not have gotten off the ground without the enthusiasm and network of Yosemite Conservancy's past president Mike Tollefson. Thank you, Mike. Tony Sisto and Deanne Adams were instrumental in enlisting and organizing the review team, broadcasting the call for stories, and providing their wise counsel on any number of topics related to this project. The story reviewers gave freely of their time, their National Park Service experience, and their powers of critical thinking to this endeavor; we could not have accomplished this project without Holly Bundock, Colette Daigle-Berg, Mack Shaver, Bill Tweed, and Bill Walters.

Yosemite Conservancy is grateful to the National Park Service in Yosemite National Park for its assistance and guidance. We congratulate the National Park Service for one hundred years of service to the nation and look forward to partnering for the next one hundred years. Yosemite Conservancy also thanks the Coalition to Protect America's National Parks (CPANP), the Association of National Park Rangers (ANPR), the Employees and Alumni Association of the National Park Service (E&AA), the George Wright Society (GWS), and the Association of Partners for Public Lands (APPL) for their kind assistance with publicizing our story quest to their memberships.

Finally, one more thank you to the writers who submitted photographs to include in this book. While we were unable to use them all, we appreciate the time and effort spent providing them to us for consideration. It is our intention that the photographs of the writers connect faces to the experiences, linking the people with the lands that they steadfastly and ably preserve, protect, and interpret to the benefit of all, for all time. To all National Park Service employees, current and former, and to the volunteers, *thank you.*

"Thoreau read Wordsworth, Muir read Thoreau, Teddy Roosevelt read Muir, and you got national parks."

—ROBERT HASS, FORMER U.S. POET LAUREATE, 1997

THE WONDER OF IT ALL

1

Getting Started

Yellowstone National Park, 1923.
Stephen T. Mather, founding director of the
National Park Service, in a motorcycle sidecar.

A Campfire Program

Rose Rumball-Petre

The sky glows and darkens. The sun is setting. Campfire smoke drifts through the campground. Lanterns are lit. The sounds of dinners being prepared and cleaned up emanate from adjacent campsites. Children and adults gather themselves, their warm coats, flashlights, and blankets and begin walking.

From the silence of the road parade, footsteps grow louder as they crunch gravel along the lighted path. Sounds of anticipation arise as noisy children and adults gather and wander toward the ring of seats. The campers are seated in small clusters of twos and threes and family groups. Latecomers straggle in. Hushed conversations and occasional strident tones and laughter radiate throughout the amphitheater.

Near the front, a ranger is stooping to light the community campfire. Children begin to direct their attention to the action. There is rustling in the back as a beam of light is projected onto the giant screen and the first slide appears. The night air is chilly.

Onto the stage walks the ranger! A hush spreads over the audience, and the program begins. The story of the national park proceeds. Bears? Glaciers? Volcanoes? Battles? Wildlife? Plant Adaptations? History? What's on special tonight?

During the presentation, I am enthralled. There is so much to see and do and learn. Where shall we go tomorrow? What shall we do?

Afterward, the campfire, which was a formality in the beginning, shares its warmth and light to encourage the inspired in the audience to ask questions as they stop to stare a moment into its glow, chatting with the ranger, who seems happy to stay late into the night to engage the children and enlighten the adults.

People begin to drift back to their temporary homes in tents and on wheels. They walk in the dark into the cool night air as if they do it every day, holding the young ones' hands or snuggling them close. Snatches of conversation mirror the program or invoke excitement for tomorrow's adventures. There is community and a shared experience, and it lingers as the participants rejoin the bustle of evening preparations continuing in the campground. Perhaps there will be a story or game before bed; or perhaps they will just huddle together in the tent, musing over the day's adventures and the preparations for tomorrow's hike, climb, departure.

The quest for learning in this place is satisfied for a while. As the night air chills the tip of my nose and I gaze up at starlight through the tent skylight, there is a sense of being satiated, fulfilled, and inspired. This is the place for me. Today, here in nature—ever learning, peaceful, cold night air, serene, beautiful—is where I want to be. Ideas have been shared and passed on. There's more to explore in the morning. It is in this moment that I decide I want to be a ranger. I want to live in and to know national parks!

Badlands National Park, 1958. Evening campfire talk in the amphitheater at Cedar Pass Campground.

Northern Lights in the Northwoods

Eleanor Hodak Siebers

I'm a city girl. And not just any city but a big city: Chicago. I took two trains and a bus to get to high school every morning, and my bike was stolen twice from the backyard until my parents refused to buy me another one. A clear viewing of the night sky meant three stars—bright amidst the endless airplanes taking off and landing from O'Hare.

College came and quickly went, and graduation loomed on the horizon. Sometime in the spring of my senior year, an SCA (Student Conservation Association) representative handed me a booklet chock-full of internships and volunteer opportunities in far-off places with bears, big trees, and geysers. Someplace a little smaller and less well known caught my eye: Isle Royale National Park. Its short blurb "leave your car at home, but bring your kayak" spoke to me.

My parents drove me to the Upper Peninsula of Michigan; and on the sunny Monday of Memorial Day Weekend 2005, I boarded the largest piece of moving machinery owned by the National Park Service—the *Ranger III*—and sailed six hours to my new home for the summer.

Except that summer would turn into three summers. And from there, seasons would follow in the southern swamps of Florida, the rocky coast of Maine, an island five hundred feet from Lower Manhattan, and to the southwestern deserts and canyons of Utah.

What was it about the National Park Service? How did it root itself so deeply and quickly in my psyche, in my bones?

It was August of my first summer at Isle Royale, and I had just wrapped up my evening program (shipwrecks, a crowd pleaser). After changing out of my uniform and plucking some beers from the fridge, I left my house to join some of the other island residents for a campfire. But on the way, looking up, I saw something I had never seen before: the northern lights! They weren't brilliant green colors that enveloped the whole sky like you see in postcards from Alaska; instead, they were a very pale white. But they were moving. And shimmering. And they were *spectacular*!

A short recruitment process and a small hike to the dock found me sitting in the middle of a canoe with a park ranger twenty years my senior paddling in front of me and the deckhand from the Rock Harbor Lodge steering in the back. We glided across Tobin Harbor in the darkness, with nothing but the northern lights and the stars as light. We dragged the canoe on the rocks, turned on our headlamps, and began the hike to Lookout Louise.

Eleanor Hodak Siebers in Isle Royale National Park.

Imagine sitting on a cold, basalt outcropping covered in lichens, wrapping your light fleece tighter around yourself.

Lake Superior spread before you.

The northern lights dancing above you.

Looking down onto the lights of Thunder Bay, Ontario.

This city girl had finally found her stars. (And is never going back.)

"Thousands of tired, nerve-shaken, over-civilized people are beginning to find out that going to the mountains is going home; that wildness is a necessity; and that mountain parks and reservations are useful not only as fountains of timber and irrigating rivers, but as fountains of life."

—JOHN MUIR, NATURALIST AND WRITER, 1901

Forget the Supervolcano; Let's Talk Buckwheat!

Daniel E. Winkler

There is knowledge in these mountains. I was drawn to the romanticism of America's national parks from a young age, after spending countless hours with my face buried in issues of *National Geographic* magazine. It was not until my first stint as a researcher in Yellowstone National Park that I realized how powerful these treasured places truly are. Most of the things I was enthralled by as a child lost their magic as I grew up, but not the parks—they became even more magical.

One bright morning near Old Faithful, I was conducting plant surveys and wondering, "What if today is the day?" I spotted a group of visitors through the hydrothermal steam just as they spotted me. I wondered if they were asking the same question. One group of visitors had already asked me if I was checking to see if the Yellowstone caldera was ready to erupt.

The Yellowstone caldera (also known as the Yellowstone supervolcano) has sparked the interest of researchers and Yellowstone visitors alike over the past decade. Justifiably so! Visitors are often intrigued by these natural wonders as a result of the difficulty in predicting these rare, earth-altering events. It adds mystery to any visit to Yellowstone.

Instead, as they approached, I heard, "What's with the orange vest?"

"This is to make me look official, so no one thinks I'm a visitor breaking the rules."

Daniel Winkler in Yellowstone National Park.

I also told the visitors that I was studying the endemic Yellowstone sulfur buckwheat (*Eriogonum umbellatum var. cladophorum*). I quickly added that "an endemic species is one that is only found in a particular area and nowhere else." Their wide-eyed gazes told me that they loved this new vocabulary word.

From multiple experiences, I have gleaned that people love learning the word "endemic" because it relates to rarity and uniqueness. This is another reason why our national parks are so valuable: they often contain species of plants and animals that can be found only within park boundaries.

"This buckwheat . . . why do we care about it?" one of the visitors asked politely. He appeared to genuinely wonder why I would be spending my summer wandering around this inhospitable area studying this tiny, uncharismatic plant.

"There are so many things we can learn from this one species!" I exclaimed. I went on to share with them that this type of rare species is perfect for studying not only how plants adapt to extreme environments but how sensitive they are to disturbance.

"This type of knowledge can often be used to better understand many other species and their interactions with the environments they occur in. They also inform us on how concerned we should be about plant responses to climate change. More than enough reason to endure a little sunburn and lug around a backpack full of survey gear all summer, no?"

The same visitor asked, "Do you think your buckwheat's going to go extinct?"

"I certainly hope not! There would be terrible consequences if that happened."

"Really?"

"Yeah, definitely! Humans are dependent upon biological systems in so many ways, from the food we cultivate to the plant-derived compounds used in our medicines. You're also currently dependent on biodiversity in two additional ways: recreation and tourism. You get to experience all the beautiful variation in nature as you travel around the park."

"Can we eat this buckwheat?"

"Well, no, because it's protected here in the park. But there are buckwheat plants in the same family as this one that are cultivated for food, and even beer and whiskey. I highly recommend buckwheat soba noodles if you ever get the chance to try them."

All of these dependencies serve as arguments in favor of understanding and conserving biodiversity in parks. Through research, scientists contribute to the ever-growing body of scientific knowledge that fuels modern society and ensures opportunities for future visitors to observe the wonderful diversity in our parks, including the unique Yellowstone sulfur buckwheat.

I consider opportunities like this "teachable moments," and I continued to talk, telling the visitors more about the plant surveys I was conducting. For a brief moment, their excitement shifted from geysers and volcanoes to scientific research. I was proud to share my enthusiasm, inciting their curiosity about this place and a plant that had gone unnoticed to their eyes before. I was in one of the most historically important and picturesque landscapes in the United States, surveying rare plant species. "This is my dream job," I often told myself and happily confessed to the visitors. I especially value experiences like this because they act as opportunities to educate people that might not have access to environmental education, and our national parks are ideal settings for this type of informal education to take place. The parks contain within them living laboratories and rich histories that are housed not only within their buildings and historical collections but also within the mountains and species they were created to protect.

Before parting ways, I smiled for their camera as one of the geysers erupted behind me. There is more knowledge in these mountains now because of my conversation with those visitors.

I finished my surveys that summer and, since then, I have worked in an additional twelve National Park Service units. When given the opportunity, I smile for the camera and toss in a fascinating fact or two about the plants that surround visitors as they hike and explore their parks. These experiences have and will undoubtedly continue to shape my career as a scientist and an educator. Research conducted on federal lands provides the public with accessible science via interpretative talks, classroom fieldtrips, and even through encounters with scientists wearing bright orange vests.

A Structural Connection

Larry Reynolds

When I was a youngster, my parents would often take our family to Rocky Mountain National Park; we lived in Denver, and it was an easy drive. We weren't a hiking or camping family, but we still found ways to enjoy the beauty of the park during our visits. It was through those visits that I began to understand the value of places like Rocky Mountain National Park.

A few years later, around 1978, I was an engineering student at the University of Colorado at Boulder and had come home for a weekend visit. Our neighbor, storied Denver Service Center (DSC) structural engineer Maurie Paul, called one evening and said he had some drawings he thought I might like to see. The drawings were of the Cape Hatteras lighthouse, and Maurie was involved in early feasibility studies regarding moving that structure.

Maurie held my undivided attention for several hours, explaining both the details of the lighthouse and the generalities of structural engineering in the National Park Service. By the end of the evening, I knew I wanted a career as an NPS structural engineer.

I got that opportunity in 1985, when I was hired by the DSC. Now, more than thirty years later, I look back on a career filled with incredible projects: from designing visitor centers in several parks to participating on the Hurricane Andrew damage-assessment team; from helping out in Oklahoma City after the Alfred P. Murrah Federal Building explosion to working on the initial assessment of the Washington Monument after the 2011 earthquake; from moving the Three Sisters lighthouses at Cape Cod to performing condition assessments of the Mormon Row barns at Grand Teton. I have had opportunities that other structural engineers could only dream of. Most important, I've been able to contribute to the mission of the National Park Service.

Yes, I found my park. A whole bunch of them, actually.

So, This Is Bush Alaska

Erica Francis

I arrived in King Salmon on a cold, gray, early May afternoon in 2007. From the small prop plane from Anchorage, I had glimpsed a land still locked into winter. My seat neighbor was dressed in a camo jacket, his fly rod in the overhead bin.

I was nervous. A couple months prior, during my only phone interview, the supervisory interpreter talked at length about the job, the remoteness. "Are you still interested?" he asked after an hour.

The floatplane to Brooks Camp was fully loaded. A few of us left the mounds of boxes and our fellow interpretive rangers waiting on the porch of Katmai Air, and jumped aboard. The flight was only twenty minutes. We circled down to Naknek Lake, still mostly frozen, then landed and glided

Erica Francis in Katmai National Park and Preserve.

to the beach in front of the closed visitor center. The pilot hopped off, lake water splashing his hip waders. He graciously piggybacked us to shore.

Here I was, Katmai National Park and Preserve, my home for the next five months. The only way out was to make friends with someone who had a nice boat or floatplane. Or to have a small fortune to pay for a plane ride in and out of the park. That would dramatically increase the price of groceries. And I had already said my last good-byes to a grocery store several days ago, when we had done our first and last summer-grocery buy. Five months of ice cream (two tubs) sat in the freezer at Katmai Air, waiting with everyone else's frozen food. Everything you hadn't bought earlier could now only be ordered over finicky satellite Internet. A Fred Meyer employee in Anchorage would pack your groceries for you, and two weeks later (sometimes four, if they got lost), you would have Christmas in the mail.

I walked past the yurt, ranger station, laundry room, bathroom, a couple wooden cabins, and finally came to the seasonal interpreter quarters. Canvased-walled tent cabins, cozy and quaint—each with a small kitchen, a small couch and table, a bed downstairs, and a bed in the loft. The "Princess Palace," as my roommate Nicki called her, came with her own "his and her" double toilet seat in the outhouse out back. Safety in numbers.

There was only one bear hanging around the lower Brooks River, a short walk from Brooks Camp, when we wandered around later that evening. He quietly grazed as we quietly watched from the Brooks Lodge porch.

July was upon us fast, and with it, the sockeye salmon. As they migrated up the mile-long Brooks River, they congregated beneath Brooks Falls, all waiting in turn for their chance to plunge forth to upriver, fishy-making freedom. Most needed numerous attempts.

With the smell of fish in the air, it didn't take long for word to get out. That's when they came back—back to their park. The brown bears. There were bears by the mouth of the river; bears by the ripples downstream of Brooks Falls; bears below the falls, next to the falls, in the falls, on top of the falls. Bears in the long, tall grasses where the anglers walked; bears on the roads and trails where the visitors walked. Momma bears treed their cubs next to the lodge; big brownies sauntered by the ranger station. They rubbed their backs up and down, up and down, up and down on the tree three feet from the laundry room. Cubs nursed on the beach only feet from the visitor center, with the "lucky" visitors gazing through the big bay windows from inside, while the "unlucky" visitors waited inside their floatplane for mom and cubs to wander off and allow them to dash for the visitor center for their bear orientation.

Occasionally today, I lie in bed on a windy, dark, winter Skagway morning and listen to the rain fall on my roof. It reminds me of the numerous nights when I was lulled to sleep in my loft by the same Alaskan rain lightly pitter-pattering the tent-cabin canvas. In the past seven years, I've switched parks several times, changed my park career focus, and come and gone from Alaska many times over—with many more to come. And I am haunted with a few words from that first phone call on that fateful day long ago: "You will either hate Alaska and never come back, or you might very well fall in love and never leave."

"You'd be hard pressed to find something that was a purer expression of the democratic impulse, in setting aside land, not for the privileged, not for the kings and nobility, but for everybody. For all time."

—KEN BURNS, DOCUMENTARIAN, 2009

Sprouting Resilience

Mary Ann Madej

I was in the midst of throwing a birthday party for a friend and had already quaffed a beer when I got the long-awaited phone call offering me a job at Redwood National Park. It would be my first professional job after college, and I was excited to start from the ground up.

Moving to the almost mythic California was a bit intimidating for a Midwest gal, but I was ready for adventure. I had already visited many of the iconic parks (Grand Canyon, Yosemite, Yellowstone, Mount Rainier, and more), so I expected to be impressed by the redwoods. (Why else would it be *Redwood* National Park?) Standing at the foot of a gnarly-barked giant, however, not being able to spot its top and feeling ancient time wisp through the almost-silent primeval forest, surpassed any of my expectations.

Even more shocking to my sensibilities, though, was then driving farther up the road to clear-cut lands newly acquired by the park service—land that had once supported old-growth majesty but was now a barren cemetery of stumps standing like gravestones. Where swimming holes once provided fish—and people—cool respite, vast expanses of sterile gravel stretched across the riverbeds. Landslides and gullies originating from logging roads and logged hillslopes poured sediment into streams and rivers during each winter storm. Several feet of sand and gravel buried the former pools and riffles, and streamside redwoods were dead or dying from this sedimentation. An abandoned log landing—a flat spot carved into the steep hillside above Redwood Creek—provided a sobering view of the ravaged landscape; we called it Devastation Point.

And so my job began. A team of young, energetic geologists, hydrologists, and biologists strategized on how best to heal the wounds of extensive erosion. We tossed around dozens of ideas—some outrageous, some innovative, and even some that were practical and might even work. Instead of jumping immediately into river restoration, we decided to conduct restoration work from the top of the hills downward. This entailed removing hundreds of miles of abandoned logging roads, a scale that had never been attempted before. We all needed to learn new skills and jargon that we were never taught in college: How much dirt can a backhoe move, or do we need an excavator? A local unemployed logger has a dragline crane—could we use him on the job? What do we do with crushed, rusted culverts? Can we use earth-moving equipment and still preserve archeological sites? How do we revegetate the hillslopes without introducing exotic species? How will we be affecting wildlife?

Oh, we made plenty of mistakes, but it was an exhilarating time putting our scientific backgrounds to work in ways we had never dreamed of.

Over the years, young redwoods sprouted and grew quickly on the restored roads and clear-cuts, winter river flows began to flush sediment out to the ocean, and salmon began finding hospitable refuges in the rivers again. And eventually, the Redwood National Park restoration team was able to apply "lessons learned" to other parks and wildlands. National parks proved to be exceptional classrooms for a wide range of studies, from spotted owls to tailed frogs, redwood ecology to prescribed burns on grasslands, floods and droughts to climate change.

More questions about ecosystem dynamics and restoration challenges arise each year, and parks provide unique opportunities to discover new relationships among biological, physical, and yes, even social processes. The need for teams of young, creative resource professionals has never been greater.

And what became of that wasteland we called Devastation Point? Today, it is a scenic picnic area called the Redwood Creek Overlook, with nary a road or bare clear-cut to be seen. The hills are carpeted with young, green forests; and a much healthier river flows in the valley far below. Summer fog sometimes creeps over the ridge or up the valley to bring much-needed moisture to the young trees, which continue to thrive.

I marvel at the resilience of this system—the ability of nature to heal itself—especially when given a helping hand. Just like us.

At the Beginning

Steve Hurd

Last evening, the power went out in my rural neighborhood of southwestern Oregon. While waiting for the electricity to come back on, I settled into my easy chair under light from an emergency lantern. It was raining heavily, with high winds forecasted for overnight.

Sitting in the lantern light, I started reminiscing over my forty-year career to my first position with the National Park Service—a GS-4 (entry level) seasonal park ranger at Yosemite National Park. My job function was to collect fees from visitors entering the park. Assigned a roommate and a two-room tent cabin at Crane Flat—with cold, running water; a wood cook-stove; a picnic table; and two single beds—I stood with bags in hand and my jaw dropping open. At night, we were given generator power for a light bulb through the dinner hour from the nearby permanent ranger quarters' generator. There were five other tent cabins along with two porta-potties and a shower house. Living below the recently established poverty line, the good news was that rent amounted to only $7.50 per two-week pay period.

I was a city boy from Massachusetts and way out of my element: no power, a sixteen-mile hike to Yosemite Valley for food and other supplies, and, God help me, doing my laundry in such conditions. No radio, no TV, and no telephone to contact the world outside. (Cell phones and personal computers hadn't yet been invented.) But all was not bad.

The citizens of Crane Flat "tent city" were all seasonal employees—a fire crew, a road patrol ranger, and five entrance-station rangers. We came from all over the United States, and every one of us was in the same situation. Some neighbors had experience from previous years and shared their know-how. Looking back, I remember that, as a community, we hit it off right from day one, despite lack of outside amenities.

Orientation included a tour of the park, when we Crane Flat seasonals met seasonals from units around the park, but we stood out as the other-side-of-the-tracks station—with no electricity. Among us, there built a kind of loyalty and comradery one doesn't often find working summer jobs. We were to be envied. We were living and working in Yosemite—*Yosemite*, folks—fabulous, beautiful Yosemite! It was a place I'd only seen in pictures of famous waterfalls and cliff-faced mountains. To top it off, how many CEOs take the time to interact with part-time workers and encourage their entire staff to do the same? Not a whole lot in those days, but the superintendent did just that. And if he didn't remember your name the next time you met, weeks after being introduced, you never realized it.

I enjoyed what I did, standing in an entrance station, collecting fees and talking with the visitors coming into the park. I heard their excitement and expectations—the same things I was feeling. I grabbed every opportunity to take a walk to the Tuolumne Grove of giant sequoias or get into the wilderness. There are no words to describe the emotions and thrill when standing under centuries-old trees; or topping a ridge and overlooking miles and miles of Yosemite's vast, mountainous wilderness. I loved walking trails and wading streams and tossing pebbles into crystal-clear lakes. I felt captivated when encountering wild animals as curious about me as I was about them. Wilderness was grabbing hold of this city boy.

As it turned out, it wasn't all entrance-station duty. Occasionally, I found myself beating back fires, searching for overdue hikers, helping accident victims, and patrolling wilderness. Thanks to the guidance and assistance from the permanent park staff, each and every situation taught me skills that built my confidence in my abilities and in the decisions I made. As the summer slid by, I knew I had changed—in my outlook on what life offers, my view of the roll of a supervisor, and my knowledge of my own abilities.

Living isolated and working long hours isn't for everyone, but by the end of the season, I knew I was hooked and would be back.

Moose Creek Madness

Kelly Habecker

I had the good fortune to grow up with a park ranger for a dad. We didn't do summer vacations at the beach like other families, but we had something better: patrol cabins. We got to spend summers in places like Tuolumne Meadows (Yosemite) and Toklat Road Camp (Denali). When I was six and my sister Katie was three, we started the tradition of skiing to the Logan Creek cabin in Glacier—these became our family getaways.

The most memorable was an adventure with just Dad and the girls, when we were teenagers. We hiked in to Moose Creek Patrol Cabin, near the west end of the Denali Park Road. I had been on one backpacking trip and considered myself an expert. Katie was going through an anti-outdoorsy phase and had to be bribed with the promise of pizza on our return.

We shouldered our packs and made our way into the rolling hills. Denali's wilderness has no developed trails, so we traveled crosscountry, bushwhacking our way through thickets of alder and dwarf birch. It had rained the night before, and drops of water shimmered on every leaf. Within moments, our heavy canvas hiking pants were soaked through.

We squelched through squishy tundra bogs and brush that fought our every move. Shouts of "Hey, bear!" soon became our only conversation as we struggled just to keep forward momentum.

Then the breeze died down. Within moments, thick clouds of mosquitoes swarmed us. Every inch of exposed skin hosted hundreds of proboscises, and we couldn't breathe without sucking in at least a dozen. The tundra hummed like a high-tension power line. These were the voracious little mosquitoes that hatched in midsummer—the kind that show no mercy. We slapped and swatted, but it was impossible to get them all.

Where were the headnets? In the car, of course!

After about an hour of this, I was concerned. Dad had told us the hike was only a mile, and we had definitely gone farther than that.

"Shouldn't we be there by now?" I asked. "Could we have passed it?"

Dad stopped and let Katie walk ahead. When she was out of earshot he said, "It's really more like four miles. But don't tell your sister."

What? He lied to us? Lured us out here under false pretenses? But he was right—Katie would never have come if she had known it was longer than a mile.

We slogged on, an occasional breath of air giving us a break from our mosquito misery. Nothing else moved on the tundra, not even a caribou.

Finally, we saw the grove of spruce trees that sheltered the cabin. All three of us broke into a run, longing for shelter. We raced down the hill, stumbling through the brush, packs bouncing on our backs; then we danced with impatience in the shelter of the cabin's porch while Dad removed the spiked bear-proof door cover and unlocked the cabin. As soon as the door swung open, we dove inside our refuge, leaving Dad to remove the shutters.

Built in 1934, the cabin was a standard log patrol cabin, with a covered front porch, a food cache on stilts, and an outhouse. Outside were small log houses for winter visitors: Denali's sled dogs. Inside were a woodstove, two twin beds, a table, and some kitchen supplies.

We cooked dinner on a kerosene stove, using water hauled from the creek. Mac 'n' cheese seasoned with . . . mosquitoes! The cabin wasn't exactly airtight, and they had no trouble finding us. The constant whining in our ears was driving us over the edge.

After dinner, I had to face the dreaded trip to the outhouse. Denali outhouses are deluxe, with warm-blue foam seats and the best views anywhere. But this one didn't have a door, which meant fully exposing yourself to a mosquito onslaught. We took turns sprinting to the outhouse, taking care of business, and bolting back to the cabin, opening the door to the narrowest crack possible to let each other in.

Rummaging around for the Scrabble board found in every cabin, we unearthed our savior—a can of Buhach! Made from dried pyrethrum flowers, Buhach is an amazing substance. We put a little on the lid of a tin can and lit a smudge. It was like a cartoon—after a minute or so, mosquitos started falling in midair, dying right and left.

We spent the rest of the evening in luxury, sipping hot chocolate and playing Scrabble in the peace of a mosquito-free cabin. Before going to bed, we lit another round of Buhach and burrowed deep into our sleeping bags to scratch our bites and try to sleep.

In the morning, we repeated the process in reverse: breakfast, haul water, lay wood for a fire for the next users of the cabin, hike back to the road. By then, we had reached a point where we could laugh about it—or maybe we had just been driven mad. To this day, the words "Moose Creek" will produce a shudder in any one of us.

But maybe that's what makes a memory. Katie and I took plenty of other trips into patrol cabins, but that is the trip we still talk about. It prepared us for other misadventures—like the trip to the upper Teklanika River with a broken stove and a foot of new snow—and we learned to take it all in good humor as part of the grand adventure of life.

Growing up in the national parks, you have the biggest, most exciting backyard a kid could want. I was lucky enough to call Yosemite, Glacier, and Denali *my* backyard. Even as a kid, I knew the backstage access I had to these places was something special. Whether it was a ride-along in my dad's patrol car, an end-of-season potluck, or donning the uniform myself as an interpreter, growing up a "park brat" instilled in me a sense of place and community that I treasure.

Go Up the Stairs

Nancy Marie Hoppe

Chief of Interpretation and Resource Management Charles Ross had no idea that after he hired me as the park's first work-study student, I laughed, jumped, and hopped from his office on the second floor of the Old Courthouse down thirty-three stairs into the rotunda. Little did I know that Dred and Harriet Scott possibly walked up those same stairs with their two little girls 114 years before me as slaves, yet returned down them as free people. At twenty years of age, I never knew about the two parents who took their master to court with five trials over eleven years in an attempt to be free of slavery, and whose freedom was ultimately purchased, not won. What kind of fear did this family face in their lifetime? After twelve years of school here in Saint Louis, Missouri, where this historic event took place, all I remembered were the words, "the Dred Scott Decision."

What did Mr. Ross see in me to hire me at the Jefferson National Expansion Memorial? I later learned people regularly contacted the park to find out how they could work at our nation's tallest man-made monument. The Gateway Arch had been open to the public only four years, with the original small staff. This included Dick Bowser, who designed the Arch transportation system that, since 1967, has hauled millions of people 630 feet to the top. I remember the staff's pride at being chosen to work here, and I came to realize the honor of being chosen myself. I feel I grew up at this park. As a person who had previously despised history, I fell in love with it as I listened, studied, and learned from the park's dedicated workers throughout the years. I call these employees "walking history books," and I learned their contagious love and passion for history and serving people.

In my thirty-six-year career here, I find I am still learning. The National Park Service led me into a life of disciplined study—of reading primary sources, analyzing documents, and making connections to the past. I learned one historic event or building leads to another, which produced a thirsty

Jefferson National Expansion Memorial, 1968. The 630-foot high stainless steel arch, designed by the late Eero Saarinen, symbolizes the opening of the West following the Louisiana Purchase.

desire to walk in the places where others, like the Scott family, walked and left their story in the pages I was studying. In my free time, I visited many Saint Louis attractions for the first time in my life, mostly to learn how staff treated visitors and how historical tours were presented.

History came alive to me because of the National Park Service. Until I worked at the memorial, I had no interest, for I could not understand why I should care about what happened or what people did hundreds of years ago. I could not understand how it affected my life, and I did not care. That is why I love working here. Many visitors I meet feel the same way I did, and I want to be the one who reaches out and creates that spark of passion—to introduce visitors to something significant that happened right where they are standing. If no one ever told me or gave me a chance to work here, I would possibly never know or care to this day.

What did Mr. Ross see in me to choose me? Did he see my fear and lack of confidence in all of life? Did he see the misgivings produced by polio, my parent's divorce, my feelings of abandonment as I was placed in two different foster homes, all by the age of five? Did he see my lack of direction and cognitive learning skills; the attention deficit disorder; the majority of

Nancy Marie Hoppe in the Old Courthouse at the Jefferson National Expansion Memorial.

THE WONDER OF IT ALL

Fs on my grade school report cards; my past, abuse, and shyness? Did he know I had no knowledge of the National Park Service, had never heard of Yellowstone or the Grand Canyon, and that I did not know the Arch and Old Courthouse was a national park? Did he know this was my first time in downtown Saint Louis and that my world consisted of a neighborhood park; the backyard; going to school, church, and Grandma's?

Mr. Ross could not have known any of this, but the Lord did and gave me the job. Mr. Ross told me as he hired me that he liked my smile—he said I smiled the whole interview and my smile would make visitors feel welcome. My future career opened with a smile. The Lord gave me a desire of my heart before I was learned and skilled enough to even know that this job could be a desire of my heart.

I hope my story encourages youth to not give up because they have had difficult childhoods. We may not recognize it, but inside each of us are strengths and talents. Mr. Ross may not have seen all that was wrong with me, but perhaps he recognized talents I learned from my father, such as diligence; perseverance; and doing a job right the first time, avoiding the easy way out. I feel honored to have learned this from him and to have learned the mission of serving set by the example of the original crew members at the Arch—through the ranger stories in the 1972 *Oh, Ranger!* book; from park volunteers; and from many coworkers and supervisors who were very talented, encouraging, and forgiving. These people not only connected visitors to national parks, they connected *me*; they inspire people to believe in this great agency.

Retirement is on the horizon. On my last day, I will turn in my badge upstairs at the Old Courthouse. On my final walk down those thirty-three stairs, I will think of the Scott family's walk too—a journey that eventually freed them from slavery's bondage. Since I believe in the same Lord they believed in, I can only imagine they were thanking Him profusely. I, too, will be thanking Him for my career and freedom from the bondage of fear. The National Park Service and women of faith have taught me that when I have to face any fear in life, go up the stairs and face it afraid.

Pursuing a Park Dream

Steve Moore

"Dad, can we go on to Nevada Fall?" asked the twelve-year-old, wide-eyed boy while standing by the lapping waters above Vernal Fall. The family was wrapping up their first-ever camping trip and preparing to leave Yosemite that day in 1960. The father contemplated the time and declined.

"What if I go on to Nevada and back down the Muir Trail, while you go back?" persisted the son. "It won't take very long." The father thought a minute—and almost relented—but wisely said no.

The boy in this story is me. My mother saw my delight and later suggested that I might want to be a park ranger when I grew up. The seed was planted, and I knew what I wanted to do from then on.

Ten years later, I was enroute to my first seasonal park ranger job at Natural Bridges National Monument in Utah when I stopped for a cave tour at Lehman Caves National Monument. The cave was—and is—not only great but the ranger guide was encouraging when my young wife and I asked about future employment with the National Park Service.

As life would have it, I, in fact, found my career for nearly forty years with the California State Parks, a superb organization that shares responsibilities with the National Park Service in some areas and the same lofty principles.

But I have now come full circle. As of 2014, I have worked five seasons at Great Basin National Park and am leading the very same Lehman Caves tours that contributed to my inspiration so many years ago. I also take delight in conducting astronomy programs and telling the story of the gnarled, ancient bristlecone pines. I am proud to dress in the gray and green, and especially to don the flat hat. Not a day goes by that I don't look forward to sharing the wonders of Great Basin and the national parks overall!

I Look Up and I Learn

Hayley Edmonston

I am what they call a "park brat" (like an army brat, but instead of growing up on military bases, I was raised in our country's national parks). My parents are rangers—my mother an interpreter, my father a law enforcement officer—and for me, because we moved so much, home was never a place. I am from the woods and the clean air; our nation's most beautiful places were my playground.

I spent my first four years of life in Idaho's Craters of the Moon National Monument, a desolate landscape of lava lands in a community of a dozen people. I rode in my dad's backpack while he went on Nordic ski patrols and watched bears roam what I called the "cinder cone mountain" in our backyard. Once, my father discovered a new cave while exploring with me, giving him the right to name it. The park does not allow caves to be named after people, so instead, he named it after the pacifier tragically lost on our adventure. I can rest assured knowing that long after I'm gone, I will live on in obscure maps of Idaho's wilderness that show my legacy: "Binky Cave."

My parents split at Lake Roosevelt National Recreation Area in eastern Washington; and my mom and I moved across the state to Fort Vancouver National Historic Site. At the ripe old age of six, I began my own National Park Service career, playing one of the historic Douglas girls during living-history events at the fort. I treasured my basket of authentic pioneer toys. The other park kids and I ran through back passageways in the historic houses; picked wild strawberries in the gardens; and waited in anticipation for the real seven-course feast we got to eat as visitors filed through the ornate dining room, and the dancing, fiddle music, and bonfire that followed.

My dad took a job at Vanderbilt Mansion National Historic Site in New York, where we lived in the historic gatekeeper's house to the estate. After hours, we would climb the ladder to the roof of the mansion, closed to the public, and take in the views of the Hudson River. I flew between parents—and coasts—every six weeks, racking up enough frequent-flyer miles to get upgraded to first class, where I discovered they serve unlimited ice cream sundaes.

My mother relocated to Virginia's Shenandoah National Park when I was seven. The other kids and I hunted for arrowheads after the plantation fields had been turned, but I never really fit in on the East Coast. Though I was reluctant to move yet again when my mom accepted a job at Mount Rainier when I was ten, she promised this would be the last move; and Washington felt like coming home.

My adolescent Saturdays were spent painstakingly writing the weather forecast on the whiteboard in the Paradise Visitor Center, making a nuisance of myself on my mother's public snowshoe walks, then getting a cup of hot chocolate and watching the snow fall on the Tatoosh Range from

Hayley Edmonston in Mount Ranier National Park.

the observation deck. But as a teenager, I rebelled (as all teenagers do) and unilaterally declared that nature was dumb.

I did not realize how unique and powerful my upbringing was until I reached adulthood. I started hiking because I wanted to, not because my parents were dragging me along; and I found that, for me, being outside is a fundamental part of happiness, health, and being human. I moved to Seattle for college, and when I felt homesick, I simply walked to a place on campus where I could see Mount Rainier—my home, my family watching over me on the horizon. As I wrote in a poem once: I look up and I learn.

Much to my parents' surprise and amusement, I began to entertain day-dreams of becoming a park ranger myself. After graduating from college, an opportunity to intern at Mount Rainier fell into my lap, and I was hired as a paid ranger the following summer. I cannot express what it meant to put on that familiar green-and-gray uniform and go to work at the park I lived in longest of all. I have never experienced pride like I felt walking the trails wearing my flat hat, helping visitors with everything from hiking suggestions to flower names. I soaked it in. I backpacked as many miles as my legs would carry me and started to ponder the lofty goal of climbing the mountain—a technical glacial expedition spanning three days. I thought if my mom could accomplish this monumental feat at fifty, surely I could do it at twenty-three. I trained for five months, made two unsuccessful attempts, but finally, as my second season at Rainier drew to a close, my team reached the 14,411-foot summit after twenty-one hours of climbing.

It was the only time I have ever been overcome by emotion; it was the most meaningful, powerful experience of my life. As we wandered breath-lessly across the summit crater, I thought of my parents, who both worked at Rainier, and how honored I am to follow in their actual and metaphorical footsteps. I reflected on the strange and beautiful ways this massive mound of rock and ice has shaped my life, and how it symbolizes where I come from and what I hope to accomplish. I considered the importance of these mag-nificent wild places and how few people have the privilege of knowing them intimately the way I do. What an incredible life these places have given me so far—and it's only beginning.

What a Day with a Park Volunteer Can Do

Keith J. Muchowski

Five years ago was one of the most memorable periods in my life, and the National Park Service played an important part in that experience. It was in July of that year that I took the woman soon to become my wife for a picnic at Governors Island National Monument in New York Harbor. It was a beautiful summer morning. It was also a weekday—quieter than a busy Saturday or Sunday.

Because my fiancée had never visited this national monument before, we decided to begin—and work up our appetite—by taking a guided tour. And that is where we met a man who continues to play a large role in our lives. He was a National Park Service volunteer and had been giving tours of the island's historic district for several years. There were four visitors taking his tour that day—the two of us and another couple. For the next sixty minutes, our guide told us the story of the island's long and rich history. He took us inside Fort Jay, the star-shaped structure originally built in the late 1700s when it looked like the young United States might again go to war with some European power. He showed us the island's beautiful grounds and explained how what we were seeing tied in to the history of the city and the country. We ended at Castle Williams, yet another fortification on the island. This one was round and had been designed by an army engineer named Jonathan Williams. President Thomas Jefferson had appointed Colonel Williams as the first leader of the United States Military Academy at West Point.

The castle was indeed beautiful, but at this time, we could not enter. He explained that the National Park Service was restoring the old fort.

We had learned so much in that hour and were now ready for lunch. There were many picnic tables nearby, all with beautiful views of the New York City skyline. The other couple had left, and we asked our new friend if he would like to join us. Thankfully, he said yes. And so the three of us spent the summer afternoon eating, chatting, and enjoying the surrounding scenery. We agreed to keep in touch.

Summer turned into fall, and my fiancée and I married that October. It was a heady and hectic time in our lives. My new wife had recently gone back to college; work was busy. Then there was the stress and exhilaration of setting up house. Around this time, I also began to speak about volunteering myself. With this in mind, I reached out to friends in the National Park Service for advice—including our friend the volunteer from Governors Island.

While all of these things were happening, there were sadder events taking place as well. My mother was suffering from cancer and undergoing treatment. That November, just three weeks after I married, my father passed away. As one might imagine, these events led me to reassess what is important in my life. It also seemed that if I wanted to contribute in some way, now was the time to do it. So, I made that phone call—I had decided to volunteer at the Ellis Island Immigration Museum, part of another national monument located in New York Harbor. I began in February.

I jumped in headfirst and knew right away that I had made a good decision. Eventually, I was giving tours, manning the information desk with the rangers, and making myself helpful to the boatloads of visitors who arrived hourly. One of the wonderful things about the Ellis Island museum is that the entire world comes to *you*. I met people from around the country and around the world. It was exhilarating.

Keith J. Muchowski on Governors Island.

Castle Clinton National Monument, 1961. Four forts were built to defend New York City just prior to the War of 1812, including Castle Williams on Governors Island and Southwest Battery on the southern tip of Manhattan, shown here and renamed Castle Clinton in 1817.

Then began my next chapter with the National Park Service. And fittingly, it involved our friend the volunteer from Governors Island.

One late winter's day, a year after I began volunteering, our friend accompanied my wife and me to Fort Wadsworth, part of the Gateway National Recreation Area on Staten Island. We met at an old-style coffee shop in Brooklyn, chatted a bit to catch up, and then took the bus across the Verrazano Bridge. We had a wonderful tour with a ranger who really knew his stuff. It was fascinating to learn more about how the many fortifications in New York Harbor had once worked together to keep the city safe. That evening over dinner, our friend recommended that perhaps I might enjoy volunteering at Governors Island. I was hesitant at first but then realized that a change might allow me to reach more of the public. With some regret, I decided to move across the harbor.

So that Memorial Day weekend, there I was in my volunteer uniform at Governors Island National Monument. I sat in on ranger tours and soaked up all I could. As the weeks went by, I learned more and more. Soon, I was given more responsibility to work with the visitors; and by summer's end,

I was giving my own tours of the historic district. That was four years ago, and I have been there ever since.

Many exciting things have happened in the meantime. My mother's cancer went into remission and she is doing better; my wife graduated from college; we are settled in to our home. The work continues at Governors Island. A few summers ago, the National Park Service completed its renovation of Castle Williams, and the old fort is now open to the public—it is one of the most visited spots at the national monument. My friend is still there too. Every time I see him, I can't help but think of everything that has happened since we first met. It gives me a warm feeling when I see him leading a group around the historic district, just as he had done for us all those years ago.

The Natural World and All Its Glory

Janet Rogers

After many attempts at applying for jobs within the National Park Service in the 1980s, I received an offer to begin working as a part-time secretary GS-3 at the Wawona Wastewater Treatment Facility in Yosemite National Park. Filled with excitement, I reported to work on October 31, 1988—Halloween.

On my first day, my new supervisor told me he was leaving on vacation for two weeks and he expected me to learn how to operate the computer by the time he returned. With a great deal of overconfidence that I could do anything I put my mind to, I attempted to learn on my own. After three days of failed attempts to learn DOS or even get the printer to work—and after getting my car stuck in the ice and snow on the driveway to the plant each day, and landing flat on my backside on the ice in front of the roads crew—my young, overly confident, fragile ego began to quickly deflate. I became discouraged, wondering if this nature stuff was all it was cracked up to be.

On the third morning (and on the verge of throwing the computer through the office's large, full-length window), I decided to take some deep breaths and walk over to the window instead, to look around. There before me, no more than ten feet from the window, was a full-grown, magnificent male mountain lion! His winter coat was stunning, spotted with shades of white, gray, and brown. He probably weighed close to 150 pounds. He was so large and so muscular he could have passed for an African lion!

We stared at each other for what seemed like an eternity, and I didn't dare make a move. He was majestic, stately, strong, and powerful; and his eyes seemed to speak to me directly. I wanted to call out for someone else to see him and experience the joy I felt, but my voice faltered. I was mesmerized, shocked, excited, and filled with something I had never experienced: the natural world in all its glory. And it filled me with a love so intense it changed me forever. I knew at that very moment that this was where I was supposed to be; this was what I was meant for; this was my life's calling. I was in the mountain lion's world and would do anything to protect it for as long as I was alive.

I will never forget that day or the seven different parks I've worked in since. The National Park Service and its mission are still, to this day, my life's mission, my passion. I have raised my two beautiful children in three of those parks and am now passing this wonderful experience on to my two grandchildren.

I've been in some of the most beautiful places on Earth, and they are right within our national parks. I've worked with the best people, made lifelong friends, and learned so much. The more I learn about our parks, the more I realize we have so much more to do. I can say from the bottom of my heart that I am blessed to be part of the National Park System and am so grateful for all I've seen, all I've received, and all I have yet to give.

"Our glorious task is, in John Muir's words, 'To entice people to look at Nature's loveliness.' Our statements must be exact and cautious beyond possibility of question. And we mustn't hesitate to show our boundless delight in the marvelous and beautiful world we have to interpret."

—HORACE M. ALBRIGHT, SECOND DIRECTOR OF THE NATIONAL PARK SERVICE, 1927

2

Life-Changing Moments

Oxon Run Parkway, 1965.
Ranger Susan Gail Estes introduces
a snake to day campers.

Rangers Don't Eat White Bread

Jim Milestone

It was the summer of 1973; I was a park aid working in the Yosemite Museum. I had been hired as a taxidermist to stuff birds hit by cars and shuttle buses, for study specimens and exhibits.

Shortly after my arrival, however, it was discovered that I knew more about Yosemite than most visitors. So, beyond my duties as the valley's resident taxidermist, my supervisor chose to put me at the front desk of the visitor center to provide basic information to the multitudes of park visitors. (The visitor center staff was being slammed with millions of visitors, and rather than have one of their talented park interpreters taking up their time explaining where the bathroom was located or how to drive to Glacier Point, they thought this young nineteen-year-old college student from San Francisco could do the job just fine.) This assignment required a park-ranger uniform, so I was driven down to Merced, California, to visit the Alvord and Ferguson Company uniform store.

I was proud to wear the National Park Service uniform and especially enjoyed wearing the ranger hat. One day in the visitor center, with nearly a hundred people surrounding the information desk, I pointed my left arm to a bookshelf across the room. As my eyes followed my extended arm, I caught site of the National Park Service arrowhead patch sewn onto the shoulder of my gray, short-sleeve shirt. It gave me pause that I was wearing this historic and iconic arrowhead. I was part of a mission associated with a great agency that managed these spectacular lands—the finest landscapes of America.

One evening after work, I headed back to my tent cabin in Camp 6 and stopped at the ever-crowded grocery store in Yosemite Valley. It was August, and I had been working in Yosemite Valley for over two months. Being a park aid meant minimum pay, and I had a very meager diet. My menu consisted of peanut-butter sandwiches and chicken pot pies.

Having just come from work, I was still wearing my ranger uniform. As I reached up to pull a bag of Wonder Bread off the shelf, a large man's hand grasped my thin wrist. I heard him say from behind me in a deep, controlled voice, "Rangers don't eat white bread!"

Turning around, expecting to see a park-staff friend, I was surprised to see a tall, bearded fellow who appeared to have just come out of the park's wilderness. Still holding onto my extended wrist, he directed my arm to the whole-wheat bread section and released it.

"Rangers don't eat white bread!" he repeated. And with that, he walked away to the cash-register line.

I looked at the loaf of whole-wheat bread in my hand and realized that I could eat this. I collected my Concord grape jam and peanut butter, and headed to the registers, seeking this man out.

Catching up to him, I was laughing to myself at what had just happened. "So where are you from?" I asked him.

He told me he was from downtown Los Angeles. He said he was a computer programmer in a skyscraper overlooking the city, and his dream job would be that of a park ranger. He saved up all of his vacation time so he could go backpacking in Yosemite every summer. He told me that he would love to have my job in Yosemite; and his image of park rangers involves people who take care of themselves, are in great physical shape, and eat wholesome and healthy food.

On another day, a young maintenance woman came into the Happy Isles visitor center and pleaded with me to scare off a black bear that had climbed into her large garbage dumpster. I shut down the center and walked outside to the dumpster. Thirty to forty visitors were standing around it with their Kodak Brownie cameras, taking photos of the bear on top of the large open garbage box. I really didn't know what to do! But I was wearing a National Park Service ranger uniform, flat hat, and gold badge. So I stood akimbo, with my hands on my waist; and in the deepest voice I could muster, I said loudly, "Bear, get down from there!" The bear heard my voice, looked over his shoulder at me—the ranger—and fled immediately off the dumpster like his life depended on it. The visitors turned to me in awe.

"The Ranger has spoken," I thought to myself. "This is the coolest thing I have done all summer!" And I turned and walked stoically back to the visitor center without saying another word.

The summer of 1973 left a strong impression on me as to how the public views the perception of the National Park Service ranger. Rangers are composed of an elite group of men and women who have many responsibilities and duties, one of which is upholding the traditions and image of the National Park Service ranger. It is wrapped in the fleeting myth of the Wild West and is as important as any iconic landscape or cultural monument found within the National Park Service's system. The image of the national park ranger is one of high standards and integrity that we must live by every day as we wear the National Park Service uniform.

Jim Milestone in Whiskeytown National Recreation Area.

Since the summer of 1973, I only eat whole-wheat bread.

Fish Hooks Girl
Not a Catch-and-Release Story

Karen Haner

Each summer, various groups of kids come to Lassen Volcanic National Park from different cities in Northern California to experience camping and/or a visit to a national park for the very first time. Many of these young folks are from broken homes or underserved communities; so it's a big adventure to come to a volcanic landscape of forests, lakes, and meadows to sleep under the stars and hike in a foreign place.

When a group arrives, they are greeted by Ranger Jeff, who welcomes them and shares stories about this wonderful place they have come to experience. The group leaders have already selected the different programs and activities they would like for their kids. One group, Youth for Change, had chosen a nature walk around Manzanita Lake, one of Lassen Volcanic National Park's most beautiful lakes.

At the beginning of this field activity, Ranger Jeff brought the group together in a circle so that each member could feel equal, be heard, and feel connected as a community. One particular teenager steadfastly refused to gather into the circle, however. The leader expressed to Ranger Jeff that she was one of the "most difficult cases" he had ever dealt with. With each stop on the walk, she would exclaim, "I hate nature" or "This is stupid." Always hanging in the back of the group, she was cajoled by Ranger Jeff, the leaders, and other group members to join in.

Walking along the lake, they came to a place where the group had gathered, amazed at how close they could see trout repeatedly hitting the surface, gulping insects. Everyone attempted to capture an image of this natural drama with their cameras, but no one got that split second when the trout surged above the surface.

As usual, their difficult case had lagged back—but the leader and Ranger Jeff noticed that the predatory drama had caught her interest. As they let the

Lassen Volcanic National Park, circa 1930. View of Lassen Peak and Manzanita Lake.

group move on, they shared in her amazement. Then it happened! She took a picture just as the trout chomped down on an insect. "I got it! I got it!" she announced. Sure enough, there was the moment in the camera viewer, captured.

They made their way around the lake and gathered into a circle to debrief their adventure; and there she stood with everyone, in the circle.

Yosemite Is My Backyard

Bob Roney

I've always been interested in animals but never truly understood wildlife until I spent time in Sequoia, Kings Canyon, and Yosemite. While growing up in suburban Southern California, I knew animals mostly as pets, captives of zoos, or characters in movies. My first encounter with a real wild animal was with a frog I found in my backyard. While I was pretty young, I still remember the delight I felt as I held that cold, green, bulgy-eyed creature in my small hands—that was the first time I recognized life in another species. I could identify the frogs' voices brightening the spring nights near my home and would smile myself to sleep as they sang their lullaby from the storm drain.

Yes, this frog was a wild creature, but it was harmless; and I was in the safety of my own backyard. But "nature," I thought, is different. It's scary. Wild places like our national parks harbor terrifying beasts like bears, mountain lions, and wolverines—or so I thought.

I first encountered animals in the wild while backpacking in Yosemite National Park with two of my best friends from high school. Warned to be wary of bears trying to steal our food, we hiked up the trail and into the wilderness. I had never seen such raw beauty. I was, at once, in awe and in fear of what dangers we might encounter. We made camp, and ate our bread and salami as the sun settled in for the night. Meanwhile, I worried about the bears.

When darkness fell, we decided to bed down. I cowered at the bottom of my sleeping bag, hoping that the bear would devour my friends and not discover me. Eventually, I dropped off to sleep, but I didn't stay that way for long. Every snap of a twig and every pinecone that bounced through the branches on its way to the ground woke me with a start. Were these sounds made by predators?

There were other noises too. A raspy voice cried out in the distance—*IEY-EEEET*—then another nearby—*IEYEEEET*—so strange, so foreign. Over there, I could hear the footsteps of a large animal or animals. Something smaller bounded onto the scene accompanied by a weird *MAAA-MAAAH*. That raised the hair on the back of my neck. How strange that, during the day, we saw very few animals. But now, in the dark, the woods were crawling with creatures of every sort; and they sounded awfully dangerous.

The human mind does terrible things to us. If we don't know what something is, our imagination fills in the blanks. I had come about most of my knowledge of wildlife by watching movies. Unfortunately, the movies rarely tell the truth about animals. If you believe the movies, bears growl their way through the forest, looking for people to attack; all the predators are that way too—mountain lions, coyotes, wolves. If you believe the movies, plant-eating mammals are the sweet children of nature. In my mind, all of the bad animals I had ever seen on TV suddenly surrounded me.

In spite of being scared, a part of me was curious. I wanted to know what was out there. I had forgotten to bring a flashlight, so my ears continued to scan the scene. Then a familiar sound wafted up from a distant pond: frogs? My old friends the frogs were beginning their chorus to the stars. This little bit of familiarity helped me begin to relax. With my old friends out there, the woods weren't quite so scary.

I awoke to some of the same sounds that I had heard that night—sounds not quite so harsh and intrusive when I could investigate them with my eyes in the predawn light of the Sierran forest. I heard that *IEYEEEET* close by. My head jerked up, and I heard it again. This time, I saw what was calling out: a great horned owl. And I have since learned that the young of this species make that *IEYEEEET* to keep in contact with their parents. This large bird lives just about everywhere there are trees and open areas in Yosemite and other places. Like other owls, it makes no sound as it glides on silent wings, helping it descend undetected on its prey—usually mice and other small mammals. The great horned owl, one of the largest owls, has been known to carry off skunks and even porcupines, but not people.

I learned that the footsteps I had heard were those of mule deer browsing the fresh leaves of lupines and grasses. I learned that the creatures making the jumping sound also made that weird *MAAA-MAAAH*. They were spotted fawns following their mothers about their new world, and I watched as they nursed.

"That's all fine. These are harmless animals," you say, "but what about the bears, mountain lions, and wolverines?" Well, yes, they live here too. But consider this: the only animal to have ever killed a person in Yosemite was a deer. Despite of all the warnings about animals that we rangers give, there really isn't much out there that wants to hurt you. There is only one truly bloodthirsty creature you are likely to see. What ghoul is that? The mosquito.

I have called Yosemite National Park my home for nearly fifty years now. I have skied across the Sierra, walked hundreds of miles through forests and meadows, sat on the tops of craggy peaks at 13,000 feet, and climbed the granite walls of Yosemite Valley. Animals live everywhere; and as I watch them going about their wild lives, they teach me the truth about themselves. The more truth I learn about the wildlife in these mountains, the more I discover that wilderness is not so scary after all.

Yes, Yosemite is my home, and I still have animals in my backyard; but it's your backyard too. For that matter, all national parks are our backyard. Enjoy them!

"Some primitive instinct of loneliness . . . made me throw back my head and howl at the stillness. . . . I repeated the cry, trying to imitate the weird and fascinating note of a coyote. My efforts were rewarded. . . . I called again and another group joined the first and this time the echoes chased each other around the hills for nearly two minutes before they all died away and quiet reigned."

—MARGUERITE LINDSLEY, YELLOWSTONE NATIONAL PARK RANGER, 1927

In Over My Flat Hat

Jonathan Shafer

I'd wager that you could ask any ranger to tell you about the first time they put on their uniform and they'd be able to recall a flood of pleasant feelings. Wearing the green and the gray makes people feel proud and self-reliant, empowered to help and enabled to serve. On January 3, 2015, being a newly minted winter seasonal at Death Valley National Park, I felt all the things every ranger feels when they put on their uniform for the first time. After giving an interpretive program at a site called Journigan's Mill, I started up the Emigrant Canyon Road to see who I could see before giving another program that evening. It was quiet in Emigrant Canyon but not in the rest of the park.

That afternoon, I listened on the park radio as law-enforcement rangers down in the valley proper responded to a hit-and-run accident that put a motorcyclist in the hospital. I felt a little left out of the action until I reached a site called the Wildrose Charcoal Kilns, just above where the pavement ends, and high enough for there to be snow on the ground. (Lots of folks don't think of Death Valley as a place to see snow, but at elevation, we get plenty of it. And it makes the roads hard to drive on.) I parked and got out of my vehicle to talk to a hiker who had just returned from an afternoon out.

"Looks like you had a full day," I said as the sun set to our west. "Did you hike Telescope or Wildrose?"

"Telescope," the woman responded. "It's pretty icy up there."

"Was anyone else up with you?" I asked.

"There was one couple that came down just behind me. They parked up at Mahogany Flat. I'm not sure how they're going to come down though. The road's pretty slick."

"Maybe I'll go up and see how they're doing," I responded.

I got back in my Expedition and drove up the road to a spot just above Thorndike Campground where, sure enough, a couple was fumbling with a set of chains next to their car.

"Hey, you folks want a hand with that?" I yelled through the open window of my car.

"Yes, we would," they replied. "We're from Southern California. We've never done this before. We're so glad you came up!"

"Sure thing. I'll be right there," I said as I turned off the motor, took the transmission out of drive, and set the parking break. With a surge of ranger pride, I donned my flat hat, picked up my radio, and opened the door to walk the last fifty feet to the couple and their car.

But as I stepped out of the Expedition, intending to help and serve, I felt something strange. No sooner had I put both my feet on the ground than the truck's tires gave way and it began to slip backward down the hill. I watched the couple's eyes grow larger until I slipped beyond their gaze. The ice slid beneath my boots as I watched the Expedition's lights play first off

Jonathan Shafer in Death Valley National Park.

the road in front of me and then the trees to the side of the road. The car was turning as it slid.

Standing helplessly between the driver-side door and seat, I held on for what felt like an eternity as I saw what I had thought would be a long and auspicious career flash before my eyes. "So this is how it ends," I thought. "You wrecked a government vehicle."

The Expedition began to turn off axis, in what I was sure would be the motion that rolled it on top of me, when the driver-side door struck the ground. Two hundred feet from where I began, the Expedition slowly slid to a stop. As I took stock of its condition, I realized the door was bent and a taillight was broken, but it hadn't sustained any other damage. It was drivable.

I climbed back into the driver's seat, turned the key, and listened as its powerful, Ford V8 roared to life. I had to pull the car forward half a foot before I could close the driver-side door but was able to put all four wheels back on the ground.

A flood of embarrassment washed over me when I realized that I still hadn't helped the couple with their chains. After I parked farther down the hill, I walked back through the quickly fading dusk to where the couple was still standing—in the exact position where I had left them. "Are you ok, man?" they asked excitedly. "We've never seen anything like that!"

"I'm fine." I said sheepishly. "More embarrassed than anything. Do you still want help with your chains?"

To my surprise, neither asked what idiot would park on such a steep and icy hill. Instead, they answered emphatically: "YES!"

I showed them how to install their chains, and said, "I'll go back to my car and keep pace a couple hundred yards ahead of you down the hill. The last thing we need is to have us run into each other on the way down though. So, I'm going to stay way ahead of you."

Once I had backed down the hill to a point below the ice, I waved the couple past me. I followed down behind them, still embarrassed but happy to have helped. I had a lot of explaining to do when I got back to headquarters, but I'll never forget the time I let my flat hat get me in over my head.

The Wonder of It All

Tom Habecker

Fourteen excited, yapping sled dogs strained at the tug lines, eager to go. Gary and his team were ready to go as well. Just before he pulled the snub line, he said, "Whatever you do, don't let go of the sled."

I had flown out to Kantishna, Alaska, at the end of the Denali Park Road, and skied the four miles to Wonder Lake Ranger Station. Gary, the kennels manager, and I had spent a few days buttoning up the station from winter operations, preparing to take the last two teams back home; it was my first of fifteen winters in Denali National Park and Preserve. The new guy, I was eager to learn all I could about my four-million-acre district. Although I had been out on a few training runs and one overnight, this was the big trip that only a few got to make: four days and eighty miles back to headquarters.

As Gary pulled the slipknot and took off downhill, my team went wild, straining to catch up. As I bent over to pull my line, the sled jerked, catching my ungloved hand on a sharp bolt on the frame. Bleeding profusely, I shoved my hand into my mitt and hung on for dear life as we rocketed after Gary. I hadn't gotten ten feet and had screwed up already, but there was no stopping now.

Out on frozen Wonder Lake, the dogs settled into an easy pace, the sled runners hissing on the crystalline snow. As we traveled along the McKinley River bar, the Denali massif was still twenty-three miles away—but looked close enough to touch. The huge monolith loomed in the bright March sun, the cobalt-blue sky in stark contrast to the dazzling white of its glaciers.

The morning sun, with its dull warmth, felt good on my cheeks; but the air was crisp and cold. I was on a dogsled in Alaska, the place I had dreamed of as a kid. It seemed surreal—was I really doing this? Visions of Sergeant Preston flashed through my mind: "On, you huskies, on!" If only my ranger buddies in the Lower 48 could see me now.

My hand throbbed, but I didn't dare take it out of the mitt. The wound was freezing shut by now. We traveled on in near silence—just the panting of the dogs, an occasional raven squawking, and a periodic "gee" or "come haw" from Gary.

Late in the day, we climbed our way up Gorge Creek to the tiny Thorofare Patrol Cabin at the foot of the Muldrow Glacier. Getting a fire going in the stove, we heated water for the dogs, who always get fed first. After eating, each curled up into a ball, tail to nose, nestled into the snow for the night. Gary and I prepared our supper, and I got a good look at my hand. Cleaning and bandaging it, I figured I would live.

There is no quieter place than a tiny cabin deep in the Alaskan wilderness on a cold winter night. There was no sound except for the crackling of the fire in the woodstove and the periodic howl of the dogs. A primordial sound—were they howling at a nearby wolf, the aurora streaming overhead, or just because they can? No one really knows, but it was beautiful music.

After breakfast—morning gruel for the dogs and pancakes for the humans—we set off again, headed for the Toklat Patrol Cabin. We had

Tom Habecker in Denali National Park and Preserve.

to dodge rocks and brush, but otherwise, travel was easy on the river bar. It was getting late as we climbed up Highway Pass to drop down into the Toklat drainage. With the sun low behind us and ice crystals drifting from the sky, Gary disappeared, an ice ghost, into the dimming light. I could only follow the trail, hoping I wouldn't get lost; catching periodic glimpses of him and the dogs as the ice fog, with its faint rainbow, drifted in and out. As the surrounding peaks turned to gold, we arrived at the cabin for the night.

THE WONDER OF IT ALL

Sitting in a spruce forest on the banks of the Toklat River, the cabin was plush by Denali National Park and Preserve standards: it had an oil heater and propane lights. It was where I was to spend a great deal of time my last summer as a ranger—but that's another story. Again, the dogs got fed. We had our supper, talked about the day, and wrote in the cabin's logbook. Every cabin has one, and there is history in those books that needs to be preserved. Reading them is like going back to another time.

A crisp morning found us moving gingerly up an infamous frozen tributary of the Toklat. Bluish-green glare ice challenged the dogs as they tried to get a toehold and ascend the creek. The sled skidded wildly, and I just tried to hang on and not crash. Flocks of ptarmigan erupted from the brush; wolf, moose, and caribou tracks flew by; brush slapped me in the face as I struggled to keep the sled from rolling. Along the East Fork, I peered down into the maw of rushing water that would surely swallow anyone who fell from the shelf ice. Climbing Sable Pass, we dropped down to the Igloo Patrol Cabin for the night.

Another night—our last—in a quiet cabin. The dogs were fed and staked out for the evening. The cabin was warm and the woodstove crackled. There was warm food, hot coffee, and a good friend to share it with. Tomorrow would bring the dreaded Teklanika drop-off, a notorious cliff that eats rookie dog drivers. Tomorrow would bring us to the road where the plows were grinding their way west. Tomorrow, we return to the world of people, meetings, computers, and phones. But for a time tonight, we stood in awe of the aurora as it danced overhead and the dogs sang their mournful song.

Teaching the Teacher

Timothy S. Good

We, who wear the gray and green, are educators for the American people. We educate through interpretive talks, waysides, brochures, pamphlets, films, web pages, and social media.

I have had the fortune to serve at nine different sites within the National Park System, and have served on details to many others. Yet when I reflect on my memories of the educational moments that I have had, I don't remember those times when I taught a visitor but those times when a visitor taught me.

The Civil War Soldiers and Sailors System (CWSS) is an Internet-based system that currently holds over six million American names. The first part of the project involved the collection and digitization of the United States Colored Troops by hundreds of volunteers nationwide. When that was completed, the National Park Service hosted an event to publicize it in conjunction with the African American Civil War Memorial dedication in Washington, DC.

We had set up four computers for visitors to use inside a nearby school-room that day, and there were hundreds of people and long lines all day. Yet of all the people I saw, I remember one particular woman most of all. She was African American, frail, in her 70s or 80s. She attempted several times that day to search for her ancestor but without success. The system had been taxed, and the computer had frozen for her each time. At the end of the day, when we were starting to pack up, she was still there, holding a small scrap of paper that had the name of her ancestor written on it. So I shut down three of the computers and sat down with her at the remaining one. I typed in her ancestor's name and pressed "enter." It was probably only a few minutes, but it seemed like an eternity; and then, the name appeared.

She stared at the screen for a moment, and then slowly raised her hand to touch it with her outstretched fingers. Tears began rolling down her cheek.

It was not that we had more information on her ancestor—she had, by far, more. It was that someone cared. Someone she would never meet, had, one day, sat down at a computer and entered her ancestor's information. And while I had continually touted the CWSS for its information, she taught me that it was something more. It was also a memorial to all Civil War veterans.

Another memory: I was standing at the top of the steps of the Lincoln Memorial, facing the Washington Monument. It was near dusk. I was constantly surveying the visitors, seeing if anyone needed help, looking for someone who might have a question, until my eyes fell upon a father and his young son. He was obviously telling a story of great importance. I was not close enough to hear, but Dad was clearly conveying the story's significance through his attention and his gestures. And then he pointed to a particular step, and I knew the story that he told. It was the step upon which King had stood and had delivered his speech. The step was unmarked at that time, but for the father, he did not want his son to pass this moment without knowing the importance of that step and its story. And then he pointed to Lincoln,

Lincoln Memorial, circa 1990. Robert Todd Lincoln, the only surviving son of the sixteenth US president, attended the dedication of his father's memorial in 1922.

and the father made the connection for his son—a connection of the hopes and dreams of two Americans.

One night, when I was standing alone by the Vietnam Veterans Memorial, a middle-aged man approached me. We exchanged greetings and then he walked me over to a place on the wall. He pointed above my shoulder to a particular name and told me a story of an American hero. It was about a hill, a group of Americans, and a battle. At the end of his story, he reached out, shook my hand, thanked me, and walked away. After a few steps, he turned and added, "That's the first time I have ever told that story." I nodded, so did he, and he gradually disappeared from my view.

The man had obviously carried that story for many decades, and I had been honored to be there at the moment when he had decided to share it.

A Story from the Cold

Daniel Williams

When I was a young ranger working at Calaveras Big Trees State Park, I was mesmerized by the story of Chief Tenaya, his tribe of Ahwahneechee, and their inevitable clash with pioneer culture in the form of James D. Savage and his Mariposa Battalion. Lafayette Bunnell, physician for the battalion, kept a diary of the events that transpired in 1851, when nonnatives got their first glimpse of the awesome wonders of Yosemite Valley and indigenous people got their first glimpse of nonnatives. What transpired was tragic: Tenaya's son was shot by a member of the battalion; and the old chief made a deal that he and his people would surrender and move to a reservation if he were allowed to collect his son's body, to give it a proper cremation and keep it from the depredation of bears. After Tenaya gave his son ceremonial passage, he and some of his tribesmen were made captive and escorted to the reservation from which they soon escaped, returning to Yosemite, the place of their birthright. These people were the "first people" in Yosemite with a material culture and a system of belief that tied them to all the cycles and rhythms of the Earth.

As a young poet struggling to express the Sierra in adept images and fresh language, there was something attractive to me about this story, the feelings it evoked, and the wild environment in which it took place. I felt almost immediately that I needed to be in Yosemite to hear the mythos-poetic voice with which such a place expresses itself—by speaking or singing or weeping or even crying out. I arrived in dark March and had a cold camp out near the Merced River, just below the El Portal Bridge. That first night was freezing, but I stuck it out and have made Yosemite my home ever since.

Perhaps it was the father–son thread woven in this matrix like a split redbud twining in a sedge basket; but whatever it was, I felt a deep need to introduce my nine-year-old son to the world in which his father lived and worked. Accordingly, I planned for us to follow Tenaya's route up Indian

Canyon on the northeastern edge of the valley, the ancient escape route of the native people—a series of various-sized boulders leading like broken stairs all the way to the rim. From there, the old chieftain and his tribe climbed over the top to Tenaya Lake.

Near the bottom of this talus slope, with Indian Creek on the right, we discovered what we thought was the huge boulder by which Tenaya would have climbed down to an oak tree, then used the ladder-like branches to climb down to the valley floor on his return from the rim. This realization of historic possibility filled us both with such excitement that we climbed our way to the top of Indian Canyon where it touched the very rim of the valley, to where Tenaya himself might have once stood before descending. On the way, we stopped on one of the granitic shelves to sit under a laurel tree and eat our lunch, sharing the shelf with three deer who were eating theirs, and appreciating the fantastic views down the valley to the west and down Illilouette Canyon to the south.

On our way to the top, we bounded from boulder to boulder—some smaller, some as big as a house—not seeing them as merely rocks but as a historic pathway that would somehow lead us back to a place where others had trod in order to trade or to make their way to the highcountry; or to escape whatever threat remained below. Our breathing was hard, and we had some hard knocks as well; but we believed this to be the way we were meant to be at times and in this vibrant, green place.

We started our climb back down to the valley floor just as the sun stood in the canyon mouth to the west and was lowering, painting the stone walls a gorgeous apricot. Halfway down, we rested under a bay laurel, gratefully breathing in the spicy air as we sat in perfect stillness with Venus showing in the purple sky. It was then that we heard the haunting lilt of a wind flute. My son and I looked at one another, and we both seemed to understand that we must remain quiet and listen. And so we did, sharing one of the most amazing moments of our lives. Our tired feet were light for the rest of the journey down. An American Indian at the Miwok Village had told us about the wind flute, how it was made from natural materials and used for ceremonies. She then placed it to her lips and created for us its lovely sound. She showed us how to purify with laurel leaves, then she cautioned that if we should ever feel a chill on a warm day, it may be caused by the presence of a spirit of one who had gone before us.

Daniel Williams in Yosemite National Park.

We made camp in the backpackers' campground that summer evening and enjoyed our supper of jerky, crackers, and fruit. Lying in our sleeping bags, we discussed what had happened until both of us dropped off into a deep sleep.

Sometime in the middle of the night, with Ursa Major hanging over the falls, we both awoke, a slight incense of wormwood in the air. Both of us were quaking with a surprising cold that seemed to surround our camp. That August night, I hugged my son to me as we both looked around for some sign of our unseen visitors, both of us grateful for their visit but both of us chilled to the bone.

Then it was I who thought of Tenaya saying good-bye to a son that he could no longer hold, making a sacrifice to preserve what remained. I thought about how it was all part of the wondrous bio-matrix that is Yosemite National Park: human history, biodiversity, DNA, mystery, water's miraculous sculpting, primal darkness and amazing light, geospatial wonderment and hope for the future of our planet—all that is truly sacred—pressed together in a seminal, blossom-like pattern of life that cold Yosemite night under the stars.

The Moose and Me

Carol L. Hines

I was eight years old and quite small. The moose was much older and quite large.

I stood frozen on a small point of land in the middle of the marsh as this majestic animal slowly plodded through chest-high water. Slow, sucking, and soft splashing sounds alerted me to the arrival of the behemoth. Each step he took pulled up muck and mud as he plodded forward. He would pause now and then to dip his head down into the morass. Then his head would reappear with a mouthful of dripping greens, some even dangling from the formidable antlers crowning his head.

I had wandered along a sodden pathway, jumping from one patch of dry land to the next. I was now out on a tiny peninsula of land in the marshlands of Yellowstone Lake. I had bent down to examine the tiny minnows skittering among the reeds when I first heard the sound. Now I was stunned with shock and fear. And I was isolated, with a huge male moose between me and dry land. Mother thought I had followed Dad along the river to watch him fly fish; Dad assumed I had remained in camp. It was just the moose and me.

He paused and glanced my way, a great brown eye fixed upon me. But apparently sensing no threat, he dipped his head again for another mixture of mossy goodness. For some time, he remained there, sampling his garden of greens. Then he simply continued peacefully on his journey. For what seemed like forever, I watched as he slowly moved along, selecting the delicacies of the marsh.

Carol L. Hines

As my panic waned, it was replaced by admiration—even reverence—for this handsome creature. There I was, less than fifteen feet from one of the largest beasts in North America!

Finally, my path to freedom was clear and I retreated, step by cautious step to safety.

While my parents only saw my adventure as a danger from which I had escaped, I was filled with wonder and awe at what I had been privileged to witness. Now, seventy years later, I still remember that encounter. I still recall those moments with a mixture of delight and wonder. It was the beginning of my lifetime of adventures in the national parks.

As a full-time volunteer in the National Park System today, I am forever thankful to a moose who allowed me to exist in his space, in his marsh, and in his world for a few minutes that would last a lifetime.

"Someone, somewhere, sometime had to stand up. . . . Wouldn't it be a tragedy if because we didn't pay attention and raise the specter . . . that tomorrow or fifty years from now [Yellowstone] is no longer here?"

—LORRAINE MINTZMYER, FORMER NATIONAL PARK SERVICE REGIONAL DIRECTOR, 1992

The Season of Renewal

Jason Ransom

In this early morning stillness of Denali National Park and Preserve, redpolls and crossbills call forth the light from a shorter night. Snow flurries fall gently on the tundra. Most spring mornings in Denali are serene and quiet, and reach deep into the human soul with whisperings of peace and solitude, but life is all but silent here.

It is the day before Easter, and the park has yet to greet its summer visitors. A young cow moose has survived winter and smells the promise of spring willows. She bedded for the night near the famous Denali Park Road, in the same place that another lone wanderer of winter was also looking for life. He is the ghost that slips quietly past you when you are hiking, and you never even know he was there. Wolves rule the winter here; I am simply watching, as park biologists often do.

On this morning, the wolf is winding his way through the spruce and frozen dwarf birch. He finds opportunity and slips silently into cover. His great sinewy mass crouches to the ground and with slow, liquid motion as he inches his way through the crunchy snow. His eyes stare intently on the young resting moose. One step . . . then crouch to the stillness of stone. One step . . . stone. Then quickly, with a burst of calculated power, he leaps and takes the moose.

Very seldom does a wolf kill a moose on its own, but this lone hunter found an exception to the equation. Exhausted and uninjured, he eats his fill and then melts into the trees. He lies down in the snow to rest, his nose tucked under his tail for warmth. He becomes a stone once again.

For nine hours, the moose is left to the birds. Gray jays and ravens have come and gone with trophies of nourishment clutched in their beaks. It is silent here, and every flap of wing and crunch of foot carries the story far across the tundra.

Morning arrives with a fresh blanket of white. The blood is gone. It is Easter; and the world celebrates renewal, life, and fertility. The wolf has fed on the moose during the night, and the snow tells of a lynx who visited under the cover of darkness. Ravens and jays are feasting until, suddenly, they flush to the trees. A shadow falls upon the morning snow. It is always amazing to me how silently the great mass of a wolf moves, slipping in and out of trees, and vanishing just before you know what you are seeing. The wolf sniffs around the carcass, reading the signs of those who came before and standing tall with a posture that leaves no doubt as to the provider of this feast.

Snowflakes fall gently onto the gray and white fur of the hunter as he buries his muzzle into the soft underbelly of the moose. Sounds of flesh and bone, tearing, rise above the chatter and gurgle of ravens. His winter fur becomes pink with life. The birds dare not land on the carcass now. Even with such authority, the wolf never lets down his guard. A light breeze ruffles his fur as he cocks his head to the west, fixing ears on some creature moving in the snow. His intense stare leaves no doubt of intention to whoever gazes back. Nothing approaches.

The wolf feeds for two hours, periodically carrying away pieces for later. In his brief absences, the ravens seize morsels. The threat from the west finally appears on the horizon, bouncing with a light and comical prance upon the snow. It is a red fox, and despite its name, this one is all black with just a flare of white on the tip of its tail. It seems the jester has arrived in court. The wolf is on his way out and only briefly bothers to chastise his smaller cousin. The fox ducks away into the rocks for just a moment, and then the wolf is gone.

Foxes never pass up the opportunity to dance their way into a free meal. For a brief moment, this fox reigns. Even the raven, which almost surpasses the fox in size, backs off when the scrappy little scavenger nips. The fox wastes no time tearing away little scraps of meat to carry away. She comes and goes only twice, each time trotting off to the horizon with a light step and swaying gait—as if the wind might blow her over. She has found life in the moose and seems content to get away with it.

The wolf appears one last time to feed. He holds his head up into the wind and smacks his jaws, trying to get moose hair out of his mouth. (It looks like a dog does when he gets peanut butter stuck in his teeth.) Hair is also stuck on his nose as he puts his head up to survey the land. He bites into the snow and chews the crunchy ice with one last cleansing of the palate. The snow falls heavier. The image of life and death becomes obscured with white, and the hunter turns and vanishes quietly into the alders. One last glimpse of his tail, and he is gone.

The moose will slowly be reduced to bones; and over time, those, too, will be taken away by rodents in search of calcium and fox kits in search of toys. Life is renewing on this Easter in the far reaches of Alaska. The moose has not died on the last of winter's snow; it only changed its path of life . . . to the running gait of a wolf, the wings overhead, and even the funny prance of a fox. By my account, the moose has become part of a magpie, two gray jays, three ravens, a lynx, a fox, and one very capable hunter . . . the wolf.

It is dark now, and as each and every night gets shorter, each and every morning brings life. It is the season of renewal. It is finally spring.

"We come to Denali to watch; to catch a glimpse of the primeval. We come close to the tundra flowers, the lichens, and the animal life. Each of us will take some inspiration home; a touch of the tundra will enter our lives and, deep inside, make of us all poets and kindred spirits."

—ADOLPH MURIE, NATURALIST, 1962

Mount McKinley National Park (now Denali National Park and Preserve), 1966. View of Yenta Glacier from the south.

Two Tourists, One False Belief, and a Moment of Joy

Jef Wilhelm

Their car zipped confidently past the "Authorized Vehicles Only" sign. It motored a couple hundred yards along the freshly paved approach, then parked in front of the dorm building that houses seasonal employees who work at Great Basin National Park. It was late enough in the season that the building's last tenant had left three weeks earlier, so the parking lot had been empty before this car arrived. A young couple hopped out of the car almost as soon as it stopped. They were excited, even exuberant. After all, they were now in one of the most remote national parks in the continental United States.

Or so they thought. Actually, they still had about six miles to go and were presently in a residential area that was off limits to the general public.

I was in a building smaller than the dorm and located along the approach to the parking lot. From my open window, I watched the couple enthusiastically take pictures of their surroundings—the guy employing a high-dollar camera, the woman snapping pics with her phone. Each shouted out to the other—not in English but in their native tongue—when they saw something particularly photo worthy, hollering out like prospectors stumbling upon a mother lode: "Hey, look what I found here!" The fact that they weren't speaking English hinted at a possible explanation as to why they'd barreled past the "Authorized Vehicles Only" sign; and perhaps why they hadn't followed the other park signage conspicuously posted along the one road that transects Baker, Nevada.

The man bounded around the parking lot, ecstatically capturing images of the dorm building and then features of the building, like windows, doors, railings, and decks. He shot the picnic area, the valley beyond, and the mountains in the distance. Then he asked the woman to pose with 12,000-foot Mount Moriah as a backdrop. She cut a striking image with her black shoes and pants, and black blouse elegantly covered by a deep-orange shawl.

This scene sparked a full-on photo shoot with a host of creative poses over a variety of backgrounds. The two of them let loose, having fun in the uninhibited manner of kids loving the moment.

Before seeing the couple in this moment, it had occurred to me to go outside, approach them, and let them know that they were not yet in Great Basin National Park—to point them in the right direction. But to do so now would mean the unnecessary and premature end to the experience of two people who were enjoying themselves as much as I've seen any tourists enjoy themselves throughout the five national parks I've worked in.

Even if I told them they could stay there as long as they wanted, a certain magic would have been lost, stolen from the moment. And I'd have been its thief by virtue of uttering a truth and, consequently, would have found myself ensnared in an ironic quandary: to right someone's wrong belief at the expense of extinguishing their joyful moment, or let them relish the moment at the expense of truth.

There was a line to walk here, and it ran parallel to the line that guides the National Park Service itself. The line is, I suppose, more of a fulcrum—a point of balance between two objectives: to preserve natural and cultural resources on one side; and on the other side, to promote the enjoyment of and education about those resources, with the hope of inspiring present and future generations to value our national treasures. The easiest and perhaps most effective means to accomplish the first objective would be to bar public access to our cherished resources, yet doing so would all but preclude fulfillment of our second aim.

The National Park Service mission, then, is the counterbalancing of these goals on both a large and small scale: managing the park system as a whole on an intergenerational time frame and on the smaller scale of daily interactions with park visitors. The macro mission is informed and guided by policies resulting from, essentially, professional crowd-sourced knowledge and decision making over decades. However, the micro mission, though directed along established guidelines, frequently calls for individual discretion.

In my own case, I did not go out and interrupt the misplaced visitors. This was partly because their obvious elation had gotten me pondering the parking lot paradox I was witnessing: Here, ostensibly, were two people reveling in a true joy based on a false belief about where they were; here was a case where the truth would not set anyone free but, rather, euthanize their insouciance. After all, being wrong about something is—to most people most of the time—the consummate killjoy. And rumor has it that ignorance is bliss.

Besides, I'd wager my life that all of us hold some false belief or other; and I'd conjecture that most of us have experienced joy or wonder, gratitude or connection, inspiration or perhaps even a sense of enlightenment from a belief that is, ultimately, incorrect. How much of what we believe is false . . . ? Well, who knows. How many false beliefs have we ferreted out over our lifetimes and abandoned in favor of a true (we hope) belief? Again, who knows, because we have a penchant for forgetting the times we were wrong.

Yet, we're also pretty good at remembering the good times, since these are part of what make our lives worthwhile. So if some of those good times happen to owe their very existence to a false belief—whether in whole or part—then, from time to time, false beliefs actually enrich our lives. I believe that. And I believe that the photo-happy couple will later recount fond memories of having arrived at the vacated dorm building that just might have been the Great Basin Visitor Center—perhaps not yet open for the day, perhaps closed for the season.

Of course, I may be wrong.

Jef Wilhelm at Lake Meredith National Recreation Area.

THE WONDER OF IT ALL

"Thank You for Your Service" (and Other Rewards)

Steve Blizin

Sometimes you don't know where life will lead you—maybe that's the allure of hiking a new trail or trying something different. When I began volunteering with the Mountain Bike Unit (MBU), part of a multiagency effort to service the Santa Monica Mountains National Recreation Area near Los Angeles, California, I had no idea where that might take me. I did it for selfish reasons. I was overweight, out of shape, unfamiliar with my local mountain-bike trails, and not very happy with my "real" job. What happened next still surprises me.

My wife and I were out riding our mountain bikes in a local area park when we ran into a group of guys in bright-yellow jerseys who had just completed a "patrol." I asked them how they got to park their vehicles in this area of the park. (I was already thinking, "Maybe I can park here too!") Next thing I know, I'm a park volunteer. I thought, "If I do this, I'll get in shape and I'll ride more often. I'll learn new trails, and best of all, I won't have to do it alone!"

I convinced my wife this would be great for us, and she agreed. We went through orientation and training, learning about the area parks and trails, and how the National Park Service worked hand in hand with our state and local park systems. We were amazed to learn how the MBU program came to be and how many other volunteer programs across the country are currently being modeled after ours. And we rode—we rode farther and longer than either one of us ever thought possible. We would ride on a Saturday and spend the entire week recovering! Then we complained vehemently—until the next Saturday rolled around.

As it turned out, we loved it. The experience of learning something new; and the excitement of completing a challenge, surpassing a personal goal, and making or sharing a discovery with someone else along the trail became intoxicating. Soon, we were patrolling nearly every Saturday and Sunday, and sometimes during the week. We jumped at the chance to ride because it gave us so much in return. We found out we worked well as team, and it strengthened our marriage. Being ambassadors for the parks, we also found that we could share our different perspectives and passions with visitors and connect with more people.

Now, I could end this story right here and tell you that we finally came to realize that we get more out of volunteering than the time or money that we have put into it. But that is not where this story ends.

Over time, we've had a chance to work closely with National Park Service rangers, assisting with both interpretative and law-enforcement activities. We have been honored to represent the National Park Service at county fairs and family recreational activities, and we've helped rescue an injured mountain biker that needed emergency medical attention. (I guided the helicopter to our location.) Because of the training we received, we were congratulated by the rescue personnel—and thanked by the patient! We've protected wildlife and witnessed things we could have never imagined: a tiny coyote-cub howl, a rattlesnake stalking a rabbit, two bobcats strolling about and exploring their woods. We once stood silently, one misty morning, watching a small herd of deer graze in open grassland when a huge, majestic buck emerged from the trees. And when that buck proudly and loudly passed wind, we nearly doubled over laughing while struggling not to make any noise.

Steve Blizin in Cheeseboro Canyon at the Santa Monica Mountains National Recreation Area.

We've helped countless people find their way home, discover new trails, see wildlife they may have otherwise overlooked. We've given treats to horses and water to thirsty dogs. In addition to our Mountain Bike Unit duties, we have had the privilege to represent the National Park Service exclusively.

So why do this? What is so rewarding about telling people to put their dog on a leash, or educating them about not removing plants or property from parks? Why get up early on a weekend and spend your free time doing something that you don't even get paid to do?

Call it karma or whatever you want—there is truth to the old adage, "what goes around comes around." When you help someone else, you help yourself. When we see someone stopped along the trail, we ask if we can help. If they say yes, we feel great! But even when we don't find someone in need, we get positive encouragement from nearly everyone we meet. We have made new friends and strong bonds with like-minded people from all over the world. People yell, "Thank you for your service!" as they pass us on the trail. They say, "You have the best job in the world!" even though we don't get paid. But we do get paid. And we get paid handsomely.

At the beginning of this story, I told you I was overweight, out of shape, and unhappy with my job. Through volunteering, I have gained knowledge, lost pounds, achieved better fitness, and along the way, gained experience that my job didn't offer. I learned to manage people, and deal with confrontation and conflict more effectively. I have faced challenges like landing a helicopter near an injured person; and I have also gained administrative knowledge, been involved with training new volunteer recruits, developed systems to inventory supplies and uniforms, and become a more effective communicator. All of these things have helped me become a happier, more confident person—a happier, more confident person who has become more successful at work, which helped me negotiate a better benefit package— and all while I continue to explore new challenges and opportunities that my workplace can't offer.

Volunteering is the best thing I could have ever done for myself, my marriage, and my career.

Grabbing the Bull by the Antlers

Peter Christian

It's September in Kobuk Valley National Park. Ice is starting to form along the creeks that feed the Kobuk River as it winds down to the Chukchi Sea. The Western Arctic Caribou Herd migrates south across the Brooks Range to their wintering grounds. I land my boat at the Onion Portage Ranger Station, where I have been patrolling to prevent incursions into the park from sport hunters. Kobuk Valley has been set aside for an older drama to unfold—Eskimos hunting caribou.

For millennia, the Inupiaq Eskimo people have waited here to intercept caribou as they swim, sometimes by the hundreds, across the Kobuk. The river has an aura, as if it has absorbed and radiates back the desperate life-and-death energy of the hunt; as if the land itself has soaked up ten thousand years of blood and fear. A silent watchfulness hangs in the air, permeating the willows that line the banks. When the caribou cross, stepping noisily into the cold water, it is as if the river is holding its breath at the first breaking of the silence since the world began.

The people of northwest Alaska still rely heavily on caribou for food, as well as for cultural connections to their ancient past. Because the pressure on caribou is growing and population numbers are in decline, the herd bears monitoring. Hiding in the willows is a team of biologists that makes a different type of annual trek here—to capture live caribou, draw their blood, and place tracking collars around their necks. I get to talking with Jim, the leader of the project, a big man with red hair and blue eyes. "We're a bit shorthanded this year," he mentions. "If you're not too busy, we could use some extra help."

Catching live caribou is as much athletic event as it is scientific endeavor. Like Eskimo hunters, we conceal ourselves in a log blind on the south bank. Out of sight, we wait for caribou to enter the river. They emerge warily out of the willows, but once they're in the river, they swim with intensity. Bulls and cows form a swimming wedge of bodies, followed by their tiny cargo of calves. When they reach midstream, we burst from cover, holding hypodermic needles like spears, and chug across the sand to tumble into the boats.

Jim gives the engine full throttle toward the caribou, now in the center of the river, while the crew clings to the bow. Skillfully cutting a bull out of the herd, Jim joins up with the other boat to form a corral. Two biologists grab the bull by the antlers while another draws blood and applies the collar. A bull caribou can weigh as much as three hundred pounds; he has hooves the size of buckets and antlers four feet high; and his ancient instincts compel him to *Run! Fight! Escape!* The men holding the twisting antlers struggle to maintain their grip. A cold arctic wind whistles across the freezing water, dousing us with icy spray. Soon, my arms are heavy and my feet are numb, as we repeat our task from dawn to dusk over the course of three days.

On a break, we watch as three boats come downriver from the nearest village. Several Eskimo men and boys beach their skiffs and sit upstream from us. The men smoke cigarettes, drink coffee, and talk quietly among themselves. Unlike us, decked out in warm, modern gear and orange PFDs (personal floatation devices), these hunters are dressed only in jeans and light nylon windbreakers.

Without warning, the men jump to start their motors: just upriver, perhaps twenty caribou have entered the water and are swimming hard for the south bank. There are several large bulls out in the lead, their brown coats gleaming in the fading light. I watch intently through my binoculars as, with shocking efficiency, these Eskimo men become what they have always been—predators. Using rifles at close quarters, all of the bulls are shot. They tip over in the water and drift downstream. When it's over, the hunters turn their boats downriver, and those bulls that are still alive are quickly dispatched. It never ceases to stagger me when I observe this timeless event enacted as it has been for uncounted generations of men and caribou. In the long current of time, these two life-ways have become entwined in a dance of death and life. It is as intensely beautiful as it is brutal to watch.

On the last day of the project, we capture a bull with a milky cataract over one eye. This caribou is calm, perhaps because the cataract interferes with his vision. As I handle the animal, I warm my frozen hands in his thick fur. He

Peter Christian in Wrangell-St. Elias National Park.

jerks wildly and tosses his head, but then submits to my touch. What a privilege it is to feel this wild and vibrant life force! Every muscle in the animal's body is taut with energy, as if it's a high-voltage wire. It occurs to me that I am actually brushing against the raw and quivering tip of wilderness itself. Drawn to stare into its one, clear, deep-brown eye, I detect an unfathomable secret there. In the gaze of this one-eyed caribou, I am aware of being observed, not simply by a single caribou but by the eye of the living world itself. I sense this world is conscious, knows I am there, and is staring back at me. Then the boats drift apart, nearly pitching me into the frigid river.

I yank my eyes from the bull's gaze and catch Jim's bright blue eyes regarding me. A blush rises in my cheeks—like I've been caught reading a secret diary or a forbidden book. A smile erupts from Jim's red-bearded face as if he intuits my thoughts and perhaps remembers his own reasons for searching for answers to unanswerable questions.

There is a saying here that "no one knows the way of the wind or the caribou." As people of science, we can study their blood and follow their movements through GPS satellites. Science has told us where the caribou are but not, I think, the "way of the caribou." We can know everything there is to know about individual caribou and still not understand their essential caribou-ness. They own forever their own mystery. It is the mystery of wildness, and it will surely elude us the more we seek to know it.

Then it's over. The blood has been drawn and the collar bolted into place. The bull is released, and we dive out of the way. The caribou surges forward like a racehorse out of its gate and swims for the bank. On shore, he frantically shakes the water from his pelt, lunging with a crash into the willows. Lasting no more than a minute, I have been blessed with the opportunity to touch a piece of the living wilderness as few people ever do.

And besides, it's not often you get to grab the bull by the antlers!

THE WONDER OF IT ALL

Roving at Old Ferry Landing

Don Winslow

I started volunteering at Assateague Island National Seashore about fifteen years ago. After several years of working at the visitor center information desk, I was introduced to conducting scheduled interpretation sessions on the island. These were planned, rehearsed programs that were interesting for a few years but, eventually, too repetitive for me. Burnout? Perhaps. I was looking for something that was not only new and fresh for the visitors but stimulating for me too. That's how my job as a "roving interpreter" started.

Old Ferry Landing is a site on Assateague Island where, before the bridge from the mainland was built, visitors would arrive. With the bridge in place, there are no ferries, just lots of visitors. Clamming, crabbing, fishing, kayaking, looking for ponies—all here, in one place.

On any given day, I may field questions about clamming, crabbing . . . I never know—and that's the exciting thing about roving. Depending on the weather, tides, my current interests, I can be prepared to: take a few people for a walk through shallow water to collect mussels; or help an individual or group experience using a clam rake to collect hard clams; or have a child tow a plankton net through the water to collect a sample, then look through my microscope to see what they've collected; or bait a crab trap so that a visitor can experience catching a crab.

At eighty-five, I still look forward to Fridays at Old Ferry Landing and have no thought of stopping these days of my very enjoyable continuing education—that's what it is for me: I learn more than the

Don Winslow at Assateague Island National Seashore.

visitors do. Through my involvement with them, they also teach me by asking questions to which I don't have answers—*yet*. (See me next week; I'll have the answer then.)

Several years ago, I wrote a poem about my roving experience. It's called "The Two Naturalists."

The Two Naturalists

We knelt together, me at 80, she at 3
Both looking in my pail
A pail of tidal water filled with salt marsh creatures.

I led her hand to pick up a clam
She held it, turned it over and over
and smiled—a beaming, radiant smile.

How could she smile
I hadn't told her yet about *Mercenaria mercenaria*,
About its life span, reproduction, and value to the Marsh.

I placed a silverside in her palm
She giggled as it wriggled back into the pail
And smiled—a freeform, joyous smile.

How could she smile
I hadn't told her yet about *Menidia menidia*,
What it eats, and what eats it.

Now it was her turn
She reached down and put a tiny grain of sand in my hand
Looked up at me and waited, patiently.

She waited for me to look as she would look
No words, no books, no cataracts of the mind
Just a simple "what is," clear and uncluttered.

I saw what she saw in that piece of quartz
A world of worlds, an infinity of infinities
In silence we looked at each other—and smiled.

Pine Siskins Make History in the Canopy Overhead

Marci Spencer

During the springtime, black bears attract attention on Clingmans Dome, the highest mountain in Great Smoky Mountains National Park. By late April, mothers and cubs depart their winter dens hollowed out of tree snags, rocky cliffs, or root balls of spruce trees toppled by the Dome's strong winds. Pulling up roots, digging for grubs, and breaking off tender new shoots, they replenish calories lost during winter's long sleep. Preoccupied by nature's nutritional urge, the bears seem oblivious to curious, admiring tourists.

When educating visitors about bear biology and safety, National Park Service volunteers maintain a safe distance between bear and man. On May 23, 2013, while a two-hundred pound mother bear foraged beside her ten-pound twins, a tiny, nondescript little creature, no bigger than a teacup, made history in the canopy overhead.

"Do you have pine siskins here?" an Ohio couple asked. Preparing to leave, they'd loaded scope, binoculars, and field guides into their car.

"Yes, I've seen them here and heard their lively chatter," I answered. "They eat seeds of the red spruce at this altitude. Did you see siskins?"

"We think so, but we don't have siskins in Ohio. Are you a birdwatcher too?"

"Yes, hopelessly so," I admitted. "I'm addicted to the little guys too. Let's go check them out."

The gentleman reshouldered his telescope; and with binoculars in hand, the three of us climbed Clingmans Dome Trail.

"We think she's building a nest," the lady said.

During my years of volunteer service at Great Smoky Mountains National Park, I'd often seen pine siskins feeding in the conifers but never observed nesting activity. Arthur Stupka, the park's first naturalist, monitored siskins for years, comparing their arrival and feeding habits to those of their finch cousins, the red crossbill; but he never witnessed nesting behavior. More recently, the park's literature described identification, habits, and habitat of the species but stated that scientists had not confirmed nesting here.

On that clear, cold day, though, approximately one hundred yards up the paved Clingmans Dome Trail and twenty-five feet down the southern embankment, a tiny brown, heavily streaked body—the size of a goldfinch—flew into a dense, wind-tossed spruce branch, clutching grassy tufts of nesting material in her beak. The short stalks blended perfectly with her drab color. For thirty minutes, the Ohio couple and I silently watched in respectful reverence as the mother-to-be diligently flew from brambles to bough, crafting her cupped nest. Her bill, slightly thickened at the base, seemed more pointed than most finches. But a faint, tannish eyebrow stripe and two white wing bars confirmed the sighting: a female pine siskin.

The female lacks the male's yellow wing bars that often flash across pointed wings in hurried flight. Although she was silent as she sculpted her nest, she sounded alarm notes when she departed to search for more building supplies. Strong winds made it difficult to assess her flight pattern. In such blustery conditions, we were amazed that she never faltered, never missed a wingbeat, and never lost a shaft of dried vegetation.

"Where is her mate?" the Ohio gentleman criticized. "He should be here guarding her!"

"Or helping her out!" his wife chided. What fun!

Tucking their email address in my pocket as they departed home, I vowed to follow the nesting progression.

Although pine siskins are known to nest in southern, high-elevation coniferous forests, they primarily breed in the north, especially Canada. There were no records of siskins nesting in the Smokies, the Park's science coordinator stated. "For me," he said, "the key observation would be the female sitting tight on the nest to indicate she has eggs."

Three days later, I arrived at Clingmans Dome at 8:45 AM to a misty, windy forty-three degrees. The unoccupied siskin nest looked larger and higher than when I last saw it. Rejected nesting material piled loosely on the limb. Had the female scolded her mate for not helping and he overreacted? Ten or more siskins were flying in the area, chattering in song and call.

I pushed through thick brambles of thornless blackberries to stand underneath the curved spruce branch cradling the nest. Straddling fresh bear scat, I determined the nest's GPS coordinates. Overhead, I imagined three adults standing on shoulders above shoulders—like acrobats in a circus—to estimate the aboveground height of the nest at twenty to twenty-five feet.

Within thirty minutes, the nesting pair flew into the red spruce multiple times. The female entered her nest. Rotating and pushing with her breast, she perfected her design. She remained cuddled inside for about ten minutes while her mate perched three feet above her. When she flew to the ground to pull seeds from a dandelion's head, he followed, flew around her, and foraged nearby. At times, other males flew in combat circles with the mated male.

Biologists and others helped monitor the siskins over the ensuing weeks. The incubating female "stuck tight" to the nest, adjusting her position periodically. I caught a glint of her soft eyes when fleeting rays of sunlight spotlighted her coveted spot. Turning south, she rotated out of binocular view. Was she hiding her eyes to conceal her position and protect her vulnerable brood? Or was she just redistributing her life-sustaining heat? Through rain, sleet, and bitter winds, she rode out the weeks in her compact nest tightly bound to her spruce branch, like a rock-a-bye cradle in a treetop.

Soon, the adults became active. The silent nest was growing in size. After the first few days, when the parents ingested the nestlings' waste, a towering fecal rim accumulated around the open-cup nest. Healthy baby siskins were growing. Parents tipped forward with seed in beak to feed hungry mouths safely hidden in their well-constructed home.

On Clingmans Dome that spring, large, majestic black bears foraged in the underbrush while tiny, often unnoticed pine siskins tended to domestic duties. A visiting couple from Ohio noticed, providing a new scientific record for the Smokies. Now, the deserted nest that made history rests in the Great Smoky Mountains National Park museum.

Dining Out

Amy Mattix

It took me a shamefully long time to make the connection between the weightiness of my pack and the fleetness of my feet. New to backpacking at nearly thirty, my excitement bred a naive optimism: as long as I could lift my bag onto my back, there was no reason for me to believe I couldn't go where I asked my legs to take me. Thirty-six miles later, when I had eaten my food and drank my drinks and felt a lightness on my shoulders, I did not recognize that the unloaded pack made for easier walking; I sincerely thought that in four days, I had simply gotten stronger. And the beneficiary of my cluelessness was the wilderness ranger I was in serious smit with.

He had legs that came up to my chest and were each the size of a tree trunk. He telemarked on the snowfield above his yurt; and after a summer of patrolling between sea level and alpine, his thighs grew out of his park-service pants. I was five foot three on my tiptoes; he was a Sasquatch.

Even he did not carry beer into the wilderness.

I know this because those were his words to me when I reached deep into my pack at his yurt, eighteen miles up trail, and pulled out multiple pounders of Cold Smoke to share. It was an unwritten rule that any ranger who called upon the hospitality of those stationed in the wilderness huts had to leave alcohol as an offering. There were two wilderness ranger stations in the sodden rainforest district I worked in—one posh and picturesque, historical log cabin in a clearing of a river valley; and one bare, canvas yurt many miles and a few thousand feet beyond. It was at the latter where, under the shadow of a round, smooth glacier the shape of a buttock, we clinked our aluminum cans and the Sasquatch gave the toast: "I don't even pack in my own beer!"

It was true. The rangers preferred the weight-per-punch ratio of whiskey, which, on a side note, fueled long and introspective entries in the wilderness station logs that I would read later with an almost guilty sense of voyeurism.

But I brought beer.

Olympic National Park, 1955. Hikers resting on Mount Angeles Trail near Hurricane Ridge.

I packed beer because of how crushed the ranger was who, as a treat, packed in two cans and sank them in the cool creek behind the ranger station in a bear box. He'd spent a humid day brushing trail, looking forward to an aperitif, but when he opened the box that afternoon, found instead two dollars. A bear can't use a quarter, but jerk hikers can. I packed beer because of the instant gratification I got from watching the furrowed, brooding, bearded face of my crush light up with smiles. I packed beer because I still didn't know any better.

Soon, my beer offerings turned to vegetables. The wilderness rangers were sitting on a glut of whiskey due to an uptick in weekend visits from the frontcountry staff, and I imagined what I might miss most on a ten-day tour: a damn salad, that's what. So instead of beer, I came to the cabin bearing gifts of zucchini, onions, fresh herbs. There were lemons and sweet potatoes; I brought milk to store in the bear box sunk in the creek; and I carried in Yakima peaches swaddled with newspaper to eat sliced and wrapped in prosciutto with white cheese.

By this time, I started to see the correlation between the weight of my pack and ache in my feet, but I didn't much care because the ranger I kept coming out to see was falling in love with me. So I just padded barefoot in the dew around the cabin after the sun went down to cool my throbbing toes. And I was happy.

The heaviest my pack ever reached was fifty pounds. It was for one week in the fall when the weather was changing, the elk were bugling, and I was newly laid-off with all the time in the world to waste in a log cabin. None of that fifty pounds I carried was due to the essentials I would find four hours ahead: nearly my entire burden was edible. I arrived the night before a three-inch rainstorm, which kept us cheerful prisoners in the cabin while the river nearby swept away established campsites. We had two woodstoves going at opposite ends of the ranger station—one with the dual purpose of baking brownies as well as providing crackling, cozy heat. We played cards and ate salmon sandwiches grilled in the bacon grease left over from breakfast. We toasted our stormy confinement with hot buttered rum.

My growing love of the outdoors could hardly be separated from the love of the food I ate in the wilderness. A fine meal with fine friends only served as an exclamation point to the sublime setting in which we dined; and this did not diminish as I was forced to give up my ridiculous extravagances to wander farther out into the park than what I could explore using a wilderness station as a base camp. When having to carry my own sleeping bag, fuel, and filter, more of my food was dehydrated, more of my drinks were powdered, and each meal was the loveliest meal I had ever eaten. I even switched out the beer cans for a plastic bottle the length of my finger filled at home with whiskey for a campsite toddy. I had succumbed to the economy of liquor.

But it didn't matter when I sat on the rock outcropping on top of the buttock-shaped glacier on which I would spend the night with my Sasquatch, the two of us sipping from a small plastic bottle of whiskey and sharing a cigar, toasting the constellations above the crown of Mount Olympus; and toasting our lives that we were lucky enough to eat, to drink, and to live in such a place as this.

Dinosaurs, Deep Time, and Deeper Lessons

Dan Chure

Dinosaur National Monument is a remarkable place to explore the Earth's past. The monument tells a tale of massive physical, environmental, and biological change over a billion years of Earth history. Whether standing on a 300-million-year-old sea floor dotted with fossil shells or peering into the face of a 100-million-year-old dinosaur skull entombed in rock, these are things one never forgets.

Most remarkable is the great wall of bones within the glass Quarry Exhibit Hall. This sandstone face—140 feet long, 40 feet high, and tilted 60 degrees—contains 1500 dinosaur bones left in place just as they were deposited on an ancient river floor. Working on this ancient dinosaur log-jam, wandering amongst the remains of ten species of dinosaurs, is a stirring experience.

Over the decades, I have accompanied numerous paleontologists studying and photographing bones on the face for their research. Many have hunted dinosaurs in the most remote and difficult places imaginable. Yet at some point, each stops for a moment, looks across the jumble of bones, and says how being on the quarry wall is one of the most remarkable things they have ever done. Then they ask to have their picture taken.

I enjoy sharing my enthusiasm for Dinosaur National Monument with the public as a paleontological intercessor, turning dry scientific publications into living, breathing dinosaurs. In my many years here, I have talked to every conceivable visitor, from elementary school classes to politicians—even the secretary of the interior. However, my most profound moments involve Make-A-Wish children.

As a Make-A-Wish participant, the monument has hosted several families. The children are invariably young, often have very serious health challenges, and sometimes face an uncertain future. It is sobering to be with such a child, watching their excitement as they scratch away at a dinosaur

Dan Chure at Dinosaur National Monument.

bone or visit an excavation site, knowing the difficulties that lie ahead for them. As a parent myself, I cannot imagine the heartbreak of such a situation. So we do all we can to make their visit an exciting one and participate in special activities.

The most memorable visit was when we hosted the McDermott family. Nathan, the son, was the Make-A-Wish child. Nathan dreamed of becoming a paleontologist and spending his life studying dinosaurs, just as I had at his age. He wanted to come to the monument, see our fossils, and help with a dinosaur dig. We were more than happy to host him, but there was one major problem: the Quarry Exhibit Hall had been condemned and closed because of structural instability and the threat of imminent collapse. With the building closed, the bone wall was out of bounds, and our paleontology preparation lab was out of operation. We would, of course, be taking Nathan on a hike to see dinosaur fossils out in the field and would show him some of the spectacular ancient treasures in our museum collections, but we wanted to do more to make the visit all he hoped for. Who would want to disappoint a Make-A-Wish child?

Fortunately, we have a long-term paleo research collaboration with the Museum of Paleontology at Brigham Young University. I called Dr. Brooks Britt there and explained our situation. After a short chat, we put together a plan. The McDermotts first went to the Museum of Paleontology, where Nathan worked in the lab, removing rock from dinosaur bones; and then they came out to the monument, where we took Nathan to wilderness sites and on a museum-collections tour. Finally, the museum crew came to one of our excavations; and Nathan got his wish to dig fossils in the field and used a truck crane to lift large fossils onto a truck bed. The whole family shared this great experience, doing paleontology among the rock slopes and vast skies of rural Utah. Nathan got the chance, if only for a couple of days, to live his dream of being a paleontologist—a little bit of the future he would have had if illness hadn't ultimately snatched it away from him.

One day, I had asked Nathan which was his favorite dinosaur. Without hesitation, he'd yelled out, "*Compsognathus!*"

Compsognathus was a rare, small, meat-eating dinosaur a little bigger than a chicken; and Nathan knew everything about it—how rare it was, how small it was, what it ate, where it lived. He talked about it like a pro. And it was a great choice for a favorite because I happened to have a personal cast of a *Compsognathus* skeleton hanging in my office. I slipped it off its hanger, and we looked at it closely, chatting about this little dinosaur and pointing out details of the skeleton. In Nathan's eyes, I saw that same focused and excited look I see in the eyes of other paleontologists when looking at an important fossil. I was determined that if Nathan couldn't see the wall of bones, he would at least get his favorite dinosaur. So I placed it in his hands and told him "I've had this cast for several years and have enjoyed it; but you are the *Compsognathus* guy, and it should really be yours." The look in his eyes was unforgettable. Later, the family wrote telling us that the *Compsognathus* cast had assumed a place of pride in Nathan's bedroom.

By the nature of our profession, paleontologists continually come face to face with the ephemeral nature of life. This is a constant reminder of our own inevitable, forthcoming personal extinction. I have spent a great deal of my life among forms long dead, puzzling, speaking, and writing about them and the world they lived in. Discovering Dinosaur National Monument and sharing it with others is a remarkable and humbling thing. But the deep time experienced in the rocks and fossils here is also a stark reminder of how fleeting our own time is.

My Memorable Memorial Moment

Cheryl A. Schreier

My brother, who is my only sibling, was visiting from Minnesota; and we attended the Evening Lighting Ceremony on Flag Day, June 14, 2013, at Mount Rushmore National Memorial. My brother is a Vietnam veteran who served as a gunner on a gun truck in 1970–1971 with an army engineering battalion.

At the end of the program, we have active and retired military come down to the amphitheater stage to be recognized for their service during the retiring of the flag. I told my brother that he needed to go down to the stage.

There were about two hundred military people on the stage that evening. They all introduced themselves and stated which branch of the service they served in or had served in. The flag was lowered, then folded; and I stood nearby in my National Park Service uniform, on the left side of the stage near the flagpole.

I was introduced (my brother was not aware that I was going to speak), and I publicly thanked him for his service to our country, presenting him with the flag. It was one of the highlights of his trip and his life to be thanked for his service by his sister, the superintendent of Mount Rushmore National Memorial.

Cheryl A. Schreier at Mount Rushmore.

There were four young men in attendance from an army engineering division who asked my brother if they could have the honor of refolding the flag—and they refolded it perfectly. Later, I gave him a beautiful walnut flag case with a brass plaque engraved with his chosen words, to display the flag and commemorate the ceremony.

A very memorable moment in my life and my career in the National Park Service.

Mount Rushmore National Memorial, 1971. A summer crowd enjoys the Grand View Terrace.

A Close Encounter with Silver Beauty

Linda C. Mazzu

I loved working at Yellowstone National Park. The wildlife observations were astounding. From elk circling my house during rut to gangs of young bison roaming the roads right after spring opening, to the river otters that once shared Boiling River with me—all of these remind us of why we work in national parks, at places like Yellowstone: to constantly challenge our sense of wonder in so many ways. But the one encounter I will never forget was the day I came face to face with the most beautiful wolf I have ever seen.

People follow wildlife in Yellowstone; it's part of the experience to try to get the perfect photo. Sometimes, though, the point where enjoyment reaches harassment comes quickly. It was a situation like this that led me to my encounter.

One day, while in the Tower-Roosevelt area of Yellowstone National Park, my husband and I came upon such a situation. We inadvertently became a part of a hoard of people in their cars following a pack of wolves as it pursued a herd of mule deer—we were caught in a wildlife jam. Admittedly, seeing such a spectacle from afar was amazing; but quickly, I felt we should break away from the mob. We pulled into a parking area and let it all go by us. It felt like the right thing to do.

How fortunate for us, though, that we decided to break away. As we stood in the quiet and watched the line of cars and craziness fade further away, a deer suddenly came bounding toward us in the opposite direction of the rest of the pursuit. I knew in an instant what was likely occurring. I remember thinking to myself, "This deer is being chased—the wolf pack has split."

Not seconds after seeing this deer, a beautiful silver wolf—one we had been watching moments ago from a distance, through a long line of traffic—came heading straight past the parking area. I tried to find my voice to alert my husband, who was on the other side of the parking lot, but words escaped me. My camera hung useless in my hand, by my side. I had no time to think but definitely had time to absorb what was happening.

The wolf came within twenty feet of me in full stride. She passed by me in silence, but not before she turned her head toward me to look at me. (I can say "she" since her identity was confirmed to me later as the most photographed wolf at that time.) We locked eyes momentarily.

When a wild animal exchanges glances with you—when two species acknowledge each other's presence through their eyes—it is something (at least for us humans) that we will never forget. When humans pass on the street, we sometimes lock eyes with strangers and nod, smile, maybe say hello to acknowledge this; these everyday courtesies are typical. How atypical, though, to be acknowledged by a wolf.

And in a flash, she was gone. I was stunned.

Because there was snow in places, we immediately walked to where this great silver beauty had passed. The tracks left behind were huge and unworldly in their size. We took photos, but somehow the context was lost within the greater moment.

When I left my job at Yellowstone, I was given a plaster cast of a wolf track to thank me for my work in protecting the park's resources. To this day, I keep this wolf track in my office as a reminder. It is a reminder of a magical moment that can only come from extended time in a park. It is a reminder of why I have spent my career in the National Park Service. It inspires me to hold the course, and to work to create opportunities for others to build their own moments of transformation and inspiration.

All I know for sure is this: every time I look at that plaster cast, I am transported back to the day when a silver beauty of a wolf looked me in the eyes and burned her image forever in my memory.

A Funny Thing Happened on the Way to the Wagon Tour

Robert Scott Vierick

The Union soldier guided the wheelbarrow down Shenandoah Street, moving the precious cargo toward its destination. Suddenly, it dipped down, the private lost his footing, and the rations he was carrying spilled into the street.

Unfortunately, this wasn't the result of some Confederate trap but my own clumsiness, as I failed to notice the wheelbarrow slipping away from me. I wasn't paying enough attention, and as a result, I hadn't even hit the ground before I was mobbed by visitors—some inquiring as to whether I was alright, others reaching for their cell phones to snap pictures. Luckily, the only thing hurt was my pride; so I picked myself up, dusted myself off, answered a few questions about the Civil War, and headed back to make some more lemonade.

Missteps in nineteenth century clothing in front of hundreds of visitors isn't exactly fun, but if that was the price I had to pay to help make the past come alive, that was fine by me. Besides, I didn't have time to mope about my fall. As a National Park Service intern, I had tours to give and lemonade to deliver.

After refilling the container, I began moving down the road again. As I walked, I mentally rehearsed a new part of the park's horse-and-wagon tour. Such animal-assisted expeditions were a relatively recent addition to Harpers Ferry that allowed visitors to travel through more than two hundred years of history. Two living-history interns were typically assigned to handle the tours each day, and I was on my way back to my fellow intern when I took my trip.

The tours, which focused on the history of Harpers Ferry from the American Indians to the devastating floods of the early twentieth century, offered visitors an idea of the political, social, natural, and economic history of the town—all in the space of a half hour.

That weekend, visitors on our wagon tours were in for a special treat, which was why I needed to learn some new facts for my presentation. While we normally had interpreters working in the paymaster's garden, the addition of a reenactor unit that was visiting for the weekend created yet another potential glimpse into the past. The soldiers' tents, set up along the wagon route, allowed visitors to literally pass through a Civil War campsite. And the reenactors were a committed bunch, as I found out when one of them walked toward me with a sign around his neck that stated "sleeping on duty."

"It's not true," he told me. "I've been framed."

"Well," I said with a grin on my face, "if you have, in fact, been wrongfully accused, I'm sure that your superior officer will make the proper decision and remove your punishment. As for myself, I have rations to deliver."

"What sort of highfalutin talk is that?" he replied as we both tried to stop ourselves from grinning. As I headed on my way, the reenactor began to speak to the smiling crowd about how he was innocent.

I continued to push my wagon back to the camp, the lemonade swishing back and forth in the cooler, and a number of visitors stopped me to ask about a rather strange sight on Maryland Heights. (A faded inscription remains on the mountain, and many visitors are curious as to what it is.) While many guessed it was a monument to John Brown, the old writing is actually a century-old advertisement for toilet powder, an early form of deodorant. When informed of this, some of the visitors laughed, some expressed admiration, while others thought that I was pulling their leg; but the truth was there, carved into the rock. Leaving them to point and laugh at this early billboard, I pushed my cargo toward its destination.

After I delivered the lemonade, I returned to the wagon tours. My final tour that day consisted of a family with two kids, and an older couple. We started the tour and moved to the point—the place where the Shenandoah and Potomac rivers meet. As I talked about Thomas Jefferson coming to the area, I could see the one kid's eyes light up. As we talked about slavery and John Brown's raid, he leaned in closer to hear every word. Passing through the Civil War campsite, he moved around as he tried to take in every single tent and soldier. By the time we returned to the drop-off point, I was absolutely certain that he had become hooked on history.

At the end of each tour, I talked about how each visitor contributes to the town of Harpers Ferry and adds to its history; and by supporting the National Park Service, they are preserving it for years to come. As the family stepped off the wagon, the little sister, who might have dozed off a little during the ride, asked her brother what she had missed, and he jumped into an explanation. At a time when too many kids think history is just a set of events in a dusty old textbook, to see the two of them get excited about the past is enough to bring a smile to any ranger's face.

At Harpers Ferry, some visitors will be most interested in a conversation between two soldiers, others will laugh and take pictures of a rock billboard, and others will want to get as much history as they can while being pulled by two horses—we have all kinds of visitors. What is important is that when they leave, they have a greater appreciation for the past and for the mission of the National Park Service. And that's why I always finished each day of work with a big smile across my face. Despite the occasional spilled lemonade, the privilege of seeing people fall in love with history is something that I wouldn't trade for anything in the world.

A Little Ranger Romance

Rick Jones

In the 1970s, being a seasonal employee in the National Park Service was an effective way to eventually gain the coveted permanent-employee status. Competition was fierce for almost every position; and the more experience and qualifications you accumulated, the better your chance of becoming a permanent park ranger.

At the time, this was not a bad option for many of us who were fresh out of college and had pinned our employment hopes on the National Park Service. Seasonal work was fun and exciting, especially if you had the travel bug. You could migrate every six months or so to another area of the country, and increase your skills and pertinent contacts as you went. These trips between seasons were a coveted time to explore new places and parks.

One of my most intense memories of my seasonal migration was a night of camping above Bishop, California, on the east side of the Sierra. I set up my tent in a campground surrounded by towering granite spires and cliffs, and practiced rock-climbing moves on one of the erratic boulders that had plunged down from the cliffs above. Finally, I perched on a freezing-cold picnic table as I cooked up some ramen on my MSR stove and watched the pinkish-orange alpenglow crawl up the rock faces as night descended.

I was heading to Lava Beds National Monument for my second season there, working at Saguaro National Park in the summer and Lava Beds in the winter. It was a perfect seasonal rotation in my estimation. Although I was employed as an interpretive ranger, this was the era of the generalist ranger; and I had the opportunity to also fight fires, assist with search and rescue, and do other cool ranger stuff.

I worked at Lava Beds for a number of years, experiencing more adventures in my time between seasons, and eventually, went through the seasonal law-enforcement training academy at Santa Rosa, California. At that point, I began to get serious about looking for that permanent ranger position, as

I had seven seasons under my belt and felt that I would compete well with all those scrambling for these positions.

In the early 1980s, shortly after I had started yet another season at Lava Beds National Monument, my new supervisor grabbed me and asked if I had put in applications for the next season. This was very early in the year for him to be asking that question, so with trepidation, I asked why.

He hesitated and said, "You know, Rick, you're a great employee; and if you had permanent status, I would willingly hire you into the permanent position that I just created using 'your' job. But because you don't have status, I've already hired an extremely qualified woman from Jefferson National Expansion Memorial in Saint Louis to fill your position." Blindsided by bureaucracy, I would have to devise a new plan of attack.

One option for gaining this coveted status was to enter federal service through another agency and/or position and then hopefully move back into a permanent National Park Service position. This was problematic at best; but if you had some experienced help in your corner, it could happen.

Meanwhile, the new ranger arrived. She was a tall, slim redhead whom I unexpectedly met in the parking lot just when she pulled in. Things were looking up, as I was the only other single person for thirty-five miles in any direction. Of course, I was actively looking for other jobs at this time and didn't necessarily expect to be around much longer.

The employee housing apartments at Lava Beds were designed with adjoining doors in the bedrooms so that any two apartments could be two one-bedroom apartments, or an efficiency apartment next to a two-bedroom apartment. Unforeseen circumstances (I blame the superintendent) placed the new ranger in the one-bedroom next to my one-bedroom, and gave us adjoining doors—locked, of course.

Meanwhile, the monument's administrative officer (AO), who was a friend, told me that, serendipitously, her clerk was going to step out of her position to have a child, which created an option for me to move into a clerk/typist position there, if everything worked just perfectly. So, I traveled to Sacramento to take the clerk/typist test, achieved an adequate score to be hired with direct-hire authority, and—*boom!*—I'm a part-time GS-2 clerk/typist with status in the federal government!

Unanticipated by either of us singles, my redheaded neighbor and I became "involved" within two weeks of her arrival (maybe the adjoining doors helped), bolstered by our joint affection for the parks and each other, along with me being able to remain there due to my new position.

We have now been together for almost thirty-three wonderful years and married for over thirty. Both of us have had challenging and successful careers with the National Park Service; although sometimes, it was tricky being a dual-career couple. I retired a couple years back, after thirty-four years with the National Park Service (and a couple other land-management agencies). She continues to pursue the ranger craft in management, as the superintendent of a large western park. Meanwhile, I still volunteer on occasion for this park or other parks (old habits die hard).

Our love and admiration for America's parks and their protectors remains strong as ever. Trips to the wild still make us smile.

The Lesson of the Flower and the Fish

Daniel R. Tardona

As a park ranger for twenty-seven years and counting, I have had the good fortune of gaining wisdom about our natural and cultural resources. What may seem surprising is how much of this wisdom is gained from interactions with very young visitors about the meanings and values associated with those resources. The children's questions are usually in simple form, requiring profound thought in order to provide an adequate response. It is one of those times that I will now share.

On a beautiful spring afternoon early in my career, while on a roving assignment along Little River in Great Smoky Mountains National Park, I came upon a youngster, approximately nine years old, who was walking with his mom and admiring the plethora of wildflowers. It was April—

Daniel R. Tardona in Great Smoky Mountains National Park.

the height of wildflower season—in the park that is a world-renowned preserve of wildflower diversity and is sometimes referred to as Wildflower National Park. I observed the boy admiring a small patch of yellow trilliums.

As I made my way over to talk to the boy and his mom, he bent down and gently plucked one of the flowers at its base. It was not a careless act, as he was tender with the flower, obviously admiring its beauty. His mom, however, noticed me; and I could see the horror on her face as I drew near. Seeing the opportunity to provide some great interpretation (in a meaningful but gentle way) on the importance of not picking flowers in the park, I approached.

The boy was very respectful and responsive to my explanation and interpretation; and his mother was obviously relieved at how I handled the situation. She was apologetic and thankful for my sensitive explanation to her son. Feeling quite proud of myself for another job well done, I started to continue on my way.

Suddenly, I felt a little tug on my daypack and a determined voice: "Mr. Ranger, sir."

I turned, knelt down to face him, and said, "What can I do for you, young man?"

The boy told me that he had been watching a man fish in the river. He went on to explain that the man had caught a fish and placed it in his bag, looking like he was going to keep the fish. Without thinking through my answer thoroughly, I said that it was okay "because the man has a license to fish in the park."

The young boy pursed his lips and thoughtfully asked, "Can I get a license to pick flowers?"

At this point, I noticed a concerned look on Mom's face, but I also sensed that she was thinking, "How is this ranger going to handle this one?"

I went on to explain that the rules for fishing and flower picking in the park were different. Of course, this serious youngster then asked why the rules were different, and my mind raced to try to respond to this apparent contradiction of my previous explanation.

"Well," I said, "fishing is considered to be a traditional use by people in the mountains. One of the things we try to preserve and protect are stories about people of the past and how they lived. We call such stories 'cultural resources.'"

I should have quit at this point, but I made the error of adding, "Besides, we only allow people to catch fish that don't belong here. We call them 'exotic,' or 'alien,' fish."

When he asked why the fish don't belong here, I explained that the National Park Service is trying to protect brook trout, the native fish. I told him, "You can't catch brook trout but you can catch the rainbow trout, because they did not originally live here."

"How did the rainbow trout get here?" was his next question, and I suddenly felt I was digging myself into a bigger and deeper hole.

"Since fishing had been an important way for the mountain people to find food in the old days, the National Park Service thought it would be nice to bring fish so that people could keep up the tradition; but this turned out to be a big mistake." I went on to explain all the reasons as best I could.

The boy drew a deep breath, and then let out in a sigh.

"I see; but the mountain people liked flowers too, didn't they? Another ranger told us that some mountain people would pick flowers to make themselves and their cabin smell pretty."

"Yes, I suppose so." I answered and attempted to explain to this bright young boy that sometimes it is difficult to balance how we preserve and use resources we value—in a nutshell, the National Park Service mission.

The boy eventually appeared satisfied, but I could tell he was still thinking after his mom finally said they had to go. While I was then off the hook, I puzzled over my encounter. It was the first time in my career that I realized preserving and protecting natural and cultural resources was even more challenging than I thought. The experience this young boy bestowed gave me the opportunity to reevaluate my understanding of managing and interpreting park resources.

As an interpreter, my job is to provide opportunities for visitors to make their own emotional and intellectual connections, finding personal meaning and value in our resources. Often in my career, however, it is the visitors who have provided me with the same opportunities in the course of my daily work. It is top among many reasons why being a National Park Service ranger has been the joy of my life—even though it's sometimes downright challenging!

"The Stars, Man, the Stars!"

Don Falvey

In 1991, shortly after I came to Zion National Park to be its superintendent, Larry Van Slyke, the park's chief ranger, came to my office to relate an incident that had occurred the previous weekend and illustrates the best of what national parks should be.

He had encountered three Hispanic youths who were camping along the Virgin River in an out-of-bounds area in Zion Canyon. As he approached, they were pointing up in the sky; and with great excitement, they said, "The stars, man, the stars!"

Coming from the inner-city area of Los Angeles, they had never seen the majesty of the night sky and were awestruck by its beauty.

Larry used the opportunity to chat with them and get them relocated to an approved camping site, but no citation was issued. What they did receive was a welcome to the national parks, an appreciation for this park and its resources, and a good feeling about an encounter with a park ranger that they'll never forget.

"Because I wanted to come in contact with a larger Great Nature . . . I came to America."

—CHIURA OBATA, PAINTER, 1965

3

People to Remember

Yosemite National Park, 1970.
Ranger naturalist Carl Sharsmith shows
how to make a monkey flower move by
tickling it with a pine needle.

Finding Hikoji
Illuminating History through His Story

Alisa Lynch

In 1942, the US government forced more than 110,000 Japanese Americans—two-thirds of them US citizens—from their homes into ten camps, including Manzanar in California. Today, Manzanar National Historic Site's main theme is "One camp, ten thousand lives; one camp, ten thousand stories."

Here is one of those stories.

Two young men were shot and killed during the Manzanar Riot in December 1942—I'd read about it. But Archie Miyatake told me the story of another young man who was shot months earlier and lived. I wondered what became of him. Archie wasn't sure.

Like Archie, Sue Kunitomi Embrey was confined in Manzanar. She spent the last decades of her life fighting to get the site preserved, and she also heard the story of the young man.

"My brother saw him in Japan," she said. An American soldier in the Military Intelligence Service, her brother was riding in an army truck in occupied Japan one day when a voice called out, "Hey, Kimbo!" No one in Japan knew that nickname. It was 1946, and it was the voice of the man who had been shot in Manzanar.

In August 2002, I was heading to lunch with Archie and Sue after an exhibit-planning meeting in Little Tokyo in Los Angeles. As we entered the restaurant, an older man was coming out. Sue and I headed to our table; Archie stopped and talked to him.

The waitress had brought the menus and tea by the time Archie joined us. "Hey, Sue," he said, "that was Hiko."

"Hiko?" she looked surprised.

"That's *him*," she told me. "You better go after him!"

"Huh?"

"That's the one who was shot!"

I was stunned.

"You better go," she insisted.

At Manzanar, we approach people slowly and respectfully. We don't chase them down the street. Then again, here was a man who had an experience few live to talk about. The waitress looked puzzled as Archie and I hurried out.

The man was already half a block away.

"Hiko!" Archie called out. The man turned around. When we caught up, Archie said, "This is Alisa. She's from Manzanar."

I saw Hikoji's surprise.

"Oh," he said.

"I would love to talk to you someday," I blurted out.

"Oh."

"I'll still be here Monday!" I offered.

Hikoji later said, "Archie told me about you. I said, 'No, no, no, Archie, no, no.' He said, 'No, she's okay.'"

Archie's endorsement worked. By Monday, I was sitting in Hikoji's dining room with a tape recorder. He told me about his life: how his parents had immigrated from Hiroshima, Japan, and opened a sushi restaurant in Los Angeles. How, standing at his father's deathbed in 1939, Hikoji promised to take care of his mother and kid sister.

He was keeping that promise on May 16, 1942, a week after he'd been forcibly confined in Manzanar. He wanted to build a table and chairs for his mother, and there was a pile of scrap wood nearby. An MP gave him permission to go to the pile. After picking up the wood, Hikoji turned back to the MP: "All of a sudden, I see this guy here lowering his rif—his rifle and aiming at me. And I thought, 'What the hell is he doin'?' you know—and that's when I heard it go off . . . and I found myself picking myself up. Oh, as soon as I heard the gun—gun go off—I felt things going through my body—like [a] hot iron rod running through me, you know, and when I started picking myself up . . . that's when I realized 'My God,' I was—I was full of blood. I thought 'My God, I've been shot!'"

Alisa Lynch at Manzanar National Historic Site.

Six decades later, as Hikoji struggled to find the words, I found my own eyes burning and my throat tightening. I asked if he ever thought about the MP. He said, "I feel sorry for the guy. He had to live with what he did—as long as he lived . . . "

I later read that the MP bragged in local bars that he'd "shot himself a Jap."

After talking for nearly five hours, Hikoji said, "Thank you for giving me the opportunity to talk about it and uh—it felt good, getting it out— the whole load off my chest. A lot of these things here I never even spoke [about] to my kids." He pointed to his heart. "I kept it in here—'cause a lot of things that had happened I—I did not like, but now it's gone . . . "

Two months later, Hikoji was at a soundstage in Burbank, recording his memories for our introductory film *Remembering Manzanar*. He recalled his first night in Manzanar, seeing stars through the unfinished barracks roof. "I thought, my God, it's so beautiful. That is the sky, the first night sky that I experienced . . . . No matter how bad things get, you know, there are good things happening too. The beauty of nature—that's one thing that no one can take away."

On April 24, 2004, Hikoji returned to Manzanar for the first time since 1944. His daughter cried when she saw his photo in the exhibit. She'd never seen him as a young man because his family lost everything—including photos—when they were forced into Manzanar. Hikoji signed the grand opening guest book at the bottom of page four—ironically, next to a man who had been another MP at Manzanar. I'm sure neither man had any idea as they stood in line to sign. Hikoji gave me a card that day in which he wrote, "The beautiful cranes are flying overhead on this auspicious day. Let's hope they're here to stay."

Hikoji Jack Takeuchi passed away on February 17, 2014, but I still hear his voice in our film and see his youthful face in our exhibits. I think of him often, especially when I see the stars and think to myself "My God, it's so beautiful."

A Message in a Bottle

Jenna B. Sammartino

On Cape Cod, the month of April is a fickle beast. On this particular day, the weather was racing out of the north, a raw wind was blowing the rain nearly horizontal, and the sky and sea blended seamlessly along a steel-gray horizon.

So I suppose I wasn't terribly surprised that no one showed up for my beach hike program, but I was a little disappointed. After all, it was the perfect day for a walk on the beach; my group would have had Mother Nature on hand to help form some great connections about the constantly changing character of our shoreline.

I decided to take advantage of the fine weather and struck out north along Nauset Light Beach. The beaches here are never the same place twice, and I was sure I'd find something to make my soaked boots worth the while.

I soon came across a plastic water bottle partially buried in the sand, rockweed and finger sponge strewn about it. Trash collection being a reflexive habit with any park ranger, I kicked the bottle free, noticing that it seemed to have some sort of paper inside. As I knelt to pick up the crumpled bottle, I realized that, along with a goodly amount of sand and pebbles, it did indeed contain a piece of green paper carefully wrapped in a Ziploc bag. My heart raced . . . I'd found a genuine message in a bottle!

And just in case I had any doubts, scrawled on the outside of the green construction paper in white crayon were the words "Message In A Bottle." The letter itself, neatly printed with red and blue crayon, was brief and to the point:

> *4-8-05*
> *If you find this message, contact me.*
> *—Tyler*
> *Sent from Nauset Light Beach, Cape Cod, MA*

I was thrilled—you'd think I'd found a gold doubloon from some ancient treasure wreck! (My colleagues back at the visitor center obliged me by acting like they were excited too.) The fact that I'd found the bottle on the same beach from which it had been thrown into the waves only a few short days earlier mattered nothing to me. I was a girl who'd grown up in the Colorado mountains only to fall in love with the ocean; and messages in bottles were the stuff of Robinson Crusoe and Treasure Island.

Thus began my continuing relationship with then nine-year-old Tyler. I did wait about a month before writing him back; I didn't want to totally take the wind out of his sails by telling him his letter was found so soon after its voyage had begun. And I used the fact that the bottle had traveled a total distance of, oh, say, twenty yards, as an example of how the ocean works.

"Sometimes things will get caught up in currents," I wrote, "and carried all over the world." I told him how I'd learned in school about a ship's container of Nike shoes that got dumped overboard and how those shoes ended up in countries all over the Pacific. But I also told him that sometimes the

Jenna B. Sammartino at Cape Cod National Seashore.

ocean puts things right back where it found them. "This is important too," I continued, "because this is how a lot of our sand gets put back onto the beach every summer after big winter waves eat the sand away."

I may not have had any takers for my beach walk that wild April day in 2005, but lasting connections were made with a visitor nonetheless.

A decade has passed since our initial correspondence, and Tyler and his parents have continued to stop in to say hello when they visit Cape Cod National Seashore. It means more than I can say that they do this. Several years back, they told me that Tyler had given the message in a bottle another try. That time, he asked a surfer to carry his bottle out past the breaking waves before throwing it in. He'd probably given the surfer a lesson in coastal processes before he paddled out! These days, Tyler's taller than I am; and on their visits, we occasionally discuss the constantly changing coastline in the park. After all this time, Tyler has the long view now too.

At its essence, interpretation is not really about information—it's about inspiration. In a place as dynamic as Cape Cod, there are endless opportunities to connect both intellectually and emotionally. And like the Cape's shifting sands, inspiration can go both ways. Whatever intellectual connections I may have precipitated for Tyler, he's more than returned the favor, providing an emotional connection to my work that has stayed with me to this day.

"Wherever a National Park is we find the most delightful sort of education . . . a wholly painless experience of such inspiration and spiritual renewal."

—GENEVIEVE GILLETTE, FOUNDER, MICHIGAN PARKS ASSOCIATION, 1962

Turning the Tables at Grand Teton National Park

Doug Crispin

One of the best parts of living and working in a national park is being surrounded and inspired by the outstanding park resources. Lately, I have encountered special park visitors who have changed this notion—the park *visitors* have inspired me!

I was leading a nature hike one day. Toward the end, I always pause at a stop where the view of the mountains is breathtaking. Here, I remind visitors about the importance of national parks and how they inspire us.

We all lead busy lives. We have daily woes and concerns: housing, transportation, education, work, family, and other demands. And what about health and health care? I tell visitors that at some point, cancer will touch our lives. We will all know someone who is facing this insidious disease. Especially at times like these, we need the refreshing and healing spirit of our national parks—to help us get through life's problems and challenges.

I end each hike with a John Muir quote. A visit to the mountains of Wyoming (Yellowstone) in 1885 inspired Muir to write: "Climb the mountains and get their good tidings. Nature's peace will flow into you as sunshine flows into trees. The winds will blow their own freshness into you and the storms their energy, while cares will drop away like autumn leaves."

I ended the guided hike and was walking back to the visitor center when a visitor caught up to me. He said, "Ranger Doug, I really appreciated what you had to say about inspirational views at our last stop. You see, I have been diagnosed with cancer. In fact, I should be in the hospital right now. But I told my doctor I am delaying my surgery and treatment; I decided to visit Grand Teton National Park first. I need to get my head on straight before facing what I know will be pretty tough times for me. Thank you for your inspirational words and for sharing that great John Muir quote."

He asked me to write down the quote for him, which I did—he wanted to hang it above his hospital bed. He thought the memories of Grand Teton National Park and John Muir would help him through his ordeal.

Wow, what a story. I thanked him for inspiring me.

He wasn't the only park visitor who taught me to keep an open mind.

Last summer, an elderly man walked feebly into the visitor center, asking about hiking trails. I directed him to our easiest hike, a simple one-mile loop trail. As he left for his hike, I wondered to myself, "This poor guy, I hope he makes it without collapsing or getting injured."

Later that day, the same gentleman approached me about joining my three-mile guided nature hike. I thought back to the previous summer when my coworker performed CPR on a seventy-two-year-old man who was on her guided nature hike. He collapsed and died right there. I politely tried to dissuade the older gentleman, telling him the hike was a full three hours long, traveled over rough terrain, and had no water or bathrooms available. The gentleman joined us anyhow.

He struggled with the hike. Soon, he lagged behind the group. Luckily for him, I planned eighteen stops along the way, where I talked about the park resources.

At each stop, the older man would catch up to the group, then continue on nonstop to get a head start on the rest of us. This continued through the entire hike. Even though he never stopped to hear what I had to say, he was able to complete the entire hike. I was impressed, especially after his wife told me he was ninety years old! I learned not to prejudge folks based on appearances.

On another guided hike, a fellow was struggling with what appeared to be an artificial leg under his pants. I told his wife how impressed I was he could complete the three-mile trek. She said, "Actually, my husband is a paraplegic—he has two artificial legs. And he is seventy-three!"

On another hike, I watched as a blind man guided his fingers over bear-claw scratch marks scarring a tree. "How high do the scratch marks go?" he asked as he stretched his six-foot-long guide pole up along the tree trunk.

"About twice that high," I responded. That day I learned a new way to communicate about park resources.

Inside the visitor center, I reviewed the junior ranger worksheets of two brothers from California. They waited patiently for my reply.

"You boys pass," I announced. "Time to take the Grand Teton junior ranger pledge."

I grabbed my park ranger hat and stepped into the lobby next to them. Mom and Dad beamed with pride as the family camera flashed. I presented each boy with his official Grand Teton National Park Junior Ranger badge. This was junior-ranger badge 169 for this dedicated pair. I shared their pride.

An eighty-year-old woman from Canada came up to me in the visitor center. She wanted my signature. She was on a quest to visit each of the fifty-nine US National Parks in one calendar year. She claims it has never been done before.

Beaming with my own National Park Service pride, I pulled out my pen and signed her Grand Teton National Park stamp. Grand Teton was park number thirty-two on her journey. I wish I could visit all fifty-nine national parks.

We hear a lot about how our national parks inspire us—and I agree, they definitely do. But lately, the tables have turned. I have met some truly exceptional park visitors who have inspired *me*!

Doug Crispin at Grand Teton National Park.

I Still See Her

Chris "Tarbrush" Jannini

It is her first day as a fourteen-year-old volunteer. We are forty-five feet up in the rig of *Balclutha*, a three-hundred-foot merchant sailing ship from 1886, and this tiny girl is telling me that she is a dressage queen and will ride in the Olympics someday. She seems so sure of herself that I don't dare doubt her.

Over the next few weeks, Ali Immel quickly learns some basic traditional sail-seaming techniques; and a few months later, I watch her take a canvas ditty-bag project out of a startled Luc Maheu's hands (another teenage volunteer), proclaiming: "Let me show you how to sew that." One year later, she and Luc bring me their latest assignment. It is an absolutely perfect, totally handmade canvas sail for one of our small sailing craft. It brings tears to my eyes.

Today, when I pop in to the San Francisco Maritime National Historical Park Visitor Center, I can't help but see her sitting on her sailmakers' bench, carefully weaving the intricate beckets (rope handles) for the sailors' sea chest we have displayed there.

While walking down Hyde Street Pier, I gaze up to the very top of the mainmast on *Balclutha* and there is Ali, on holiday from Mills College, age twenty, securing the Christmas tree that she insisted that we had to have. When I turn around and look down at the small boat docks, there is the little *Merry Bear* with the miniature one-eighth-inch wire splices that Ali made for the mast rigging last summer. And when I look up at *Balclutha* again, there is the giant splice in 1⅜" wire that she finished just a few weeks ago. I showed her how to splice wire when she was sixteen and these are done to her usual standard. I never tell her that they are as good, actually better, as any I have done.

In *Balclutha*'s shelter deck I see Ali again, now twenty-five years old, in her wedding dress, dancing with her new husband, Luc, who's looking very handsome in his Merchant Marine officers' uniform. Happy as she is, she can't wait to change into more comfortable clothes and escape for a honeymoon sail on their beautiful schooner *Tiger*, which they are rerigging in a traditional style with the skills that she and Luc learned here as volunteers.

And now, at twenty-six, Ali (Immel) Maheu, Phi Beta Kappa, *summa cum laude*, the girl who can be anything she wants to be, is standing in front of me absolutely covered in sticky Stockholm tar and grinning from ear to ear, because she is working as a historic ship rigger at San Francisco Maritime National Historical Park—her dream job.

Ali Maheu is not at work today because she and Luc were in a pedestrian accident that took her from us last Christmas.

I see her meticulous craftsmanship in canvas, wire, wood, and even varnish on every vessel in our fleet. You may not see Ali here at the park every day as I do, but you will see her handiwork here for many, many years to come.

"I know that the strength of our park . . . lies in the people who protect and serve them: these men and women are truly special. They are devoted to the past, vigilant in the present, and optimistic for the future."

—FRAN P. MAINELLA, SIXTEENTH DIRECTOR OF
THE NATIONAL PARK SERVICE, 2003

The Lure of Yosemite

Don Neubacher

I still clearly remember the day my father drove our family to Yosemite Valley for the first time; the towering trees and lush meadows, the crystal-clear blue sky, the scent of the cedars and pine are all images permanently secured in my mind. And of course, seeing for the first time the majestic Half Dome, El Capitan, and Bridalveil Fall are lasting, embedded memories. It was spring; and the waterfalls in Tamarack and Cascade Creeks were going full roar, the water flowing like cascading columns of beauty. Some of the details are lost, but the awe-inspiring nature of the images remain.

During my childhood, our family frequently camped in Yosemite Valley. We hiked the trails, plunged into the icy Merced, and gathered to watch the now historic "firefall" from Glacier Point. One of my earliest Yosemite memories is of being held by my mother in Stoneman Meadow as a bear passed too close. These types of experiences have become the fabric of my life, and I am forever privileged to have had so much time in such an incredible place. From those early days in Yosemite, I dreamed of one day working there.

There are countless stories about how this sacred place, with its sacramental waterfalls and cathedral walls, has changed and transformed individuals. The reverence of the place forces one to reflect, focus on hope, and find good in the world.

The most memorable story I want to share about Yosemite is from the day we swore in eight-year-old Honorary Ranger Gabriel Lavan-Ying from Florida. Gabriel had a dream of becoming a National Park ranger, and loved the outdoors, adventure, and national parks. On a June 2014 day in Yosemite, with the help of the Make-A-Wish Foundation and over one hundred park staff and partners, his dream came true. As a long-time employee working in many spectacular parks, this event was one of the finest days of my thirty-two-year career—an incredibly proud moment for the National Park Service and Yosemite National Park.

Ranger Gabriel suffers from a life-threatening connective tissue disorder called Ehlers-Danlos syndrome, which results in chronic inflammation, loose joints, and skin that breaks open at the gentlest bumping. His body is often marked with black-and-blue hematomas; and someday, it is likely he will have to undergo major heart surgery.

As superintendent, I really wanted to make the day very special. Everyone—including education and interpretation personnel, law enforcement and fire, and other park staff—kept telling me the day was going to be spectacular. And, simply put, it was.

The ranger training activities included Gabriel racing to a small grass fire in a meadow with sirens and lights flashing. He was one of the ranger team, in full firefighting gear, that suppressed the fire with water from one of the park's wildfire engines. (By the way, no one had told me we were going to light a real fire!) The day continued with Ranger Gabriel rescuing an injured climber who needed to be safely placed on a litter and loaded in a park ambulance, and then into the park's emergency helicopter. He also did nature walks and got to meet the various talented staff at Yosemite in all disciplines.

The highlight of the day was the formal ceremony in front of the visitor center, before a crowd of nearly two thousand, to make Gabriel an honorary park ranger. More rangers were dressed in parade-formal uniforms than I had ever seen in Yosemite. They proudly marched in at the north edge of the stage to create a scene of green and gray. In the distance came Gabriel and family in a formal procession down the main path toward the podium, with towering Yosemite Falls in the foreground. A procession full of ranger vehicles (with emergency lights flashing and sirens going) and an honor horse patrol (in full regalia, carrying our sacred flags) led the ranger parade. To top it off, there was a cadre of joyful supporters cheering Gabriel on. The local schools adorned the area with large signs honoring his day.

To make it official, our local judge, Michael Seng, with his court gavel and in his official robe, performed the swearing in before an adoring and

Don Neubacher and honorary ranger Gabriel Lavan-Ying in Yosemite National Park.

cheering crowd. I had the honor of presenting Gabriel with an official ranger badge; and welcomed him to an elite group of wonderful, caring individuals who are dedicated to preserving sacred places for the American public. He wore a uniform that one of the staff had lovingly altered to fit him, and we found a full-brimmed ranger hat (with some stuffing inside the hatband to make it fit snugly on his little head). Yosemite had a new ranger that day—one that will never be forgotten.

As you might expect, the day was full of cheers, joy, hope, and countless tears and weepy eyes. The National Park Service staff amazed me, offering such love and caring for someone they had never met before—someone who needed a magical place for a day full of joy.

Sometimes these special moments are the ones that really matter. Moments that last forever.

Cattail Man

Jari Thymian

Seven hundred years ago, the inhabitants of the Gila Cliff Dwellings lived very close to nature. Many plants still growing in Cliff Dweller Canyon and nearby were used for food, medicines, and dyes. Some, like yucca, were used for many things: food; medicine; soap; and fibers for baskets, paintbrushes, mats, cords, and sandals. Daily life was tightly woven with nature through every season of life.

I can't think of anything from nature to which I've been that deeply connected. The chances I will live that closely with nature in my lifetime are slim. By comparison, I'm reminded daily in the cliff-dwelling village of how my footprint on the Earth is very different.

One day, while working at the trailhead to the cliff dwellings, a visitor caught my attention. He looked like he followed Henry David Thoreau's "beware of all enterprises that require new clothes . . . ." It was refreshing to see someone who doesn't get his wardrobe from Walmart, Kohl's, or Target. His shirt and pants looked like they were entirely hand-stitched. My eyes felt a new awareness, like when I have traveled to a foreign country for the first time.

I won't reveal the man's identity or where he lives, but you could choose a name similar to his from this list of elements: earth, wind, fire, or water.

"I like your hat," I said. It had a wide brim and looked very lightweight. "Did you weave it?"

"Yes, I did." He smiled, so I asked another question.

"What is it made of?"

"Cattails."

I've not seen many cattails in New Mexico or Arizona (except those planted by landscapers in a high-end part of Tucson), so I was surprised. I hadn't thought cattail leaves could be used for anything except hide-and-seek and playing with the dry heads when the seeds burst into the autumn wind (reflections from my childhood near the swamps and lakes of Minnesota).

Turns out, I was blinded by my own past experiences. I thought the Midwest had the majority of cattails because of all the lakes. I was even more surprised when he told me his house has a thatched roof made of cattail leaves from the Southwest.

"How often do you need to replace it?" I asked.

"I've had the same roof for five years. Snow and rain slide right off."

I admired his lifestyle. "It's great you live off the grid."

"It's not about being off the grid," he disagreed with me bluntly, and with very clear and direct eye contact. There was a pause. "It's about being close to nature."

In the next pause, when I stopped to realize the difference, I had one of those pleasurable moments of epiphany that seem to come with little lightning bolts. I had the impression he'd never been entangled in the wires and cords of the grid. He wasn't fighting against the grid so much as voting for nature. The same type of comparison as "against war" versus "for peace."

Meeting Cattail Man (not his real name either) is one of the many benefits of volunteering here at Gila Cliff Dwellings National Monument—a shift in perception a day. And I received a vivid reconnection to nature through a window into a park visitor's life choices that I hope will shape my lifestyle in the future.

"My Grandfather Worked on the Railroad . . . "

Patrick McKnight

Steamtown National Historic Site was created on October 30, 1986. Its enabling legislation stated the goal of furthering "public understanding and appreciation of the development of steam locomotives in the region." The park's mission was further defined in a Comprehensive Management Plan in March of 1988, and four major interpretive themes were outlined in the Railroad Yard Design Program/Interpretive Concept (August 1989), with the last one being, "people who worked for or whose lives were influenced by the railroads and the values they represented."

It is this last point that leads to this story. Not only did the National Park Service get a railroad yard and rolling stock, we also acquired paper documentation from the railroads that operated in the area—many from the old DL&W (Delaware, Lackawanna, and Western Railroad) passenger station that is now serving as the Radisson Lackawanna Station Hotel.

I was brought in as the park's historian and archives manager around the year 2000. What I found onsite were nearly a thousand boxes of railroad records with little organization. They had been reboxed according to a very rudimentary filing system developed a few years earlier, but the system was pretty much useless for specific searches. I also found, as the park historian, that when questions were forwarded to me, the most common one was, "My grandfather worked on the railroad; can you tell me anything about him?" I like to compare this question to the most-asked question of front-line rangers: "Where is the bathroom?" My problem was that while most front-line rangers had the answer, I did not.

The park's archives did have personnel files, accident reports, and other people-related documents mixed in with the thousand-box archival collection. One person researching his grandfather asked to look through these boxes for more information. It became immediately apparent that the papers were a hodgepodge and needed organizing to ever be useful. I apologized and bemoaned the fact we did not have the staffing to get this collection properly organized. The researcher then volunteered to help organize these files, and the work began.

Ultimately, ten thousand files were identified and processed relating to people that worked for the DL&W and Erie Railroads. They were entered into the archival management program, and the information disseminated to a number of railroad-related websites. One of these websites even posted the employee ID pictures with some of the basic information. It was this website that Ginny Dudko stumbled across one night in April of 2005 when she did a search on her grandfather's name. She also found a young picture of her grandfather, Matthew H. Vollmer.

Ms. Dudko immediately contacted Steamtown and a copy of the folder was sent to her. Upon receipt of the package, she sent this heartfelt response:

Dear Pat,

Thank you, thank you, thank you a thousand times over for sending the vast folder on my grandfather, Matthew H. Vollmer. His picture that was available on the website traveled to members of the family from Maine to Florida and from New York to Alaska. Others are now eagerly awaiting copies of the folder, which we have promised to send them (my brother works in an office where he can get the copying done).

I enjoyed looking through all of the information, but most precious to me were copies of handwritten notes from my grandfather to his employers during the period that he was out on sick leave. As with most families of that era, the women did [the] writing, signed birthday cards, etc. I don't think I ever saw anything my grandfather wrote until the folder arrived today. To sit here and say, "These are my grandfather's words, written by his hand sixty years ago,"—you can't imagine what a gift this is to me.

We lived right next door to my grandparents when I was growing up, and I was always his "right-hand gal." I was the tomboy of the family so would get up at 6:00 am to help him milk his few Jersey cows (by hand) that were his retirement project. I would row the boat on the lake for him to fish—and later fished with him. And I was the one who helped him with cutting wood for the winter. We all got pressed into service at haying time—and not with the modern equipment of today!

He was such a special part of my life. You have opened a door for me on a part of his life that he never talked much about. Once he retired on disability (a year before I was born), he went on with retirement and never talked to me about the railroad—other than an occasional "I was in charge of building that bridge" as we would drive along the Delaware River that the railroad ran along.

My husband, on the other hand, is enjoying the folder from a whole different perspective. My husband was a promoted engineer when we married, and worked both west from the Port Jervis hub and east and west from Scranton. When Conrail took over, he was no longer able to hold a job locally (and we were not willing to move to Elizabeth, New Jersey). He has always loved the railroad, though, so is thrilled to look over all the information.

Grandpa died in the '70s and Grandma in the '90s. She was the glue that held the family together. Finding that picture has rekindled an interest in the family to get together. It seems we may have a family reunion project brewing—and it started with the picture of Grandpa on the computer.

Bless you for your work.
Sincerely,
Ginny Dudko

The family reunion was held later that summer in Lackawaxen, Pennsylvania, within sight of the railroad where Matthew Vollmer once worked. While family members from throughout the country attended, one nonfamily member was invited and attended . . . me.

Moments on the Mall

Mike Vouri

Memorial Day belongs to the fallen. It is for them we mourn and for them that we search our hearts for a deeper meaning that is never fully satisfied. Those of us who have been on the point of our nation's interests know this.

For me, it was the Mekong Delta in the old Republic of Vietnam, 1968–1969. Most of us didn't give a damn about politics beyond embracing the dim hope that, by some miracle, our leaders might bring us home before anyone else was killed or maimed. What we really cared about was each other, on the left and the right.

I would give everything I have for the life of my pilot, Frank Birchak, who was killed on January 11, 1969, while on a reconnaissance of the Tap Moi (which now, incidentally, is a nature preserve for redheaded cranes).

Vietnam Veterans Memorial, undated. Visitors reflected in the Wall.

His name is on the Vietnam Veterans Memorial in Washington: Panel 35 West, Row 69. I go there and run my fingers over the letters of Frank's name and one other on the same panel each time I visit the capital on business for San Juan Island National Historical Park—a park that was created to commemorate the peace that was maintained at crisis point more than 150 years ago. The reflection I see in polished granite grows more silver by the year, and now I am nearly twice the age of Frank when he died.

The one comfort I take—and I am certain it is the same for all veterans and the families of the fallen—is that a part of him lives within me and will do so until I am no longer here. Then we both will carry on in the memories of my son, who has heard all the stories.

Before leaving I quietly share the poem a brother vet posted on the Virtual Wall for Frank Birchak on the fortieth anniversary of his death:

> Do not stand at my grave and weep.
> I am not there; I do not sleep.
> I am a thousand winds that blow,
> I am the diamond glints on snow,
> I am the sun on ripened grain,
> I am the gentle autumn rain.
> When you awaken in the morning's hush
> I am the swift uplifting rush
> Of quiet birds in circled flight.
> I am the soft stars that shine at night.
> Do not stand at my grave and cry,
> I am not there; I did not die.

—Mary Elizabeth Frye, 1932

Mud Balls and Feathers

Deb Liggett

Gabriel stands in his front yard. I squat down to get acquainted.

Gabriel is five. His eyes are blue, his hair dark. He has some delicate scrapes on his face and needles in his T-shirt. He looks like he might have tangled with a tree in the not-so-distant past. His clothes suggest some time spent crawling around on his belly. Gabriel's hands are muddy, and with them, he is working an egg-shaped mud ball. He tells me that there is an oak seed inside; and he is going to get his mom to plant the mud ball and water it, so it will grow into a tree. He is intent upon his work.

I am a guest instructor at Horace Albright Training Center, the so-called "ranger factory," on the South Rim at Grand Canyon National Park. Gabriel's mom, a park ranger, is a trainer at Albright and has been kind enough to invite several of us to dinner. I am the first dinner guest to arrive.

As Gabriel and I talk, I pick up and cup a ponderosa pinecone in both hands. I have played with the cones since childhood and studied the fire-adapted tree in college. The cone is closed as it matures; and the sharp spurs on the tips of the scales keep would-be seed stealers away. But the cone in my hand has opened and the seeds are gone. I tell Gabriel that I have never seen the seeds of a ponderosa. He pauses and thinks about my admission, then kneels down, dusts away the pine needles, and without saying a word, points to the ponderosa seeds. Gabriel is casual about his knowledge.

I tell Gabriel I live in Alaska. He wants to know if there are bald eagles in Alaska. I tell him, "Yes, we have lots of eagles."

He states, "I'm a bird expert," and proceeds to tell me that here on the rim of the Grand Canyon, they have "eagles, mountain bluebirds, jays, juncos, ravens—oh, and condors." He is very matter-of-fact.

We form a shy, easy friendship, but we are still a little awkward with one another. Gabriel asks if I want to meet his dad and starts to take me inside. I suggest that since I have never met his dad that perhaps I should ring the doorbell and introduce myself first. He nods his head. There are three small, muddy handprints decorating the front picture window.

I meet Gabriel's dad. His mother isn't home from work, but Hernan welcomes me into their home. I am just another stray on the doorstep—in this case, the two-legged variety. The other guests arrive, and Gabriel and I go back to discussing the important things we have in common.

"I have six pets," he tells me. "Two fish, two gerbils—a black one and a white one—one cat and one dog." He names them in order: "Azula and Cody, the fish (Roja, the third fish, died); Kiwi and Mango, the gerbils; Jesse, the cat; and Pinto, the dog." Only after listing his pets does he mention he has a sister.

I tell him about my eighteen-pound cat named Asparagus (Gus) and my little cat, Annie. He goes off to collect Kiwi, the black gerbil, for me to hold.

With great care, Gabriel hands Kiwi to me and points out that the gerbil has a short tail because his sister dangled the gerbil by its tail, and the tail broke. Kiwi had to go to the vet to have a tail bone removed. (I wonder how much tail surgery on a gerbil costs.)

As I hold Kiwi, Gabriel tells me about the deer and the elk he sees in his yard. He tells me about coyotes and I ask about mountain lions; and in between our spurts of conversation, he wrestles on the floor with his sister, Reyna, who's older than him.

I already know that I would like to pal around with Gabriel. I could water mud balls and put handprints on windows; I might even be able to crawl around on my belly if it were required. And I can only imagine the things that he might still teach me.

When the time comes, we say our good-byes and I step away. At a slight nudge from his father, Gabriel slips from behind his mother's leg and honors me with a gift: the feather of a mountain bluebird. We need no words.

Gabriel is the child I want to be—the child I want every kid to be. Gabriel's eyes are trusting and open to the world; he knows wonder. He takes his kinship and his knowledge of the natural world for granted. He has the freedom to get dirty and to roam beyond a sidewalk. He loves and is loved.

I think his parents have stumbled upon a secret recipe. I can only anticipate the kind of man this child will become.

A Night at the Opera with Carl Sharsmith

Bob McConnell

Ranger Carl Sharsmith was one of the National Park Service's most honored ranger/naturalist/interpreters. He was a summer seasonal ranger for sixty years—from 1934 to 1994—in the Tuolumne Meadows, Yosemite National Park. If you were one of those who ever met or walked with him, you would join the thousands who said he was one of a kind.

"He took me all he way up Mount Lyell"; "he was our guide on our week-long walk to the high Sierra Camps"; "I took a class with him in Tuolumne Meadows"—to meet a visitor who had known him is to find another member of his faithful cadre. But I may be the only one who can say, "I took him to opera nights in San Francisco."

The first child born to Karl Schaarsmidt and his wife, in 1903, was given the name Karl Wilhelm Schaarschmidt. Born in New York, Karl's family returned to Switzerland and later lived in London, Canada, and America. While living in London, young Karl asked to have his name changed to Carl Sharsmith.

In America, he worked at various jobs and found little time for a formal education. At the age of nineteen, he entered ninth grade in a Los Angeles junior high school. Eventually, he entered and graduated from UCLA. By this time, he had worked in lumbering, was an assistant chef and baker in well-known restaurants, and was a caretaker for a mountain mansion.

During this time he also visited and fell in love with the Sierra Nevada.

He worked with youth groups who took major backpacking trips in the Sierra. These trips included the Mount Whitney area and Yosemite National Park. When he heard about the field-service school in Yosemite, he applied and was accepted for the summer of 1931.

He continued as a one-man "ranger" for two more summers and was accepted into the National Park Service in 1934. In the Yosemite National Park highcountry—Tuolumne Meadows—he would spend the next sixty summers. He would be given national honors twice and was honored in the nation's capitol on several occasions.

During my summer family vacations in Tuolumne Meadows, from 1969–1993, my kids and I would often walk with Carl. I enjoyed visiting with him in his cabin and listening to his collection of operatic music records. He would talk about the days at UC Berkeley when he and his wife were working on their doctorates: "We would often go to the San Francisco Opera House—usually with standing-room-only tickets."

One summer, I told Carl that I would love to take him to an opera in San Francisco. I had done my homework and listed that season's operas. When I said *Tristan and Isolde*, his response told me that was the one we should attend.

Living just off Highway I-5, about forty air miles true east of his home in San Jose, it was an easy hour-and-a-half drive to his house. About an hour away, in San Francisco, we found an Italian restaurant near the opera house, and enjoyed some spaghetti and wine. We got to our seats at about 6:30 and relaxed. The five-hour opera began right at 7:00 PM and ended at midnight. A true student of German classics, he would quietly say the lines and softly sing the arias. He was in heaven.

Bob McConnell in Yosemite National Park.

Then it was back to San Jose, and I arrived home about four o'clock in the morning.

It was probably the next summer when I went to his cabin he was listening to *Fidelio*, by Beethoven. I didn't recognize it, but he told me about the music (the plot) and the fact that the opera was performed on two levels—on the ground level and below (there was an underground stage).

"Well, Carl, how would you like to go to San Francisco and see *Fidelio* this season?" (What would you say if you had just been invited to attend your very most favorite opera?)

Later that year, I drove to San Jose and then on to San Francisco—had pastrami sandwiches and a beer at Max's Opera Café—and did we both enjoy Beethoven's only opera!

About this same time, I went on several walks with Carl and videotaped his wonderful stories. I am working on creating a two-hour DVD of Carl's comments and will place a copy in the Yosemite National Park history files.

On October 14, 1994, Carl died in his little house just off Highway 101 in San Jose. I had been there several times. Many of us gathered in Tuolumne Meadows in September the next year to remember and say good-bye to him. All of us had memories that are lasting our lifetime. For me, it was the two days we spent together at the opera—an experience I believe only his wife and I had with this wonderful man of the meadows and classical music.

Freedom Is Not Free

John Plumhoff

"Freedom is Not Free"—so read the words on the wall at the Korean War Veterans Memorial on the Mall in Washington, DC.

The Korean War Veterans Memorial is where I spend my time during my volunteer hours. I was not very aware of the history of the Korean War or of the significance of the memorial. I have learned to deeply appreciate what our Korean veterans experienced during that conflict. The legacy those veterans left not only our country but also South Korea is one that should not be forgotten.

Every week that I am at this memorial, there is some token of appreciation in the form of wreaths, flowers, or flags from the people of South Korea; and I have attended several formal ceremonies hosted by either a Korean military unit or the Korean embassy. Korean tourists show the utmost respect during their visits, and many are visibly moved.

Korean War veterans are especially interested in the physical representations and symbols within the memorial itself. They can point out the weapons and equipment on the sculptured soldiers in the *Field of Service.* Those sculptured soldiers represent all the US combat troops that fought in the Korean War and, for the most part, are the artist's representation of those troops.

The veterans can look at the Wall of Faces and point out the various military occupations represented on the different panels. Those faces are pictures of actual people taken in theater during the conflict. They do not represent specific people but they are real people, not an artistic representation.

Whenever I am able to identify a veteran, I always approach them, shake their hand, and thank them for their service.

On one particular day, I noticed a small group of visitors, one of whom was a Korean War veteran. I could tell by his baseball cap: "Korean War Veteran" stood out boldly along with his 3rd Infantry Division patch. The veteran was being pushed in his wheelchair by a young man and was surrounded by folks of varying ages.

I approached him, leaned over, and shook his hand, saying, "Thank you for your service."

He looked at me with red-rimmed eyes, pointed over his shoulder at the Wall of Faces, and said, "That's me!"

I was certainly not going to argue with him, as this was a very reasonable claim. As I stood aside, the group was trying to arrange themselves in order to get a picture of the veteran and his likeness on the Wall. It was about this time that a small elderly gentleman approached the veteran, and asked to shake his hand and get his picture taken with him. This was a South Korean citizen who was on vacation and was visiting Washington, DC, that day. The South Korean gentleman shook hands with the veteran and thanked him "for fighting for me and my family, and keeping us free."

The elderly Korean then motioned for his wife and family to come over and get a family picture with this elderly veteran. His wife, two sons, two daughters, and four grandchildren gathered 'round; as did the veteran's sons, daughters, and grandchildren. Pictures were snapped by both families as well as by other tourists who were witnessing the moving event.

Eventually, both groups moved on. I did catch up with one of the veteran's group and expressed my amazement at the moments we had just witnessed. She, too, was moved to tears and told me that the veteran was her dad. He had a stage 4 cancer and was terminal. One of his last desires was to visit the Korean War Veterans Memorial, and this day was the fulfillment of that wish.

Certainly that veteran did not expect what had happened, nor did those Korean tourists I'm sure. But it did make for a memorable few moments for all who saw that converging of two life paths.

The Alligator Whisperer

JoAnne Merritt

Many years ago, I met a ranger who had already worked at Lake Mead National Recreation Area, Everglades National Park, Blue Ridge Parkway, and Shenandoah National Park. I met him while working as a Student Conservation Association volunteer at Assateague Island National Seashore. He was a man of principle and dedication. He truly loved being a park ranger and, several years later, would be my husband.

During his thirty-five-plus-year career as a park ranger, which began in the '60s, he worked as a seasonal interpreter, a law-enforcement ranger, a chief ranger, and a management assistant and chief of natural resources. The stories that he told about his life in the park service fascinated and deeply impressed me. Some were amusing, some were interesting, and some were inspiring. Because he had worked in so many areas, he had stories about mountains, lakes, seashores, and all kinds of human and animal interactions.

While working at Everglades National Park as an interpreter, he had learned that the alligators there had become a bit opportunistic and would come out when they heard paper crumpled. He astounded many a visitor to the park by telling them all about alligators and then proceeding to "miraculously" make one appear on command (while covertly crackling a bit of candy wrapper). The visitors were awed by this "Alligator Whisperer," and thrilled to see an alligator up close. He emphasized to me that he only did this in areas where an alligator could get out of the water and be seen easily, without being even a remote threat to the visitors. He often emphasized the importance of safety.

Early in his career in law enforcement, he told me of the days when protection rangers were unarmed and enforcement was almost entirely by education and conversation. It was a simpler time for the world as a whole.

Some rangers did have a personal weapon in their vehicles; and one day, he found that he desperately needed that protection.

At Shenandoah National Park, there were some local people whose families had lived in the area for many generations and felt that the park's designation shouldn't prevent them from hunting where they always had. This young park ranger (my husband), while on patrol in his vehicle, came across an older man and his son in possession of a deer that could only have been harvested by poaching. The park ranger exited his car with his rifle in his hand, keeping his vehicle between himself and the two men. He calmly and patiently explained that they had taken a deer illegally and couldn't keep it.

To put it mildly, these two armed and annoyed men didn't want to hear that they couldn't keep the deer they had shot. The older man raised his rifle and pointed it at the young ranger. He then went on to say that he would do whatever he wanted because he was dying of cancer anyway, and didn't need to worry about any poaching laws. This put the young ranger in a very hazardous situation. Did he want to risk his life to enforce this law? Could he walk away from the situation even if the hunters allowed him to? He told me that he had never been so afraid for his life—then or in the years since—as he was in those moments when he looked down the barrel of that hunting rifle. Luckily, he never had to make a decision because the son convinced his dad that the deer wasn't worth it.

He spent the last eighteen years of his career at the Upper Delaware Scenic and Recreational River, which is where we married. He became resource management chief, and dedicated his time to preserving the natural beauty and environmental health of an area he quickly came to love. He was proud of his years as a park ranger and, looking back, said he would not have changed anything in his professional life. He retired in 1998 with over thirty-seven years of service.

His name was Malcolm "Angus" Ross, and he passed away in 2005.

Graffiti in the Statue of Liberty

Don Frankfort

For forty-eight years, (almost all of my adult life), I have been a seasonal National Park Service ranger. I have worked in the same western national park—Wind Cave National Park in South Dakota—for forty-seven summers. But during the fall/winter/spring of 1969–1970, I had a very different national park experience. I lived in my hometown of New York City and commuted daily to my National Park Service job at Statue of Liberty National Monument in New York Harbor.

The years of 1969 and 1970 were of some significance for the Statue of Liberty. In October of 1969, anti–Vietnam War activists organized the first Vietnam Moratorium Day to mobilize protesters of that conflict. The Statue of Liberty was a meaningful symbol to both sides of this debate, allowing both sides of the debate to freely express their opinions.

In April of 1970, the first Earth Day was celebrated to promote environmental awareness, and the National Park Service, an "environmentally conscious" agency, became involved.

My job as a park ranger was to help protect the physical entity of the Statue of Liberty, and interpret its values and significance as part of our culture and history to the people who came to visit it.

This mission was tested one day in the fall of 1969. A visitor had just descended the staircase within the statue and reported to several of us who were stationed at the base of the Statue that another visitor was writing something up in the crown. This was a frequent occurrence, but that never ceased to infuriate us. People were always writing their names in the crown of the statue, and maintenance personnel were always cleaning them off. It was an ongoing ritual.

Well, we now had the chance to catch someone red-handed, and it was my turn to go. I mustered all of my indignation, and dashed up the narrow twelve-story spiral stairway, preparing to dish out a proper scolding. (We

Statue of Liberty National Monument, 1965. The statue faces the entrance to New York Harbor.

park rangers prided ourselves in how fast we could climb to the crown of the Statue. I think it took me one minute.)

At the top of the Statue of Liberty, on the tiny platform inside the top of her head, stood a man, maybe thirty to forty years of age, slightly shorter than average height, with dark hair and a big black mustache. Sure enough, he was writing something with a black felt-tipped pen on the green oxidized copper sheeting above his head. He must have been writing his name, but I do not remember that detail after all of these years. I said something like "Please don't do that," but it did not matter because he spoke no English.

The man responded to the sound of my voice and turned around to face me. He broke into a big smile, nudged me with his right elbow, and pointed with his marker to his *magnum opus* on the ceiling. He said one word and I demurred, immediately guessing the essence of his story. The word he said was the name of his native country. Phonetically, he pronounced it "Check-o-slow-va-KY-a," with the emphasis on that fifth syllable.

In 1968, there was a protest against Communist rule in Czechoslovakia; and the Czech people gained some social and political reforms during the "Prague Spring" of that year. However, this did not please the Soviet Union, and a few hundred thousand Russian and other Eastern Bloc troops were sent into Czechoslovakia to quell the protest. The reforms were rescinded and Communist rule remained.

This man—this "Check-o-slow-va-KY-an" that I was so ready to rebuke—was perhaps involved in the protests; perhaps he was an organizer, or perhaps he was a bystander victimized by persecution or violence; perhaps he barely escaped with his life, or perhaps he just needed to find sanctuary where he could pursue a greater happiness. I could only guess.

His smile had said it all. I am sure he was delighted to be in the United States of America; I am sure he was delighted to be enfolded within the embrace of Lady Liberty; and I am sure he was delighted I caught him in the act of writing his personal thank-you note to her.

Our maintenance staff probably cleaned the crown shortly after the incident, but my memory of it still remains after almost forty-five years.

Miss Minidoka

Anna H. Tamura

"Miss Minidoka," my mother said, naming the title of a play about "camp" that she wanted us to see together. I was in seventh grade and had no idea what she was talking about—and even less interest.

Flash forward to the summer of 2000. I'm fortunate to have an internship with the National Park Service in the Parks Cultural Landscape Program, surveying the Wonderland Trail in Mount Rainier National Park. What fun it is—hiking, photographing, sketching, taking notes for days to document the trail.

On a break from the internship, I'm sitting in bed, tracing my finger across a road atlas and planning my road trip from Seattle to Salt Lake City to visit friends. It will be a day-and-a-half drive through Washington, northeastern Oregon, southern Idaho, and into Utah. My finger passes over "Minidoka."

"Hold up! Wait—Minidoka? Wasn't that the 'camp' where my family was during World War II? Whoa! I'm going to be driving right by it. I must stop and see what's there." I'm now on a mission.

Unbeknownst to me, at that moment begins a new chapter in my professional and personal life.

At the end of a long day's drive, I'm finally almost there—through the high desert of sagebrush, basalt outcroppings, wide-open spaces, brilliant green irrigated fields, small homesteads speckling the landscape. No one is around; the place feels empty. A bridge crosses a rushing, gushing, river-like canal.

Now before me are two basalt foundations of old buildings with a huge red sign that reads: "This is the site of the Minidoka Relocation Center. One of ten American concentration camps established in World War II to incarcerate the 110,000 Americans of Japanese descent living in coastal regions of our Pacific states. Victims of wartime hysteria. These people, two-thirds of whom were United States citizens, lived a bleak, humiliating life in tarpaper barracks behind barbed wire and under armed guard. May these camps serve to remind us what can happen when other factors supersede the constitutional rights guaranteed to all citizens and aliens living in this country."

Actually, more than 120,000 Americans of Japanese descent spent the war years in the camps. Thirteen thousand people from Alaska, Washington, Oregon, and California were incarcerated at Minidoka, and it became Idaho's seventh largest "city" at the time.

That day, I explored the site, snapped photos, and left with a swirl of questions and a thirst for finding the answers. My grandparents passed away without ever speaking to me about it. I wondered why, and about the many hardships they must have faced. From that point forward, I wanted to speak with my family—to learn everything about Minidoka; why it happened; and most of all, to meet and connect with people who had ties to Minidoka.

Six months later, on January 17, 2001, President Bill Clinton would designate Minidoka as a new national monument. I was lucky to get the chance to help with the first archeological survey of Minidoka and inventory the cultural landscape. When I began full-time work for the National Park Service, my primary project was to develop a long-term plan for Minidoka's development and management. Being given the opportunity to help design a new national park—and one that was so important in my community's history—was incredibly thrilling, a great honor, as well as a heavy responsibility.

During the four years after Minidoka was designated, I was part of a group of National Park Service employees dedicated to engaging the public in planning Minidoka's future. We traveled from Idaho to Alaska to southern California, meeting with people who were connected to Minidoka and could provide valuable information about the site and history, and were invested in its development. Along the way, there were times when elders would say that they had known my grandparents and would proceed to tell fascinating stories about them.

As I pieced together my family's history, it became very clear why they had buried it in the past. They were immigrants from Japan; and though they had been living in the United States for twenty years, they were legally barred from becoming naturalized US citizens. On February 14, 1942, my mother was born in rural Oregon City and became the youngest of four children. Five days later, on February 19, President Roosevelt signed an executive order that eventually allowed for the mass, forced removal of all Japanese Americans from the West Coast. My family was forced to abandon their leased truck farm and move into one stall at the Pacific International Livestock Exposition building, amid the three thousand other Japanese American Oregonians. They were then sent on trains to Minidoka to live out the duration of World War II. As a mom now, I often think about my grandmother taking care of four young children, hand-washing diapers in the lavatory barrack building, and planning the future for her American-born children in the bleak Idaho camp.

With each trip to Minidoka, there is something new to see. On one memorable pilgrimage, the reestablished honor roll was dedicated. The historic honor roll listed one thousand names of young men and women who had left Minidoka to join the American armed forces, fighting in Europe and the Pacific. At the ceremony, surrounded by his descendants, an elderly man pointed to his name on the honor roll.

Some of the most memorable trips to Minidoka have been on the annual pilgrimage from Seattle to Minidoka with the elders who experienced it firsthand; their descendants and friends; and many young people who are eager to learn about this civil-rights site. For some youth, their grandparent or great-grandparent was at Minidoka. However, for many more, they are drawn to learning about Minidoka because it tells a uniquely American story.

I am proud that our country has admitted to and apologized for unjustly incarcerating more than 120,000 people. I am even more proud that Minidoka is now protected by the American people as a unit of the National Park Service, sharing this history with the world.

This Is Your Land

Nyssa Landres

"This is your land. I've done my best to take care of it, but it's not ours; we just used it."
  —Inupiaq elder in Kotzebue, Alaska

Arġaġiaq, also known as Willie Goodwin, Jr., grew up in a sod house in what is now Noatak National Preserve. Fishing for whitefish and mud shark, trapping muskrats and ptarmigan, chewing gum from spruce sap, and using local plants and herbs for medicine—this life required a holistic awareness of the landscape. Knowing the river currents, spotting weaknesses in the pack ice, and safely mushing the sled dogs downriver meant survival. In this remote Alaskan park, it still does. Life in this landscape draws on knowledge passed down from the collective experiences of past generations.

Northwestern Alaska is a severe landscape located above the Arctic Circle with expanses of open tundra, rolling beach ridges, and forests of black spruce. Northwestern Alaska is also a haven and the parklands here help sustain a people and a way of life. Subsistence uses of the land and the deep cultural connection Inupiat people share with the landscape are preserved here as an indelible part of these parks. Today, Arġaġiaq is an elder in Kotzebue and a tribal liaison to the National Park Service at Western Arctic National Parklands. His work bridging National Park Service and Inupiat values has been instrumental in the continued preservation of these lands and the subsistence way of life that continues in the parks today.

Until he was seven years old, Arġaġiaq lived in a summer camp near Aliktongnak Lake, and a winter camp in the mountains north of the Agashashok River. The change of the Arctic seasons is dramatic, quickly turning from a white expanse of snow and ice into green tussock thrumming with the activity of animals and insects. Seasonal camps were common throughout northwest Alaska as people moved with the resources. For Arġaġiaq's family, this meant using the fish and lowland plants near Aliktongnak Lake, then finding shelter and increased availability of firewood in the mountains.

Yet his parents knew the region was changing. Arġaġiaq's grandmother was born in 1884. She told stories of bringing the mail north by dog team, traveling across the frozen beaches of what is now Cape Krustenstern National Monument. She also told stories of people starving and other stories of ships arriving with nonnative peoples bringing crackers, flour, and sugar.

"She said our way of life is going to change, but we've got to learn to adapt. There's no use fighting it because it's going to change," Arġaġiaq says.

His own father stressed education, telling Arġaġiaq that "the old ways of trapping and hunting were going away." So Arġaġiaq began attending school in Kotzebue. In middle school, Arġaġiaq got his ham-radio operator license and used Morse code to communicate with people around the world. For high school, Arġaġiaq left northwest Alaska, later becoming an electrician technician and working for NASA on Apollo I. But he always intended to come back to northwest Alaska; and in late 1969, he did.

Land ownership requirements were changing, and in the early 1970s, Arġaġiaq worked with his people to file ownership claims for the land they'd lived on for generations. When the Alaska Native Claims Settlement Act (ANCSA) was enacted in 1973, mandates required Alaska to be carved into parcels of land ownership. The Northwest Alaska Native Association (NANA) worked to assure the forthcoming land designations were favorable for the native people, including legislative language to preserve their subsistence way of life.

Arġaġiaq worked as the head of Land Selections for NANA, meeting with elders in Kiana, Ambler, Noorvik, Noatak, and each of the eleven villages to decide which lands the villages would claim. Elders shared traditional knowledge about which areas were needed for berry picking, fishing, trapping, collecting wood. Arġaġiaq listened, and those places were kept as village lands. "Today, we understand how the elders helped us make the right decisions for today," he says, "and what the land may give future generations."

Arġaġiaq's role was to facilitate these meetings, but afterward, he had to draw lines across this landscape for which areas would be owned by the villages and native corporations. The lines land managers see today are drawn by the collective knowledge of Inupiaq culture. In 1980, the Alaska National Interest Lands Conservation Act (ANILCA) was passed, and these boundaries were codified into law.

Perhaps the most important aspect of ANILCA is that subsistence rights became guaranteed in the parklands of northwest Alaska. Traditional techniques of hunting caribou in the Kobuk River will continue to be passed on to the next generation; as will setting up fish camps along the riverbanks in the summer to dry salmon and whitefish, the skill of navigating open leads in the pack ice to hunt seals and beluga, and countless other traditions passed down over thousands of years.

These parks preserve beautiful vistas and remote, craggy peaks; but they also foster a deep sense of connection. With every footstep, visitors follow the paths of ancient peoples and ancestors; shards of chert and depressions of house pits provide a glimpse into the traditions of use from countless generations. The parklands of northwestern Alaska are vital to the subsistence of a people and culture. The lands protected here are an identity.

When Arġaġiaq was ten years old, a Kotzebue elder stopped him along the town beachfront. Pointing to the shore and hills of what is now Cape Krustenstern National Monument, he told Arġaġiaq, "This is your land. I've done my best to take care of it, but it's not ours; we just used it." Almost fifty years have passed since this encounter. Still, Arġaġiaq described how he called on that conversation as he met with elders and drew land-ownership boundaries. Ultimately, the shared knowledge of the elders and his people shaped his life and the parklands of northwest Alaska.

Today, when he sees kids playing on the waterfront, he tells them, "This is your land now."

4

Stories from
the Field

Grand Canyon National Park, 1978.
Sonja Johnson, seasonal ranger, patrols
the South Kaibab Trail.

How to Talk to a "Girl Ranger"

Rebecca Bailey

I am walking the Devils Garden trail at Arches National Park in southeast Utah, nearing Navajo Arch. Just as I'm congratulating myself that I've escaped the visitors for a few minutes (I've talked with more than five hundred visitors this morning and am hoping for a little solitude), a male hiker rounds the rocks.

"Hey!" he exclaims when he sees me, his face lighting up. "It's a girl ranger! Have you come to rescue me?"

Hardly. First of all, I'm not a girl; I'm pushing fifty. And while I'm strong, I'm also small; there's no way I'm "rescuing" this big guy—unless it's to clonk him on the head with the communications radio I always carry and put him out of my misery.

Instead, I smile. "You betcha," I say, and we make small talk for a couple of minutes before resuming our respective hikes.

When I became a National Park Service interpretive ranger, about a year before, I'd manufactured fantasies about what the job would be like. It had never occurred to me that as a woman in uniform, I'd be of interest to almost every male I encountered.

Not that the park service uniform is alluring in any way. The "pickle suit," we call it—mostly green, some gray, some brown. Summer in southeast Utah can be grueling, hiking in full sun at 114 degrees Fahrenheit, my clothes and I are usually salt encrusted from evaporated sweat. Or the wind is gusting so hard that red sand is coated in the corners of my eyes and mouth, along my nose, in my ears (and, I discover at home, in my underwear). Hat hair like you wouldn't believe. While I love the work, I can't say that it makes me feel gorgeous.

But there's no accounting for the mutant that is the male species. If you're working the information desk, they'll keep asking for minute details about hikes, then wander through the exhibits until they find something else to

Arches National Park, 1950. Double O Arch, Devils Garden section.

ask about. One guy half my age, who'd been hanging around nearly an hour, was inspired to show me pictures of a gopher snake eating a rat. A surefire way into any woman's heart.

Then there are the gentlemen who want to have their pictures taken with you, and who manage to sneak a feel of your butt as they slip their arm around you . . .

Sometimes it can make you feel uneasy. After I finish an evening program in the campground, an obviously inebriated young man follows me around. "Wontcha come to campsite number one?" he repeatedly asks. "I'll give you anything you want." I doubt it. Still, I'm glad I have my radio in my hand and a car ten feet away that I can lock myself into.

Mostly, though, it's benign—just people playacting while they're on vacation. Plus, it gives us "girl rangers" a lot to laugh about. I always like being asked if I'm Anna Pigeon, Nevada Barr's fictional park ranger detective. "You betcha," I say, despite the contradiction on my name bar.

At times, the fantasy pans out better than you imagined. I'll always remember meeting another solitary male hiker on the same Devils Garden trail. I prepared myself for the "girl ranger" comment, but instead, he says, "I want to shake your hand," with tears in his eyes. "Thank you for taking care of this beautiful place. Thank you."

I have tears in my eyes too, as I do now, remembering the highest compliment I've received as a park ranger.

Yes, this is what my uniform means.

This is how to talk to a girl ranger.

"I still love this uniform. . . . Partly because there's a silent message to every little girl of color that I pass on the street or in an elevator or on an escalator . . . that there's a career choice she may have never thought of."

—BETTY REID SOSKIN, ROSIE THE RIVETER NATIONAL HISTORICAL PARK RANGER, 2015

An Owl Took Flight and Headed for Her Face!

Judy Geniac

I was one of three firefighters—all women and all from very different cultures—returning from a wildfire. (I'm changing the names to protect the innocent!) We were in Big Cypress National Preserve, on a highway that ran through the Everglades.

An owl flew straight at our windshield and hit with a thud. It bounced and sailed over our fire truck and the large trailer we were pulling. (The trailer had a large swamp buggy on it, as it was our "fire truck" in the cypress swamps.) I watched in the rearview mirror as the owl rolled down the highway, and I told Josephina, our driver, to pull over. Why? Because we could take the bird back to the park. They may want to preserve it and use it in the visitor center. (I'd worked with many wild birds at a bird hospital and sanctuary, so I was pretty comfortable doing this.)

So, we stopped and got out. I ran to the owl in the middle of the highway and picked it up. We got back in the truck. I needed my hands free, so I asked Tibah to hold it (it was a barred owl). I thought she was going to cry—it was dead, and she was terrified. What was there to be afraid of? I convinced her to hold the bird and promised I'd take it right back, just as soon as I got my seat belt on.

She stiffly held the bird in her lap, its face to the dash, with talons down—she didn't want to look at it.

As I clicked the seat belt, Josephina pulled out onto the highway. We were headed back to headquarters. Then, before I could take the bird back, I heard a very strange sound—something between a groan, a squeal, and a shaky voice. I watched as the owl turned its head almost completely back to look up into Tibah's eyes.

I gently told Tibah to stay calm; the last thing we needed in the cab of a fire truck (that was traveling down the highway!) was an owl flying around.

Josephina was startled; and it took every bit of bravery Tibah had to stay calm, because she knew the alternative would be far more frightening.

Tibah had a firm grip on the owl, so I took my hands and put them around hers. I told her to gently slide her hands out, as I increased my grip. The transaction was successful. I moved the owl to my lap. Now, what to do with an owl?

I asked Josephina to pull over and told Tibah that we needed to get out. She wanted to know what I was going to do; I told her I was going to release the owl. She was afraid, but we had to do it.

We all got out, and I went to the front of the fire truck while Josephina and Tibah went to the back, behind the trailer and the enormous swamp buggy. I swooped my hands down and released. The owl flew up, made a wide arc, and came straight back over my head and all the way back, nearly hitting Tibah in the face! She let out a very loud scream and dropped to the ground. I laughed (as I do when I'm nervous!), and the owl flew off into the trees.

We hopped into the truck, and headed home with a story even better than any we had about fire fighting.

A Good Old-Fashioned Mountain Rescue

Jane Marie Allen Farmer

In the 1980s, cell phones were nonexistent, which meant rescue could be a long way off. But I was a fresh seasonal "interp" with a new EMT certification and about to use my training.

High atop the Great Smoky Mountains at Peck's Corner trail shelter, a hiker's wilderness vacation had abruptly turned lethal. He had a spontaneous pneumothorax—a blown-out lung, and he could be dead by morning.

His friend, unfamiliar with the trails, headed the long way for help. Ten miles later, he hailed a visitor in a car, who drove to relay the critical information. It was sunset when rangers finally got the report.

Foggy weather and tall forest prohibited a helicopter; Peck's Corner was accessible only by foot or horseback. A horseback rescue team was abysmal but the best alternative. A law-enforcement (LE) ranger quickly set off on foot to triage as the rest of us prepared for the rescue.

We trailered the horses and equipment three-and-a-half miles on a rugged dirt road. As we tacked up in the illumination of the pickup truck's auxiliary lights, I noticed one saddle had no stirrups. A return to the barn would take another precious hour. It was my mistake, so I would ride the stirrupless saddle six miles up the mountain. The night was destined to be tough.

As we mounted, the triage LE ranger radioed that he had arrived at the trail shelter. He confirmed the injured hiker was in bad shape. With more than six hours since the rescue hiker had left his injured friend, the golden hour of rescue success was well behind us.

Horses like routine. We had surprised them with emergency night duty, so I worried they would be fractious and resentful. Saddle packs were loaded with bulky, heavy oxygen cylinders, and bulged with blankets and medical equipment. Our trail was rough and slinked narrowly up the steep and foggy mountain.

The lead EMT rode Charlie Brown, the most energetic horse. Charlie's quirks included a strong fear of wild hogs. Unfortunately, wild European hogs were common on this trail. They are most active at night and can sometimes be quite aggressive. I hoped we would not see any that night.

Hauling up the mountain, I had plenty of time to review spontaneous pneumothorax in my head. I wondered how long a person could survive while their ruptured lung gradually filled their chest cavity with air. It seems ironic that the act of breathing could eventually crush the heart and kill a person.

The image of us throwing a corpse over a saddle and tying it to the horse cowboy-style kept floating in and out of my mind. I wondered if the other rangers knew how to secure a corpse to a horse. It was nothing I had learned in EMT training.

The horses delivered us to the shelter in a little under two hours. The man was still alive but in a lot of pain. Via radio, Medical Command ordered us to bring him down immediately—easy for them to say, sitting in their sterile, well-equipped hospital.

Another hour passed as we rearranged our equipment and hoisted the injured man onto Charlie Brown. The guttural groans the hiker emitted as we shoved him up into the saddle made me cringe. This was no way to treat a patient.

Wilderness rescues severely warp many rescue guidelines. Taking a man with a ruptured lung on a horse ride is insane, but it was our only alternative. With an oxygen tank strapped to his saddle, he was destined for the ride for his life.

I led Charlie Brown and his rider back down the mountain. The procession moved slowly. The fog completely darkened the already dangerous mountain trail. Charlie was sure-footed, but the trail seemed to have morphed into a mass of roots, rocks, and holes. Our headlamps dimmed.

I hoped Charlie's night vision was better than mine, but I guessed he was depending on me to be his eyes. I carefully picked the way down the trail. Every time Charlie took a rough step, the man swayed dangerously and groaned painfully.

Two-thirds down the mountain, Charlie's head shot up. He stopped abruptly, his eyes widened and ears pricked—the classic symptoms of a frightened horse ready to bolt.

I gently encouraged Charlie to move forward. He tentatively took two steps forward then three quickly back. The whiplash effect elicited a near scream from the patient. What was the matter with this horse? Did he sense something?

Then we all heard it, first on the right and then on the left. The underbrush was rustling all around us. Even in the dark fog, I could see the whites of Charlie's eyes. We were surrounded by hogs, Charlie's mortal enemies.

Fearing Charlie would throw his injured passenger, I desperately tried to reassure the horse, as a frightened horse can react violently. If a hog darted across the trail, I could lose control of this animal, ten times my size.

The lead EMT shouted to get out of there. I tugged gently on the reins. Charlie had trusted me this far, and I hoped he would trust me to get him past the hogs.

With little more than a stiffening of his gait, we quickly passed the porcine-infested area. The patient groaned at the pace, but he hung on gamely.

We arrived at the trailhead at 1:30 in the morning, happy to see the lights of a waiting ambulance.

Contrary to my worries, the horses had been great. They performed well without understanding why they were required to take part in the strange nighttime duty. Their ultimate reward was returning to the comfort of their pasture.

My ultimate reward came about a month after the incident in the form of a crudely drawn crayon picture of a brown horse with a black mane and tail. In a child's block-style letters, it was captioned, "Charlie Brown." The handwritten note that accompanied it said, "Thank you for saving my daddy's life."

It was one of my best ranger days.

Jane Marie Allen Farmer

The Skunk, the Badger, and the Ranger

Patti Bacon

It was the day after Thanksgiving—a bleak, gray day. Snowflakes were in the air but not sticking to the ground, making things miserable. Not many visitors to Big Hole National Battlefield in rural Montana on such a wet, gloomy day.

It was four in the afternoon, almost time to go home. I was sitting in the front office so I could hear if anyone came in for a visit. The custodian popped her head in to inform me she was leaving unless I wanted her to stay late. I would be fine, I told her. There was only an hour left to the work-day—what could happen?

A few minutes later, the automatic door in the lobby slid open by the front desk. I got up to check it out. "That's odd . . . "—no one was there. No cars were in the parking lot. Hmmm.

Sometimes the motion of the wind or the rain would activate the door. "I should really turn that off," I thought. "Next time, if it happens again, I will."

Settling into the office computer chair, I heard the door open again.

As I bounced out of the chair and around the desk, there in the office doorway was a skunk with her little tail held proudly in the air.

"What are you doing in here, you little bugger?" I asked.

She turned promptly and pranced out of the office into the viewing room, where our video is usually shown. I quickly closed the door behind her to keep her from going into the museum area that

Patti Bacon at Big Hole National Battlefield.

was close by. Also in the viewing room was an exit door to the outside. Maybe, just maybe, I could convince her to use it to escape.

No such luck.

The room was circular shaped with cushion-backed chairs located in the center. Each time I tried to coax the skunk toward the door, she would stamp her little feet at me, then go around the chairs farther away from the door. First one way and then the other, until she took refuge in the heating-vent register along the wall, with her tail sticking out. When the heating duct got too warm, the skunk would turn around, coming out head-first. And around the chairs we would go again, bypassing the open exit door to the outside. If only I had one more person to help block the circle.

Just then, visitors arrived—a middle aged couple with two young adults. The mother reported, "It smelled skunky outside, so we left the dog in the car." I informed her that the skunk was inside the video-viewing room. Incredulously, she peeked into the room. Sure enough, there was the skunk. As her son entered the visitor center, she told him the story. Unbelieving, he also glanced into the room, asking: "Do you want to help me get her out?"

"Oh no," the father said, "we must be on our way. Good luck with your problem!"

With a wave of the hand they were gone!

As I stood at the electric door, watching them disappear down the road, I saw this rather large animal headed toward the visitor center. Could it be a dog? As it came closer, passed the flagpole and traveled straight up the sidewalk, it seemed to be a badger. I quickly turned off the motion sensor to the front door; didn't need him in here too.

The badger followed the sidewalk around to the back of the building, where the exit door was propped open awaiting the skunk's exit. Realizing the badger still had a way in, I quickly stepped inside the room—just in time to see the badger standing in the doorway. Pointing my finger at him, I said forcefully, "You are not getting in here too!" Being afraid of all five foot two inches of me, he ran back around to the front, where he peered at me through the full-length window behind the Howitzer display, his nose pressed up against the glass.

"I can still see you!" I proclaimed as he became visible under the limber. Again, he ran around to the back exit, this time I was waiting for him in the doorway but he had stopped just out of sight until he bravely stuck his neck out and peeked around the corner of the building.

"That's it, I've had it—and I'm losing ground! I'm going to close this door and wait for help to arrive," I thought.

About that time, the skunk came out from the heat register. I quickly ran around the circle of chairs, grabbed the closest one to the skunk, and laid it on its side forming a triangle shaped corral, with the wall as the third panel. There was only the length of the chair legs—a mere two feet—between me and the plume of the skunk's tail, which dangled over the edge of the overturned chair. The skunk moved inside the makeshift corral as I bent over and pushed it along the wall, until I came upon the threshold of the open door.

Now what?

I pulled the chair toward me and gave it an extra-big shove forward, which bumped the skunk out over the doorway and into the great outdoors. Mission accomplished. With the door latched and locked, I called off the rescue party. Looking at the time, it was five o'clock on the dot. Dusting my hands in a satisfied manner, it was time to close up and go home.

Just another day in the life of a National Park Service ranger.

Not His Night to Die

Colette Daigle-Berg

It was a chilly, Old Faithful morning. January something, 1980. 06:30. Morning snowmobile patrol took me north toward Madison. We had detoured traffic along the Freight Road due to lack of snow on Fountain Flats.

There was no good reason I should have killed the engine on the Arctic Cat. Back in the days of no thumb warmers, no reverse, no heated seats, and certainly no electric start, it often took seven to eight pulls on the starter cord to start the machine—even when it was warmed up.

In the zero-degree silence and the moment it took to kick the snow off the "Road Closed" sign, I heard an elk—or was it a "help"? Or was it an elk calling "help"? Must have been an elk. No—it's a "help." But where?

"Over here! I wrecked my snowmobile last night and broke both of my legs."

A recent graduate of the seasonal law-enforcement academy and suspicious about why someone was sitting in the snow under a tree twenty-five yards off the road, with no wrecked snowmobile in sight, I kept my distance. I heard an instructor's voice in my head: "Watch his hands. It's the hands that can hurt you."

There it is. A wrecked snowmobile, another thirty yards into the trees. Okay to approach. But still, watch his hands.

His helmet was off and scorched, he said, from trying to light a fire with the cash in his pocket. He had a now-dried, bloody laceration on his forehead. Both legs were turned to the right at a definitely unnatural angle. He said when he woke up, he had to pull one of his legs down from the tree he was sitting under.

So he had made it through the night—what's the worst danger now? Hypothermia. My balaclava and body warmth became his. With yesterday's alcohol still on his breath, he kept me humored with bad jokes.

The rest of the Old Faithful rangers, rudely awakened from their sleep, arrive about forty-five minutes later. They are driving a commandeered Bombardier snowcoach. (No ambulances then, much less ambulances on tracks. No helicopters either.) Our patient is gently packaged and loaded for the twenty-five mile, "washboard" trip to West Yellowstone.

His story? He and two friends drank and raced their way around the Lower Loop the previous day, stopping at Old Faithful for dinner and—more drinks. The two friends headed back to West Yellowstone and left him there flirting with one of the female waitstaff. His flirtations didn't pan out, and he left about 10:00 PM. At the road closure sign, he made a forty-five degree turn out of the ninety and was tossed over the handlebars, breaking not only both femurs but his pelvis as well.

If it wasn't for cranky Arctic Cats, he might well have been there until spring.

No, it wasn't his night to die.

"The National Park Service today exemplifies one of the highest traditions of public service."

—STEWART UDALL, FORMER SECRETARY OF THE INTERIOR, 1963

Save the Whale!

Dan Richards

On a January afternoon, I had just returned from lunch when Bob caught me in the hallway and said, "Grab your dive gear. We are going to save the whale!"

I had been diving the previous summer on the NPS Kelp Forest Monitoring Project and had recently started as a full-time bio tech for Channel Islands National Park, the only biological technician at that time. Bob went on to explain that Navy pilots had reported seeing a whale tangled in a net about forty miles off the coast. Someone got the idea that we could go cut the net off and set it free. I was dubious about how we might accomplish that, but it was a worthy cause and sounded like a good adventure.

This was the mid-1980s, and gill nets had become a popular way to catch swordfish and shark in the Santa Barbara Channel. Unfortunately, gill nets are indiscriminant and tend to tangle any marine life that swims into the nearly invisible mesh. I recall that year as being particularly bad for whales; to my knowledge, at least four or five entangled whales had been reported.

Gray whales travel from their feeding grounds in the Bering Sea to warm lagoons on the Baja California peninsula, where they give birth in the longest mammal migration on Earth. Along the way, they are challenged by rough seas, killer whales, large ships, whale-watching boats, and fishing nets. Our whale was relatively easy to find: bright orange floats were attached to the netting wrapped around its flukes. We donned our wetsuits in the crowded and noisy Navy H-46 helicopter, and tucked knives and wire cutters into our sleeves to minimize drag and anything that could entangle us in the netting.

This was only my second flight in a helicopter; the first had been a few months before, when I was asked to take some aerial photos of a structure on one of the islands. On that flight (also on an H-46), they attached the gunner's belt to me and told me I could just lean out the open door to shoot away (trust is good?). Our rangers had told me they often trained with the Navy Search and Rescue squad to do "10 and 10s," meaning jumping out of a helo in dive gear from ten feet up at ten knots. As this was only my second time in a helo, you probably realize I had never tried that stunt. On the other hand, I had jumped off the Anacapa Island dock wearing full scuba gear plenty of times (which can be a fifteen-foot drop); and this time, I would not be wearing a tank or weights.

Three of us dropped into the water, and I was able to kick ahead and catch the trailing end of the gill net (the whale was slowed by the trailing net). However, the helo hovering above us (for safety reasons) scared the heck out of the whale, and it started swimming away as fast as it could. I hung on, hoping the whale would calm down, and that I might be able to cut the net free. With several large floats tied to the net, the whale could not dive; however, with each down stroke of the flukes, the net—with me hanging on—would plunge at least ten feet underwater. Then it was back to the surface to grab a quick breath and be pulled back down.

Getting tangled was my biggest fear and a horrifying thought. Those fears were compounded with the discovery of a set of scuba gear entangled in the net. I almost didn't want to look, but I did—and it was only gear. (A few weeks later, we learned that some divers had tried to free the whale near Dana Point and that they had thankfully escaped unharmed.)

I could barely see the whale in the murky water. I remember looking at the barnacles on its skin and the deep cuts around the tail flukes from the monofilament net. Mostly, I remember seeing the eye looking back at me at one point, and I felt the panic it seemed to hold. I wanted to communicate that we were there to help, but I quickly realized we were not going to be able to remove the net as long as the whale was moving. The entangled dive gear also drove home the danger of the situation, and we aborted the effort.

Several whales were caught in gill nets that winter; not all survived. A few days after our unsuccessful attempt, we did hear that a gray whale was freed from a net in southern California. Rescue teams had learned from earlier attempts and had developed hooked knives on poles that allowed rescuers to work safely from small boats. Hopefully our whale had survived.

The remainder of my career centered more on protecting endangered species and fishery management than rescuing individual animals. Nothing was ever quite as dramatic as trying to rescue that whale. When I think back to that day, I can still clearly see that huge eye staring at me through the murky water.

Channel Islands National Park, 1939. Sea Lions on the beach, San Miguel Island.

A Brief Encounter on Kilauea

Jim Martin

The National Park Service seeks to connect the visitor with the past through programs such as living history and cultural demonstrations. Presenting the story of American Indians and indigenous people who have connections to our park areas has always been problematic and often a shallow attempt. A public hula performance or an annual cultural festival is a commendable effort but only a veneer—a brief peek into genuine living culture. Once in a while, however, both the visitors and employees may have a once-in-a-lifetime experience or interaction outside of these scripted interpretive programs. I was fortunate enough to have one of these experiences while working at Hawai'i Volcanoes National Park during the early 1970s. What follows is my epiphany experience relating to Native Hawaiians and their relationship to Hawai'i Volcanoes National Park.

It was a fall evening in 1970 at the Kilauea Visitor Center. Darkness came early during this time of year. In addition to the fading light, a rare storm with wind, lightning, and thunder raged outside. I was assigned to close the visitor center, and it had been awhile since the last visitor left. Just as I was moving toward the doors to close up, they suddenly burst open with the wind.

A rain-soaked and windblown old Hawaiian woman entered. She stopped and stared at me, and then came up to the desk. Her eyes were intense and laced with an unnatural brightness, but her expression kind, almost familiar. She asked me if I respected Hawaiians. Stammering, I told her that I had just arrived as a ranger a few months before and really did not know much about Hawaiians. She smiled and said she wanted to pray to her Tūtū Pele. She pointed at the large oil painting of Pele, the volcano goddess, rising out of the glowing lava of Kilauea. There was such intensity in this old woman's presence that I was very uncomfortable and asked her if she wanted me to leave while she prayed. She said, "No, as long as you respect Pele."

What happened next changed my life and commitment to Hawai'i Volcanoes National Park, and to the cultural connection of Native Hawaiians. Out of this frail small lady came a sound I had never experienced. Her chant, or *oli*, was powerful—a force reflecting the volcano with its flowing lava, the forests, and all that was Kilauea. For a time that seemed endless, her voice rose and fell, exposing me for the first time to the depth and power of the Native Hawaiian language and a largely hidden side of Native Hawaiian culture.

She ended her *oli*, turned to me and took my hands, and simply said, "*Mahalo*" (thank you). Then she turned and opened the door, and with the wind and rain, disappeared into the night, leaving me feeling like a wet rag—completely emotionally spent.

The next day, I contacted a friend who was very knowledgeable of the Native Hawaiian community and related my experience, suggesting that it was just like the stories where island residents encounter a young woman, a middle age woman, or an old woman standing beside a lonely road or trail who's thought to be a manifestation of Pele. He thought for a minute and then said, "No, that was 'Iolani Luahini." I was soon to learn 'Iolani was one of the great *kumu hula*, or teachers of traditional Hula, and traces her family lineage to the court dancers of the *Kaua'i ali'i* (chiefs).

I was hooked. There was a living cultural fabric woven through this park. Eventually, I would have two tours of duty here as a ranger, the chief ranger, and finally, as the park superintendent, doing what I could to ensure that the Native Hawaiian culture was preserved for future generations. And it was all because of a Native Hawaiian elder seeking a connection to her Tūtū Pele one stormy night on Kilauea.

So what is the measure of success for the National Park Service in preserving this elusive resource? My measure was witnessing those rare occasions when, in the early morning, I might see a lonely Hawaiian with his long wooden pole of *ohia*, fishing for *ulua*, or perhaps hearing the drone of the *pū* (shell trumpet) resonating around the crater; or feeling the ground vibrate from the percussion of a large *pahu* (drum), unheard and unseen but felt. The ultimate value of the living culture of indigenous peoples in our parks is much like wilderness: you might never go there and might never see it, but you are lifted by the knowledge that it still exists.

How My Park Improves My "Mooooood"

Stephanie Marrone

I find my park soothing. I am on the interpretive staff at Oxon Cove Park and Oxon Hill Farm, just outside of Washington, DC.

I became a park ranger as a second career, after fifteen years as a classroom teacher in a busy middle school. Before coming to the farm, I had never even touched a cow before! Now, I am an expert cow milker, tractor driver, and chicken feeder. On a typical weekday in the spring, we serve hundreds of happy children.

One sunny day in May, I did the cow-milking program with a small group of children who have autism. Each child had a turn squirting milk from Minnie's giant udder into a bucket. The teacher held the hand of one boy until the end of the presentation and then she approached me tentatively.

"Ryan needs lots of reminders to be gentle," she said. I assured the teacher that I would help Ryan to be gentle, and I guided his small hand to Minnie's udder.

After he successfully milked the cow, Ryan stood up and buried his face in Minnie's side. Then, with a smile on his face, he delicately smoothed her fur, using both hands, in slow, circular motions, humming a soft tune.

His teacher began to cry. Then she smiled and said, "I need to get a cow for the classroom!"

I totally get it. Being on the farm is soothing to me too.

Stephane Marrone and friend at Oxon Hill Farm, Oxon Cove Park.

Night Rescue on the Lava Falls Route

Clair A. Roberts

The Tuweep ranger position at Grand Canyon National Park has a history of dedicated individuals who worked independently at this isolated and remote duty station on the Arizona Strip near the Canyon's western end. The main attraction of this area is Toroweap Overlook on the Esplanade, which is a sheer three-thousand-foot, near-vertical drop down to the Colorado River.

From the overlook, one can look downriver, and see and hear the roar of Lava Falls Rapid, one of the biggest anywhere on the Colorado. Access to the area is via sixty miles of extremely rough road, and visitors often sustain flat tires and/or damage to their vehicles as a result. The views are breathtaking, and there is a small campground near the rim; but there is *no* water, electricity, phone coverage, or other service available—except what may be provided by the Tuweep ranger.

As the only National Park Service employee at Tuweep, my responsibilities for the area (tens of thousands of acres) included maintenance of several miles of the park road, the campground, and the historic ranger station/residence and its facilities; as well as the protection of hundreds of archeological sites and, most important, the visitors. On many occasions, someone would knock on my door after dark, seeking help—from asking for directions to fixing flat tires, to needing water or equipment, to wanting a ride or something more urgent. On the rare occasions when it was a true law-enforcement or medical emergency, the nearest backup/response was by helicopter, which was usually over an hour away!

Another little known draw for Toroweap is the Lava Falls route, which is the shortest but steepest hiking/climbing route down to the river, in Grand Canyon National Park. This is not an official park trail and was never constructed as such. The route requires using one's hands much of the way and crosses a variety of nasty terrain, including an ancient lava flow; steep and narrow, rock-filled chutes; small ledges; and generally loose and unstable slopes that hang on the canyon in the angle of repose. It is only 1.5 miles and about 2,500 vertical feet (one way), but there is almost no shade on the south-facing, black landscape; summertime temperatures can easily get over 110 degrees. The park's warning sign posted at the top of the route discourages use by all but the fittest and most knowledgeable of potential users.

As the Tuweep ranger, my goal was to talk with and educate anyone who wanted to attempt this route. Most do not attempt it during the hot summer months; but occasionally, someone thinks it's short and easily doable—only to discover it is an extremely difficult and potentially fatal endeavor.

One summer's night near midnight, two young park visitors knocked on my door: other members of their party were in trouble and needed help on the Lava Falls route. Several family members and friends, ranging from adolescent to middle aged, had gone to the river earlier in the day and started the climb back out in the heat of the afternoon. They soon became overheated, dehydrated, and exhausted; so they decided to wait until dark to continue climbing out. Temperatures were still near 100 degrees; and the two older males, who had given their last water to the younger members, were last seen about halfway out and needed help.

Clair A. Roberts at Grand Canyon National Park.

THE WONDER OF IT ALL

This was a life-threatening situation; and despite the danger in going down the route in the dark, park dispatch was notified by radio that the strongest young male and I were going down to rescue the helpless hikers. We filled our packs with EMS supplies, flashlights and headlamps, high-energy snack foods, Gatorade, and as much water as we could reasonably carry.

When we arrived at the top of the route, other members of the group were there and said they only needed water; a young boy and two older males were the only ones still missing. We started down and found the boy sleeping in a rock alcove only a couple hundred yards from the top. After giving him food, electrolytes, and water, he seemed in good condition, agreeing to wait there until more help arrived.

It turned out the two older males had decided that the only way they were going to survive was to get back to the river to get water and cool off. They did not make it back to the river! When we found them about an hour later, they were about one-third of the way out—still above the most dangerous rock-filled chute on the route. Both were conscious but extremely weak and incapacitated; they had attempted to drink their urine. After rehydrating and feeding them, and resting for another hour or so, both said they could not climb out. We decided to carefully descend to the river, where we could cool down and rest until morning.

About daybreak, a helicopter arrived and airlifted us off the river and back to the road to be reunited with the others. Medics cleared all members of the group—none had to go to the hospital.

Later that day, we met at the group's campsite to get details for my report. It was an emotional encounter, and all were very thankful for my assistance. The leader said they had overestimated their abilities, misjudged the route's difficulty, and made strategic errors. And though they had learned a valuable lesson, they would not abandon their lifestyle of adventuring outside.

I have many unforgettable and memorable stories from my time as the "lone ranger" at Tuweep. Because this incident ended positively, it is one the most rewarding experiences of my entire National Park Service career.

The Jack Main Bear

Laurel Munson Boyers

Having lived inside Yosemite National Park most of my life, I've had many encounters with black bears. Perhaps the most meaningful was with the little bear who looked down at me from the canyon wall in Jack Main Canyon, forever validating the inspiration of my life's work.

I am a Shaw woman—one of a line of sturdy woman whose families came across to the new America with the first Europeans and later fought in the Civil War. More recently, they settled in, or had significant association with, Yosemite. The following story is in part due to their inspiration, instilled in me over the last three generations—inspiration that is partially responsible for me living inside Yosemite National Park for significant portions of my almost fifty years.

My great-grandmother's family brought the first phone lines into the park and greeted Teddy Roosevelt as he arrived in the small town of Raymond for his historic sojourn with John Muir. My grandmother spent her summers at the family's stagecoach way station just outside the park, greeting early Yosemite visitors. My mother worked in the park as a young woman, and returned with her new husband to live and have her children in Yosemite Valley. She told a story of watching a black bear follow me around the corner of the house when I was a very little girl—perhaps that was when I developed my relationship with the bears. And perhaps those early experiences set my career path to protect them.

My early childhood in the park certainly affected my career choice; and I found my life's calling was to help others not just enjoy but understand this magnificent place in more depth. Instilling awe is easy here—just go outside. But understanding the complexities of the paradox of use and preservation, the importance of open space and untrammelled ecosystems, the value of wild places—these things begin with a more profound understanding of this park and of the Earth. I found myself dedicated to trying to convey that deeper message to park users from across the globe, to park- and forest-management experts, to National Park Service coworkers, to school groups of all ages, to scientists, to scouts, to politicians, and to lawmakers. And because humans seem to have an affinity with bears, these messages could sometimes be wrapped around a direct plea to protect the bears. (People *always* wanted to talk about the bears, and protecting them is an important message itself.)

However, despite my best efforts, not everyone got it about wild places; and the bears always seemed to stay one step ahead as we strove to keep them from a diet of human food, known to be bad for them in many ways. Incredibly opportunistic, they found that backpackers are a good source of lots of high-calorie eatables. As a member of the wilderness staff for thirty-plus years, and eventually serving as the wilderness manager, I spent countless hours with other experts thinking about how to keep the right animals eating the right food! Even as we promoted new methods of food storage, the bears were figuring out how to get it. Hanging food from trees no longer worked when bears figured out where the rope was tied. Bear poles didn't work because visitors couldn't position bags to avoid the bears who got a claw-hold on the joint of the pole and reached high. Counterbalancing two bags of food with no tie-off was the next "solution" until we realized it was very difficult to do.

I remember watching a group of new wilderness staff learning how to counterbalance. Those who were demonstrating committed almost every mistake possible, including the potentially hazardous act of hitting oneself with the rock used to toss the rope over the limb, followed by the really hazardous act of actually pulling the broken limb down on your head as you try to pull your bags up. Luckily, there weren't a rash of injuries park-wide with this method. The bears' system to foil the hang was to bounce on (or break) the limb until a sack came into reach. There were also bear *kamikaze* dives off the limb, tearing the bags on the way down, backpacker food raining down like candy from a *piñata*.

Many memorable "eating" incidents come to mind when thinking of these amazing and charismatic animals: the acrobatic bears of Tiltill Valley harvesting acorns from the highest branches of the oaks; the night at Matthes Lake when the bear tried all night—in the falling snow—to get our food; the bear who killed a fawn next to Merced Lake Campground; the middle-of-the-night standoff over a large stack of food at Young Lakes with a bear that looked three times my size. I've also stood quietly in awe many times, watching the bears forage for their natural diet. And I've chased, hazed, yelled, thrown rocks, and banged pots in all sorts of circumstances and at all times of the day when they were after human food. Sadly, bears sometimes spend more calories than they gain trying to get human food, and unnatural food sources affect their health and demographics. While thrilling, a bear in camp isn't optimum for people either. Something had to be done.

One of my last major administrative actions as Yosemite's wilderness manager was to finally get a food-storage system in place that the bears have yet to figure out: food canisters. As canister use became logistically possible and it became clear that this method might even work, it felt like the wild in wilderness was a little closer.

My farewell patrol (a ten-day ride all the way across the wilderness that I had worked so hard to inspire others to protect) was made even more poignant because of that little wild bear watching as I passed by on the trail—the epitome of an untrammelled ecosystem, perhaps free(r) of human food now. My great-grandmother, grandmother, and mother would be pleased.

The Motorcade

Amanda Garrison

If you close your eyes and let your mind drift through its catalog of past experiences, are you able to visualize a moment where you were breathless? A moment in which time seemed to stand still? A moment that invoked that tiny gasp, where the air was stolen right from your lungs? A moment that you will never forget?

For me, many of these moments have taken place at National Park Service sites: from the first time I tried to wrap my arms around a Redwood tree to the first time I laid eyes on the blue water of Crater Lake; these memories still take my breath away. And as I think back on my first few days as a park ranger, one moment in particular stands out in my mind.

The early morning sun had made its appearance above the US Capitol building on the east side of the National Mall. As its golden rays soaked Pennsylvania Avenue, they scarcely seemed to penetrate through the century-old willow oak trees that insisted upon shading my position near Sherman Park.

The brisk April wind whipped at me and seemed to be playing a game with my crisp, new, straw flat hat. Each time I meticulously adjusted it, tilting it so the brim was perfectly horizontal, the rough wind came in and, in one foul swoop, attempted to throw it from my head. As I repeatedly battled the weather, I did everything I could to maintain my professional ranger appearance in front of the several hundred park visitors and in front of my new coworkers, the Secret Service.

Since I had been working at the park for less than two weeks, I was not accustomed to the unique events that are so much a part of the fabric of a regular workday at 1600 Pennsylvania Avenue. Outwardly, to the visitors anxiously waiting to start their White House tour, I appeared "official" in my iconic green-and-gray uniform. However, almost every interaction was a learning experience for me, with surprises waiting at the turn of each street corner.

On this particular morning, operations began as usual: with reassurance to visitors from across the country that they were in the correct place for a White House tour, with explanation about the stoic equestrian statue of General Sherman who presides over the visitors, and with distraction as we asked impatient kids waiting in line who their favorite president was.

However, a few moments after the check-in process began, the Secret Service stopped what they were doing, and time froze. The movement of the line stopped too, which only intensified the anxiety of the already anxious visitors. As I stood in place under the oak canopy, grasping onto a handful of White House brochures, I waited and I watched. Along with the visitors, I tried to make sense of the seemingly senseless situation.

The long, slender oak leaves above me softly rustled in the wind as visitors shifted back and forth in line and the minutes ticked by.

Suddenly, directed by a voice only they could hear, several officers took strategic positions in the street. Behind them, a black bollard adorned with five gold stars receded into the ground and the southwest gate slowly opened, revealing the curving driveway on the South Lawn. The soft rustle of the leaves was overpowered by what sounded like rolling thunder as motorcycles poured out of the gate, one after the other, their red and blue lights flashing brilliantly.

As they charged past me, my attention was drawn back to the open gate just in time to see several black armored vehicles rush out. All were identical except for the second vehicle, which donned two flags at the hood, snapping in the April wind. The presidential seal caught my eye for a split second and then vanished. As more black vehicles of different shapes and sizes followed in the procession, I am sure I shared the same thought as the captive visitors: "How many more vehicles are going to follow?" Finally, the last car appeared, the black gate mechanically closed, the bollard raised into place, and the tours resumed as normal. For a single moment, I stood under the canopy of the oak trees, still stunned, excited, and impressed by the departure of the president of the United States.

Amanda Garrison at President's Park.

Over two and half years later, witnessing the presidential motorcade thundering past the stopped traffic and crowds of people waving is as familiar to me as the sun rising east over the capitol building. Although it will never be a new experience for me again, the theater of it all still stirs the same emotions I felt the first time. And seeing the eagerness and surprise in the faces of the onlooking visitors tugs at my memory of the first few days I spent in my green and gray.

Battle above the Clouds

M. Ann Belkov

I had been in our large maintenance yard many times, but still, storage areas existed that I had not yet been through. While walking with the foreman, Charlie, I noticed a very large rolled-up package that looked like it might be a carpet. I was surprised when Charlie told me he had heard that it was a painting that had been in storage there for more than fifty years.

After checking our records, we were convinced that the painting was created by the artist James Walker. We were also pretty sure that our painting was the smaller of the two he painted of the Battles of Chickamauga and Chattanooga. It was an extremely narrow five-foot-by-eleven-inch painting depicting the Battle of Snodgrass Hill on Chickamauga Battlefield. I asked Charlie to get a crew together to see if we could unroll it and take a look. No one on the current staff had ever seen the painting.

I invited the park's division chiefs to observe the unwrapping of our historical find. For the first time in a half century, we would see whatever was inside. It would be an exciting experience!

We slowly and carefully unrolled the painting, and much to our surprise, we were very wrong. It wasn't the long, narrow Snodgrass Hill painting we thought it would be (actually, I later found out that that painting is hanging in the Pentagon). It was humungous, brilliantly colored, and marvelous! We were thrilled.

We all gazed in wonder at the immense thirty-by-thirteen-foot original painting by James Walker, *Battle of Lookout Mountain* (also known as *Battle above the Clouds*). It was brittle as a crisp potato chip, and contained many cracks and some peeling.

The actual battle was fought on the north slope of Lookout Mountain on November 24, 1863. Military artist James Walker witnessed the event and sketched scenes to render this historically accurate painting. It was commissioned by the Union commander in that battle, Major General "Fighting Joe" Hooker, and was completed in 1874. The middle of the painting shows Hooker on his white horse.

We finally found the records of when it was donated to the National Park Service by Hooker's family, who had stored it for over thirty years before the donation. Fortunately, someone had the foresight to wrap it in cyanide poison—so the rats and insects hadn't touched it.

Now, what to do with this treasure? How to restore it—and if it was, where could I display a painting of such extraordinary dimensions and grandeur?

The National Park Foundation had given us a building on Lookout Mountain that we were remodeling to be our visitor center and offices. I had been involved in the new building design and exhibit planning, and I knew the center had plenty of room in front for an information desk and exhibits. The plan called for an addition to be built with a large room: thirty by seventeen

M. Ann Belkov at Chickamauga and Chattanooga National Military Park.

feet with thirteen-foot ceilings. That room was to be for interpretive talks and additional exhibits. In back, we would have offices and rest rooms.

I wondered: "Would that large room be big enough to hang the Walker painting?"

I had no idea if the painting could be refurbished or how much money it would take to do so. I consulted a few museums and they recommended Perry C. Huston and Associates, a highly respected painting conservator from the Dallas-Fort Worth area. (Perry Huston was recently on the team that restored the Gettysburg Cyclorama.) I wanted Huston to evaluate what was needed and how much it would cost (including transportation and installation).

Perry was ecstatic with our discovery and wanted to do the restoration himself. He volunteered to come to Chattanooga at his own expense—and he was wonderful. Not only was he tremendously knowledgeable about the historical painting and the artist, he explained everything in layman language. I could easily understand what needed to be done, the costs, how he would do the restoration, how he would transport it, and—after I showed him the projected space—how it could be installed.

Perry gave me a quote of $100,000 inclusive.

In 1986, the National Park Service budget was really tight as usual, and certainly couldn't appropriate the funds I needed. However, I was sitting on lots of boards then and knew most of the influential, prosperous, and philanthropic Chattanooga leaders. Maybe I could raise the money?

Much to my surprise and delight, it didn't take much effort to raise the money. On my first fund-raising attempt, I went to a very generous art enthusiast and gentleman of means who lived on Lookout Mountain, and sat on the boards of the Chattanooga Community Foundation and a national bank. Between his personal donations (and a few of his friends'), the foundation, and the bank, I got all the money we needed!

Putting the 30′ x 13′ painting in the 30′ x 17′ x 13′ room would be a challenge, but it could work—as long as I had the builders held off on constructing the wall to enclose the room until after the painting was installed.

It would be a tight fit.

After six months of construction, the building was ready for the painting to be put in place. Perry arrived the day before the delivery and was pleased with our preparations. We had installed the recommended humidifying system (to keep the painting from drying) and lighting (to illuminate the painting without harming the colors).

We all waited in anticipation for the truck to arrive with our treasure.

At last, it arrived!

I was amazed and a bit scared when I saw a gigantic spool in the back of the truck—it was at least five feet tall. The spool holding the painting was on a dolly that would be rolled down a ramp. I was afraid it was going to get away and roll right down Lookout Mountain!

The entire floor of the room was covered in special cloth so the workers could roll out the painting face down. It was then attached to a massive wood frame. The painting covered almost the entire floor. We had all of about three feet to walk along one edge of the painting.

The workers attached pulleys and rope to the top of the frame so it could be hoisted up and secured to the wall. It took four men and me (always hands-on, whether needed or not) to slowly and carefully pull the ropes— and it fit!

When mounted on the wall, it was a fabulous sight—perfect! Then the remaining wall was constructed to close off the Walker Painting Room.

Now there's no way to remove the painting until they tear down the building!

Trapped in the Woods Together

Sherri Anderson

I get to experience many amazing things as the wildlife biologist and bear management supervisor of Katmai National Park and Preserve. I spend a great deal of time at Brooks Camp, our official visitor center; and when you are there, the question is not *will* you see a bear but *when*. In the month of July, there can be anywhere from thirty-five to sixty bears in the area, which can cause quite the excitement for both visitors and staff. One of my fondest memories occurred on a July evening with four wonderful women from Australia.

Now before I go on to tell the tale, you must realize that being close to any brown bear is not a very good idea—even at Katmai, where the bears are human habituated. Staying at least fifty yards away gives the bear its space and gives you time to react if the bear does not like your presence. That being said, I will begin my story.

It was late evening, and I was monitoring bear and human activity on the Brooks River. To cross the river to the viewing platforms or to access the camp facilities, you need to cross a floating bridge. The bridge, however, is not bear safe, so the staff close the bridge when a bear is within fifty yards.

I was joined by four older women from Australia who wanted to observe all the bears fishing in the river. We started to chat, and I was telling them about the bears that were in view when a bear climbed out of the river and headed toward us. Calmly, we gathered and started walking down the trail, away from river and the bear. We waited at a spot fifty yards from the river, watching the bear follow the shoreline and then swim across the river. We moved back up to what is known as "the corner," where the trail from the visitor center meets the river and leads to the bridge.

We hadn't been at the river very long when another bear started coming toward us. Again, we backed up—this is known by the staff as the Katmai

Shuffle. When bear activity is high, you tend to move back and forth to give bears their fifty-yard space. I explained to the group that we do this dance quite often, and they could leave to go back to camp if they liked (it was getting late) or they could stay with me in the hopes of seeing more bears. The Australian women informed me that they could do the dance all night.

After a few minutes, we went back to the river to resume watching the activity. But that did not last long before a bear on the other side of the river started swimming in our direction. I gathered the group, and we again moved back—only this time, on our way back, we ran into a bear coming toward us on the trail from camp. My group started to get nervous, but I told them to stay calm and follow me.

We entered the woods along the trail with the goal of getting to the beach on the other side of the trees (we could take the beach back to camp). Half-way through the trees, however, a courting bear couple entered into the same area, blocking our way. We now had a bear behind us, a bear to our right, and a courting couple to our left. Even so, I managed to keep everybody calm.

We tightened up our group so that we looked bigger (bigger is better in bear country) and very slowly started to move through the trees toward camp . . . until we were stopped by two subadult bears chasing each other.

So there we were, trapped. The only thing we could do was stay still until an opening allowed us to move out of the way. But we were not bored. The courting couple began to mate, with the male making an assortment of sounds. The bear from the river stood up and scratched his back on a tree. And the bear on the trail—a young male—happily followed the two female subadults in and out of the woods.

Each time a bear moved away from us, I tried to move the group to a safer area. The subadults, however, split up, with one running very close to the group, giving the ladies a scare. I reassured them that none of the bears were paying attention to us and the best thing was to stay calm.

Inch by inch, we worked our way to safety, even though we were surrounded by bears engaged in all types of behaviors. And we did finally make our way to the trail and back to camp. The ladies thanked me for the most wonderful experience and for keeping them safe.

I later heard them tell other visitors that they never expected to have such an adventure, and that my presence helped them to stay calm. They could not wait to get back home and tell their tale.

"We must be refreshed by the sight of inexhaustible vigor, vast and Titanic features, . . . the wilderness with its living and its decaying trees, the thunder cloud, and the rain which lasts three weeks. . . . We need to witness our own limits transgressed, and some life pasturing freely where we never wander."

—HENRY DAVID THOREAU, WRITER AND PHILOSOPHER, 1854

All Aboard for Trails and Rails!

Robert and Kandace Tabern

For the past two years, we have been the Chicago coordinators of what we believe is one of the most unique volunteer programs in the National Park Service—Trails and Rails. Imagine being able to share history, geology, plus natural and cultural heritage with others while the subjects zip by outside your train window at almost eighty miles per hour. That's exactly what we do aboard Amtrak's Southwest Chief between Chicago, Illinois, and La Plata, Missouri.

In the mid-1990s, Jim Miculka was Chief of Interpretation at Jean Lafitte National Historical Park and Preserve in New Orleans. He would often travel by train to visit his family's ranch in east Texas. Being a professional nature and history lover, Jim would engage in conversations with fellow passengers about the landscape—from answering questions about alligators to explaining more about French influences in Louisiana. One day, an Amtrak marketing manager overheard Jim and requested ranger-led programs be developed for passengers on the train. Considering that travelers have taken the railroad to reach national parks since the start of the twentieth century, this seemed like a perfect idea.

What would later become Trails and Rails started with Jim and his fellow rangers from Jean Lafitte National Historical Park and Preserve riding the rails from New Orleans to Mississippi and Texas, whenever their schedules allowed. Passengers, often from other areas of the country, were now able to understand what they were seeing outside their window—an opportunity that was not possible until this program was developed. Instead of a family just taking the train to visit a national park site for their summer vacation, the National Park Service was now reaching out to *them* by making the journey to the park part of the overall experience. As you might guess, the popularity of this program grew rapidly, and volunteers had to be recruited to assist the rangers in presenting additional programs.

Kandace and Robert Tabern during a Trails and Rails journey.

By early 2000, Trails and Rails became a formal partnership between the National Park Service and Amtrak, with on-board educational programs expanding across the country. Today, more than 750 volunteer guides can be found on twenty different train routes—from New York to California, and everywhere in between. While all of the programs fall under the Trails and Rails umbrella, the rangers and volunteers from each park sponsor a program, developing their own themes and talks. One of the most scenic Trails and Rails routes operates from Santa Barbara to San Luis Obispo, California, with guides from the Juan Bautista de Anza National Historical Trail helping passengers spot orca in the Pacific Ocean. (Yes, the train gets that close to the beach!) A new program operates out of Washington, DC, and helps travelers learn about the various monuments before the train even reaches the nation's capital.

Our first encounter with Trails and Rails was during a trip to Alaska across the northern tier of the United States in June of 2006. A pair of volunteers with the Mississippi National River and Recreation Area, based in the Twin Cities, provided outstanding narration as we cruised along, looking at the various locks and dams, barges, and rolling hills of Wisconsin and Minnesota. Being both national-park and train-travel enthusiasts, we knew this was something we wanted to volunteer for. Luckily, the program was expanding to seven days per week the following year, and we decided to put in applications. Our involvement over the years deepened with assignments to teach new volunteers, and expand the reference manual and visuals.

In December 2012, we helped reached an agreement with the National Park Service, Amtrak, Texas A&M University, and the American Passenger Rail Heritage Foundation (APRHF) to develop a brand-new Trails and Rails program on the Southwest Chief between Chicago, Illinois, and La Plata, Missouri. For years, guides have presented talks on this train through Colorado and New Mexico, but no program had been established across the nation's breadbasket—Illinois, Iowa, and Missouri. After working closely with Jim to recruit volunteers, the first program hit the rails on May 18, 2013.

Our Trails and Rails program begins with telling passengers about the history of Chicago and why people began traveling west to the numerous suburbs the train passes through. From there, we spend a good distance traveling across the flat farmlands of central Illinois, giving travelers an up-close look at soybeans and corn, and explaining how this used to be prairie land with grasses up to twelve feet high.

One of our favorite stories is shared near Cherry, Illinois, where passengers get a clear view of a slag hill left behind from an old coal mine. In 1909, the Cherry Mine had the deadliest coal-mine fire in United States history; and passengers get drawn into our story when we pass around an authentic mule shoe that was recovered from the mine.

From there, we cross the Mississippi River, the Mormon Pioneer National Historic Trail, and historic Fort Madison—all before reaching the rolling hills of northeast Missouri.

Honestly, it can be quite a challenge for both of us to work full-time jobs and still find time to coordinate our group of thirty Trails and Rails volunteers; however, we have no hesitations, because we believe in the mission of the National Park Service and its dedicated employees, volunteers, and visitors. There is nothing more satisfying than being able to swear in a new Junior Ranger on the train after that child learns something new about our country's history; or having a family say they have ridden our particular train route dozens of times before, but this is the first time they actually learned something about what was going on outside their window—all while thanking us with a thunderous round of applause.

Wonders under Wings

Steve Hurd

A goose, beaver, widgeon, eagle, thrush, weasel, moose, otter, husky, wren can all be found here.

"What park are you talking about?" you might ask.

I'm not talking about a park! I'm talking about the models of bush planes you might find in any national park in Alaska.

Bush pilots fly the best planes for the job such as the Piper, Cessna, Grumman, and DeHavilland aircraft to service the remote and rugged areas of Alaska. As seasons change, so do the options for pilots flying the bush. Their planes are often equipped with floats for water landing, skis for glacier/winter landing, or large tundra tires for unimproved strips. Although bush planes come in all sizes and shapes, these rugged crafts are able to take off and land in short distances. Katmai National Park and Preserve in Alaska certainly meets the criteria for bush flying.

The park spans across four million acres of remote, wild, and spectacular country. Within its boundary lies the Valley of Ten Thousand Smokes, the site of the world's largest volcanic eruption of the twentieth century. In this rugged country, there is no alternative other than aircraft for searches and supplying its remote sections.

Flying in the park planes, I've had the pleasure of seeing hundreds of caribou migrating, millions of salmon swimming upstream, moose wading knee-deep in streams, even infant bears learning to fish. I've seen red fox, wolf, lynx, mink, and wolverine as they lope over open meadows. And the surrounding views are spectacular—shimmering tundra ponds framed by ridge upon ridge of snow-covered volcanoes. Katmai sports massive glaciers and deepwater Naknek Lake, which reflect hues of blue on bright sunny days under the plane's wings.

I cherish my memories of flying over Shelikof Strait along Katmai's eastern boundary. I recall a waterfall dropping straight down a vertical wall and the wind drafts pushing the falling water upward. Cruising over the coastal shore, I observed magnificent brown bears wandering freely along the water's edge and up river estuaries, clamming and hunting salmon, and feasting on berries. One can even see the footprints of many brown bears trailing along ridge edges, each print added to the first, as bears step exactly where other bears have stepped before them.

I recall one flight in the long hours of summer, following American Creek. Dozens of moose—many with gangly legged young—wading in the water, feasting on willow uninhibited, while brown bears gobbled berries only yards away. I even spotted a fox couple hunting along the creek bank. Every air trip is an adventure.

Take, for instance, flying in a Cessna 206 over the Aleutian Range southward, toward Aniakchak National Monument and Preserve. The pilot drops the plane over the volcano rim into the ancient caldera, which is six miles across, and lands on Surprise Lake. The lake is the source of the Aniakchak River, a member of the National Wild and Scenic Rivers System. Standing on the floats of the Cessna, I wonder at the power of the eruption needed to hollow out the land and ask myself, "How would we handle such force if it happened today?"

On the return trip, as on each return from every patrol, I often feel helpless to express the exciting adventure provided me.

It's hard to reminisce about flying above Katmai without thinking about the long, dark winters and the northern lights so prevalent in those months and short day flights. On one particular trip over the frozen tundra, the pilot and I followed a wolverine running over the packed snow. He snarled and flipped into the air as if he could bat away the irritant tailing him. A beautiful, bad-tempered creature. Then we spotted a brown bear taking a stroll to stretch his legs before curling up again for his long winter's nap. He paid us no attention.

Mentioning bears brings to mind my many flights to Brooks Camp, landing on the edge of Naknek Lake, where fishing is king for man and beast. And where the beast rules the fishing at famous Brooks Falls.

So you ask, "What is so special about being chief ranger for Katmai and Aniakchak—flying?"

Well, no. It's bears! Grandiose landscapes! Bears! Stately rivers! Bears! Fishing crystal waters! Bears! Superlative discoveries! Bears! Memories for a lifetime! Bears!

Wow, truly a life-fulfilling experience!

"There is nothing so American as our national parks. . . .
The fundamental idea behind the parks . . . is that the
country belongs to the people, that it is in process of making
for the enrichment of the lives of all of us."

—FRANKLIN D. ROOSEVELT, US PRESIDENT, 1936

Irrational Fears

Melanie Armstrong

I understand it is hard to find a warm place to snuggle up for the winter in Yellowstone, but I hereby modify my open-door policy to disinvite anyone who scurries under my bed and poops on my counter.

Long ago, I owned up to my irrational fear of mice; and though I can reason out that the mice are more afraid of me than I am of them, when I see one, I become that 1950s cartoon housewife, standing on a chair, shrieking and swatting wildly with a broom (and that is only a slight exaggeration).

My fear was born in government housing during my first season as a park ranger, in a creaky trailer that was so twisted on its foundation that a beaver could have snuck in through the cracks in the wall. I awoke one night with an itch on my head; and when I reached back to scratch it, I palmed a furry creature.

Out came the mousetraps, and every night I'd count "one . . . two . . . three . . . four . . . five" until all the traps were sprung. The next day, I'd shake the rodents from the traps, building a mousey mound in the backyard for the neighborhood coyotes, who weren't too interested in leftovers. For nearly a month, every shadow seemed to be a rodent scurrying behind the couch; every crumb on the counter looked like a pellet of mouse scat; and every time the wind blew, I heard tiny feet scampering up and down the hallway. My sleep was already troubled, but the night I opened my eyes to see two mice nibbling on the cord of my bedside lamp, I became convinced that they had banded together to eliminate the human who stood in the way of world domination—or at least their free run of Trailer 118.

I've made an unsteady truce with Yellowstone's rodents. At Norris, I welcomed the "squirrel on crack," who ran zigzags through my attic at two o'clock every morning. I came back to work even after I was working late at the office one night and a mouse crawled under the desk and up my pant leg—and then got kicked across the room and chased down the hallway by a crazy ranger yelling and stomping in an awkward mouse-scaring dance. I know how to handle a mouse; it just takes all my energy to suppress my desire to hop on a chair and tremble when I glimpse a legless fur ball scampering under my bed.

Which is exactly what I saw my first night in Yellowstone this winter. Just as I was dropping into bed, I saw that unmistakable motion dart between my bed and nightstand. Predictably, I screamed and banged on the walls and table, first for the mouse and then in frustration, because I was so exhausted and desperately needed a good night's sleep before work the next day. In resignation, I pulled on my slippers and went to search for a mousetrap.

I found two traps in the laundry room, which I baited with carrots and honey (I hadn't brought my tried-and-true bait of peanut butter and caramels). I had barely turned off the lights again when I heard the trap snap. Content that I'd captured the intruder, I let myself sleep. We left for seasonal training the next day and I reset the traps, just in case my unlucky visitor had not been traveling alone.

It was a full week before I returned. Walking through the door, it was apparent that good times were had in my absence. Fresh scat marked every corner; and though both traps were sprung, those slick critters had darted away before the metal bar snapped. In my hurry to pack, I'd left my new, furry slippers sitting beside my bed, two cozy little mouse houses which were now speckled with scat like chocolate sprinkles on a vanilla cupcake. I also found a curious, different scat on the coffee table: about the size of a marble, rough around the edges, and honey-colored rather than the color of dark chocolate. Too big for a mouse, too round for a squirrel, too hairless for a carnivore—I was stumped.

Determined to overcome my fears, I reset the traps with the proper, tooth-sinking caramel I'd picked up in town, put in my earplugs, and went to bed. The next morning, I'd caught one more . . . but the other trap was sprung and empty. Had the trap been sprung by the larger creature that was leaving Captain Crunch–sized turds on my end table?

Another morning, another dead mouse. Then, as I was putting my boots on to head to work, my foot jammed against something in my shoe. I overturned the boot and dozens of that peculiar scat poured out, rolling over the kitchen floor like honey-colored marbles. Finally, I realized my boot had become a convenient stash for a years' supply of dog food, which was likely being collected by the mice that were clearly still living in my house. I baited the traps again, and caught three more mice over the next few days. And then, blessedly, the night came when no traps were sprung and no mice were caught. Had I finally stopped the infestation?

While my mental state dramatically improved on mornings that did not begin with the handling of dead rodents, I noticed an odd smell in my kitchen. I emptied the garbage, sterilized the mousetraps, and did my dishes, but the odor lingered. Though I'd seen no sign of mice in days, I couldn't shake the feeling that they were just regrouping. Boldly, I decided to look again to see if I could find the hole they might be using to enter the apartment. On my hands and knees, with a flashlight, I poked around in the closet, behind my bed, under the sink, behind the heater and the woodstove, and in the kitchen cabinets. I shined the beam underneath the stove, which was clean, and then the refrigerator, which most definitely was not. Beady eyes stared back at me, frozen momentarily by the light, before dashing into the corner.

And here I discovered the limits of any tough-girl image I may have built up during the ages. I will snowmobile thirty miles in minus-twenty-degree weather, and when that snowmobile gets buried in a six-foot drift, I will shovel for hours until I can drive it out myself. I will drag a bloody bison carcass off the road with my bare hands; and I can force myself to empty a mouse trap in a howling blizzard, burying the stiffened carcass in an icy tomb so it will someday nourish a starving coyote. But I cannot, will not, shall not clean a nest of dead and dying rodents in the kitchen where I eat my Cheerios every day. I called our maintenance crew so fast you'd think women's liberation never happened.

I may not be standing on a chair and shrieking, but in my head I am; and I dedicate every good night's sleep to the kind crew who removed the rodents, cleaned out the nest, and sealed up the holes so I can sleep in peace.

Inside the Rainbow

Bill Fink

My time with the National Park Service ran from 1971 to 2004. I had assignments at park units in Maryland, Arizona, Hawaii, Nebraska, Pennsylvania, and Michigan, along with two extended details in Alaska. I found the mundane and I found great wonder.

I had some experiences that shaped the course of my life, and others that I still try to figure out. I drove over a road less than ten seconds before it split open and erupted in a curtain of lava. I saw the head of a forest fire burst over the top of my car as I sped down another road, another day. I crawled through a shallow, abandoned coal mine beneath the historic house I was charged with protecting. I received a blessing of safety from Pele, the goddess of the Hawaiian volcanoes, when I drew "tending" duty for a priestess of the old ways who had made her offering of gin to the volcano (after drinking much of the bottle herself) and was unable to drive, but too culturally important to arrest. And I stood inside a rainbow.

Except for the two other rangers who were with me, I've not heard or read of others who have had the experience of actually standing inside a rainbow. Indeed, I've read some "scientific" statements indicating it is physically impossible to do so. But we did.

We were on a patrol out to Nāpau Crater, along the Chain of Craters in Hawai'i Volcanoes National Park. At the time, Chain of Craters Road was closed due to the eruptions of Mauna Ulu.

As we stood on the rim of the crater, we looked out toward the sea, across the wide crater of cooled lava from eruptive activity of the last several years. The crater edge was perhaps 200 feet higher than the floor.

There was a bright, warm afternoon sun over our shoulders behind us. We noticed the visibility drop in the distance as a light, misty rain shower moved *mauka* (uphill) toward us.

A rainbow gradually formed. Its bands separated into vivid, distinct displays of color. It formed a perfect arch, from crater floor—up and over—to crater floor.

The shower continued quietly on its course toward us; and our view on the edge of the crater meant we were looking down, as well as out, at its approach.

As the leading edge of the shower got closer and closer, the rainbow morphed into a full circle, still brilliantly banded. It was eerily quiet and still—no wind, no trees rustling, no birds talking.

Just before the shower came over us, we looked into the full-circle rainbow and could see our shadows surrounded by its distinct, brilliant circles of color—the Brocken spectre.

Then the shower overtook us. For a brief but intense few moments, everything around us sparkled with color. Looking up, down, and all around, I saw brilliant sparkles of color. Interestingly, the bands of color were gone; all seemed random and unorganized.

In short order, the mist and rain were dominant, the sun was obscured, and we got wet.

We talked of our experience as we hiked back to the road. Did it have some profound, greater meaning? For just a moment, as everything sparkled around me, I wondered if this was the culminating act of some Hawaiian spirit or some sort of rapture.

Overall, my memories of the event are pleasant. I reflect on it occasionally and enjoy telling the story whenever I can garner a new audience. That's what old rangers do.

To me, it *was* a special moment in my life—that was forty years ago and yet *is* today.

Thoughtful Preservation the Hard Way

Laurant Pingree

"The Big Thicket National Preserve (BITH) contains remnants of a diverse ecological system and provides habitat for several threatened and endangered species. The preserve provides protected lands and waters for public recreation and for research on the rich biodiversity of the area."

This is the National Park Service statement of the preserve's significance.

Well, back in the '70s, when the first National Park Service preservation unit was being pieced together, we were given a goal to begin work on preserving something that did not really exist. The idea was to remove as much human impact on the Big Thicket as possible. As a work leader, my mission was to remove every vestige of human occupation possible in the new eighty-thousand-acre "Big Thicket National Preserve."

We were dealing with over two hundred years of human occupancy. There were dozens of old cabins, shacks, homestead sites, as well as some unfinished new construction. Litter, old roads and trails, broken-down fences, barbed wire—if you could name it, it was there.

Early on, we ran into a phenomenon that was somewhat peculiar to the area. Many of these old buildings had a garbage dump dating back one hundred years or more. They were full of cans, bottles, broken toys, and every imaginable item that was not biodegradable. They *did not*, however, have any plastic bags. The workload was heavy, but we were given a free hand to do what was needed.

Over a three-year period, we removed building after building. We wore out two dump trucks. We built miles of new boundary fence. We hauled away garbage. We reconstructed an old cabin for a visitor center. We remodeled a farmhouse for a seasonal housing dorm. Best of all, we were able to hire more than one hundred local kids to help with all this work. These were city kids from the Beaumont/Houston area in Texas. They learned first-aid,

Laurant Pingree at Big Thicket National Preserve.

a work ethic, and an appreciation for unlittered, pristine areas. They learned to appreciate each other, to work together, and to prepare for life itself.

The preserve has grown some over the years. There were eight ecosystems originally and now there are nine. The eighty thousand acres have expanded to over one hundred and five thousand acres. A beautiful new visitor center, along with administration offices and maintenance buildings, now makes the workload a little easier. But in the beginning, thanks to some local kids, a handful of dedicated National Park Service maintenance folks, and a park administration staff that gave us direction then turned us loose to do the job, the Big Thicket National Preserve is just that: a wild, natural, unlittered area tastefully preserving what is known as the "biological crossroads of North America."

The Raven

Kristin Camitta Zimet

At the winter solstice, hiking is different than at any other time of year. The sun hangs low over the mountains. Even at midday, you hover at the edge of dusk. There is a hush, a remoteness, a solemnity in the air. A farewell.

As I walked out along the Appalachian Trail in Shenandoah National Park, cold bit through four layers of clothes. The landscape was a sketch in dark tones: sepia, charcoal, umber. Only a few hemlocks held a brooding green.

But here was beauty at every step. The ridge, stripped of its leaves, was no longer a secret, closed-in wood. It took its place among a throng of ridges. A fellowship of mountains stretched to the horizon. On the ground was a scatter of snow, loosely strewn. Lifting a leaf, I could see each separate, sprawled crystal.

Shenandoah National Park, 1974. A snowshoe adventure, possibly along the Appalachian Trail.

THE WONDER OF IT ALL

The lowest boughs seemed hung with airy tufts of snow. Close up, this snow turned out to be clematis, its seeds in whorls. Each seed trailed a curled white plume; each inflorescence was a spiral nebula.

Here and there, black cohosh stood tall. Graceful stalks three or four feet high carried rows of open seedpods. Wild basil thronged the path. Each tiny dried flower curled open in a five-way arabesque.

Black, glossy seeds hung upon red threads. These were the last fruits of the maple-leaved viburnum, a treasure for the birds.

What birds? I walked in a chrysalis of silence. No chickadee sputtered; no Carolina wren clacked. I seemed to dream on my feet. Perhaps this was how the world would seem someday, with the last patch of land unfit for our wild kin, the last small voice snuffed out. A cold, fixed twilight; no breathing but our own.

Then, from the far ridge, came a cry. A rich, rollicking call; a baritone with a purring rumble to it. The rough-and-tumble mastery of one who rides the wind, slides up and down it. The raven flung four notes across the mountaintop.

Without a moment's pause, I answered it. Don't ask me how. I had such need of greeting. Four notes came throbbing out, raven to raven. They shook my throat and belly.

And the raven came, straight over the intervening ridge. Riding the updrafts like a bareback cowboy. What did he think, as he hung over me, his yellow eye staring in his shaggy-feathered head, his great wings pouched, and his keeled tail flaring?

In that eye, I saw myself. Grounded, awkward, with stumpy body, heavy boots, and pack. I named myself interloper, spreader of silence, eater of wilderness. My claws tore the wild into yards and parking lots. I named myself kin, height seeker, mountain keeper. My beak spoke all the tongues of life.

He hung above me half a minute. He called again—four rough, commanding notes—testing me. I meant to answer, but out came a half-baked croak. I heard the whoosh of beaten air, just once, as he lifted away.

I made my cold way home. The day stayed suspended between light and dark.

5

Volunteer Adventures

Yosemite National Park, 1920.
Dr. Harold C. Bryant conducts a nature
walk in Yosemite Valley.

The Sky Is Alive Again
The Redemptive Power of the California Condor

Joseph Belli

Growing up in central California in the 1970s, I became attached to the landscape and the various creatures that also called it home. Of those, none captured my imagination more than the California condor: huge, mysterious, and heartbreakingly rare. (*Huge*: with a wingspan exceeding nine feet, condors are the largest birds in North America. *Mysterious*: despite their high profile, much about them remained unknown. Although primarily inhabiting the mountains of southern California, they occasionally wandered north; and when one appeared locally in 1972, it created quite a stir. *Rare*: experts estimated the population at no more than sixty, making them one of the most endangered birds in the world.) As I hiked the hills, I was habitually looking skyward, but I never saw a condor. Not so long ago, they used to fly here. Without them, the sky seemed empty.

In 1984, a local Audubon Society chapter offered a condor-watching trip to southern California. For several days, we scanned the skies from a reliable observation post, and I saw my first condor—albeit at a distance of several miles, where it appeared as a dark, regal speck floating in the air. I vowed to return, and a year later I did.

But the intervening year had not been kind to condors. Several had been confirmed dead, while others had vanished, never to reappear. The entire population had dwindled below two dozen, with just one breeding pair remaining in the wild. The California condor seemed to be sliding inevitably toward extinction, and I wanted to get one last look while I still could.

I did get that look, but given the bleak situation, it was bittersweet. Shortly thereafter, the remaining birds were captured and taken into captivity for their own safety, where they would hopefully breed and replenish their numbers. In 1987, the last of those wild birds was trapped, and no one knew when—or if—condors would ever fly wild again.

Fortunately, those condors fared well in captivity, and the success of the captive breeding program emerged as a turning point in the condor recovery effort. In 1992, condors were returned to the wild in southern California; and in December 2003, Pinnacles National Park became the latest release site when six juvenile condors were set free after an absence of nearly a century. When that happened, the sky came back to life.

I followed the progress of the Pinnacles birds with keen interest, attending the first and subsequent releases open to the public. Early on, I asked one of the biologists if they took volunteers. He replied that a volunteer program had yet to be developed but was planned for the future. For me, "the future" came in 2010, when I responded to an announcement soliciting help monitoring condors in the park.

I wasn't quite sure what monitoring condors entailed, but I would've done nearly anything for the chance to play even a meager role in condor recovery. I figured I'd be hiking up some mountain with binoculars and tracking gear, and have at it (all condors are fitted with radio transmitters). As it turns out, that's part of the deal, but there's a lot more: observing nests, watching captives in the flight pen, trapping condors (for health checks and transmitter replacement), and assisting the staff when they handle birds. Five years down the road, I've participated in all those activities, and the experience has been rewarding and invaluable.

An unexpected benefit has been the privilege of working alongside a very talented and dedicated group of people: the staff, interns, and volunteers representing Pinnacles National Park in the California Condor Recovery Program. Through the program, I've been able to observe condors on a regular basis—something that seemed impossible thirty years ago—and I've found them to be highly social, intelligent, and comically curious. The most memorable observations, however, are the unexpected encounters in the field, when, out of nowhere, a large shadow looms, and I look up to notice a condor gliding past, just overhead, the wind from its wings sounding like waves crashing on a beach. That never gets old.

Condors have an effect on people. Besides being large and rare, they are highly visible; and that adds considerably to their charisma. In flight, condors seem oblivious to people. They aren't particularly attracted to us, but, unlike hawks and eagles, they don't avoid us either. They fly on their terms, people be damned. As a result, they sometimes fly incredibly close; and when they do, it's a powerful feeling.

When I began, I was most comfortable working alone, soaking up those experiences solo. Sometimes, though, I was stationed along a popular trail; and in the beginning, I have to admit that I tried to remain inconspicuous—pretty futile when toting a spotting scope, antenna, and beeping receiver. People flocked to that setup, eager to ask questions and talk about condors. And when I witnessed their enthusiasm, my reticence melted away.

These people came in all ages and from various places. Some were locals, some from out of state, some from other countries; and condors became a kind of universal language. Many confided that they had never seen a condor and had come to Pinnacles just for that reason. Once I heard that, I wanted them to see a condor as much as they did. And when condors did appear, people profoundly thanked me for something as simple as setting up a spotting scope or letting them use my binoculars. Best of all were the times when condors flew in close, giving visitors a special kind of experience—something no interpretive talk or television documentary, no matter how well crafted, could ever match. Some witnesses were moved to tears.

From a young age, I believed restoring the California condor was good for nature. What I've since realized is that it's good for human nature too.

"I'll go sit in front of the bulldozers to buy some time."

—VIM CRANE WRIGHT, ACTIVIST AND ENVIRONMENTAL
EDUCATOR, 1989

Mountains of My Heart
A Story from a Young Volunteer

Felix Christiansen

When my dad asked me whether or not I wanted to be a volunteer at Guadalupe Mountains National Park, I thought he was kidding.

It was October 2013. I was about to turn ten years old; and when I figured out that he was being serious, I immediately accepted. We lived in El Paso, Texas, then. Every day, my dad would drive ninety miles to the "Guads," our nickname for the mountains. My dad was a park ranger there, and he organized the Volunteers In Parks program. My younger brother was slightly hesitant about the prospect. He was a bit daunted by Dad's stories about the west Texas mountains—mostly true, but there were a few tall tales as well. But I know how my dad tells stories, so I was less hesitant.

On Sundays, I'd wake up at 5:30 in the morning to ride in the car for an hour and a half. After we arrived at the Guads, we'd check the schedule, grab our radio and packs, and head out. My mom and brother and I started our workdays with excitement. We would usually head to one of two of the historic cabins to open them up and share information with visitors.

One of those sites is known as Pratt Cabin. It was the summer residence of a geologist named Wallace Pratt in the first half of the twentieth century. I enjoyed the two-and-half-mile hike up McKittrick Canyon, especially crossing the creek, to get there. Visitors enjoyed finding the cabin open when they got there!

Felix Christiansen at Guadalupe Mountains National Park.

Guadalupe Mountains National Park, circa 1990. Old stone house ruins.

Frijole Ranch was the other site. It was a ranch owned by several families, with the Smith family being there the longest. My brother liked Frijole Ranch better because it had a cute little yard with a stone wall around it, big pecan trees, and a small irrigation canal running from a spring into the fruit orchard of apples and pears and berries. The ranch house itself was a little creepy, with dark corners, creaks, and that scary feeling of "old." There was also a cool schoolhouse nearby, which was also the old post office.

After a few months, in April 2014, we moved into the park, living for a month in a small cabin in park housing—where many of the park rangers live. This move gave us the chance to hike more often on more trails like the Frijole Trail and Devil's Hall. We even scaled the main summit of the mountains, the highest in Texas—Guadalupe Peak—at 8,749 feet! And we did some tougher hikes to Pine Top and around the Bowl, even traveling on the foothills of El Capitan, the face of the Guads.

While living in the park, I helped my dad more often. We'd open up and shut down at the beginning and end of each day—me checking to see whether anybody was in the bathrooms, and, since there never was, him locking them shut for the night. We'd check gates and outbuildings. I also worked in the visitor center, telling visitors about trails and park activities, setting up a touch table of skulls and footprints, and other cool things like helping other kids with Junior Ranger activities. I became a Junior Ranger as well, and even a Senior Ranger. I still have the patches and badges.

I also still have my old hiking stick. I still have my old volunteer cap and shirt. I still have poems about the place on my website. I still have the memories.

I do believe it is safe to say that my brother and I are the youngest people ever to work—or at least patrol—at the park. I miss hanging out with my old ranger friends, and I miss all the amazing places and features. I miss the gypsum dunes, the canyons, the history, and the elevation. I even miss worrying about wildfires, mountain lions, and rattlesnakes.

The Guadalupe Mountains were, and still are, a gem of the National Park System. That month living in the park was the end of my time in Texas. Now I live far away from there, in New York, at another park. It's different here, but I like it. And I'm eleven now.

Still, the sun and the wind and the colors and the experience of the Guads will never leave my heart.

More than Twenty Years of Friendship with Japanese Volunteers

Mika Moore

In 1993, a small group of us in Japan sent a few letters to the National Park Service in the United States, asking for it to support the group in coming to do some volunteer work. Mount Rainier National Park (MORA) was the first and only park that responded to us, saying, "Yes, we will support you!"

The very first year, in 1994, we sent about fifteen university students to MORA. They built the first ADA (Americans with Disabilities Act) trail at MORA with absolutely no previous maintenance experience. They stayed in the park trailers, but those weren't in a good condition. For the second year, the program coordinator at MORA, Tom Moore, found enough host families to support this program by asking his friends not only in the park but in the surrounding local community—so the volunteers could stay in American homes for free while they came all the way from Japan to donate their time and labor to the Mount Rainier National Park.

Over the past twenty years of this ongoing program, J-VIPA (Japan Volunteers In Parks Association) has had 386 participants, contributed 23,040 hours of service, and worked on multiple projects (such as building the popular Nisqually Vista viewpoint at Paradise; building the paved, wheelchair-accessible trailhead at Skyline Trail in Paradise; building Cougar Rock Campground, Ohanapecosh Campground, and White River Campground). This tremendous experience not only inspired all the visitors to the park but also all the participants who became part of MORA history.

I was one of the members who started this group, but I also took part in the program in 1996, 1997, and 1999. I worked building muddy trails at West Side Road and also worked in building the ADA campsite at Cougar Rock. As of this date, I can see my campsite still being used every summer, and I can proudly show my families and friends that I built this site!

Mika Moore at Mount Rainier National Park.

Through these twenty years of experiences, I fell in love with Mount Rainier, and loved it enough to give up my Japanese citizenship to apply for US citizenship—so I can work for Mount Rainier National Park. I have been involved in not only coordinating J-VIPA but also being asked to help out multiple Japanese programs, such as the Teacher-Ranger-Teacher program between Mount Rainier and Mount Fuji, the US/Japan Interpretive Training Seminar, and the Sister Mountains Exchange Program between Mount Rainier and the Fujisan Club. Our friendship between two mountains and two countries has been getting much closer and growing tremendously. Giving up my Japanese citizenship wasn't an easy decision to make, but to hear the comments of "we couldn't have done this without you" and to see so many smiling faces, I don't have any regrets.

J-VIPA is the longest-running international volunteer program in the National Park Service. I am very proud to be a part of this program and will continue to contribute to build many more small bridges between two mountains, two countries, and all over the world.

Real Work on the Appalachian Trail

Cosmo Catalano, Jr.

I'm a fifteen-year volunteer for the Appalachian National Scenic Trail. When people find this out, they often ask me how I got started.

I saw a notice in the local paper and went to the meeting place, expecting to find a lot of hard-core trail rats with callused hands and muddy boots. Instead, I found Pete and Jack, and a VW bus with a bunch of rough-sawn two-by-twelves sticking out the back. It seemed we were going to build a bridge.

We drove off through some fields and then onto what might have been a road fifty years ago, and finally stopped in the middle of the woods.

"Here we are," Pete said. "This is the trail."

It wasn't quite my idea of how one got to the Appalachian Trail, but I saw one of those white blazes I'd heard about, marking the route. I was beginning to think my assumptions about the Appalachian Trail were about to change.

Once we carried the materials to the job site, we were ready to go to work.

Since I had some carpentry experience, I expected I could be fairly helpful on this project, and asked if there was a drawing of what we were going to build.

"Nope," Jack said, "this is just a simple box bridge. Let's start with piling some rocks up here and over there, to make a place to land the bridge."

Gradually, working together, we built up some nice rock cribs and began to assemble the planks. Then we took a lunch break on the stream bank.

"Do you guys do this on a regular basis?" I asked.

"We've done a few of these over the years, but we work on a variety of projects every Tuesday and Saturday, all season long."

"Wow," I said, "that's a lot of work. Who decides what you're going to do?"

"We do, mostly. There's a committee of us that creates a work plan for the year, and we take turns being project leaders," said Jack. "Some of us lead more projects than others," he said, looking over at Pete.

"So, you basically keep the trail open and functioning for, what, about ninety miles in Massachusetts?"

"Well," Pete said, "there are maybe forty other volunteers besides us who keep their sections open all season long, and we all gather together for the larger projects."

"But who decides what to do and how to do it?" I asked. "The National Park Service?"

"Well, ultimately, yes, I suppose," said Jack, "but it's a long trail. So, locally, the management is basically up to us. We let the staff at ATC (Appalachian Trail Conservancy) and the Massachusetts DCR (Department of Conservation and Recreation) know what we think needs to be done, and they usually agree and let us do it."

"Hmm," I said. "This is pretty cool. Every person who hikes to Maine is going to be right here at this spot where we are right now. Really, each of you is individually responsible for keeping the whole trail in one piece. The work we're doing on this bridge is a link in a two-thousand-mile chain that has to remain unbroken. If it were broken, it wouldn't be the Appalachian Trail."

"Well, I guess you're right," Pete said. "The thing is, they trust us—just regular people—to do it. There are some basic standards—very few, actually, for something this big—but other than that, yes, it's up to us."

"Yup," said Jack. "If we think it needs to be done, then we do it. The National Park Service says, 'Maintain the trail and care for the surrounding lands. We're here if you need expertise, but how you do it is pretty much up to you.' And you know, that kind of trust is returned a hundredfold by volunteers like us—and now you, it would appear.

"What are you doing next Tuesday?"

"I want to see what's on the other side of the hill, then what's beyond that."

—EMMA "GRANDMA" GATEWOOD, FIRST SOLO FEMALE
APPALACHIAN TRAIL THRU-HIKER, 1955

America's Front Yard to the World

Sandy Murdock

I have the privilege of volunteering at the Survey Lodge Ranger Station, which serves as the front porch to the National Mall, America's front yard. The Survey Lodge is a place where visitors ask for information and advice about the monuments and memorials that surround the grassy expanse. The work is interesting because you meet so many people.

As a native Washingtonian, the expectations were that our "customers" would primarily be Americans. But my very rough estimates indicate that many of the Mall's guests are from abroad.

From my time at the Survey Lodge, some very vivid and interesting impressions have developed from multiple conversations. Here are a few of the highlights:

First, visitors are shocked by how beautiful the Mall is. As one visitor said, "This is awfully good for such a young country." They are really taken by the way in which we have preserved our history: "Yes, we have statutes at home, but yours have such meaning. You make the individual honoree's times and accomplishments so visible and understandable."

Second, they appreciate how open the Mall is. America is perceived overseas as having heavy security measures everywhere. The presence of the National Park Service rangers makes visitors feel comfortable without being overly intrusive. Our guests enjoy being able to move freely among all of the sites.

A frequent exclamation is that everything is *free*. In their native lands, visitors have to pay for entering equivalent facilities. That conversation easily flows into the fact that our parks benefit from the support of both the National Park Foundation and the Trust for the National Mall, which help fund these beautiful representations of our country. The restoration of the Washington Monument came through a major private donation from David M. Rubenstein.

Sandy Murdock near the Survey Lodge Ranger Station at the National Mall and Memorial Parks.

A fourth impression from our international guests is how welcoming and valuable the park rangers are. It is not uncommon to hear comments like "She was so knowledgeable about [her area of expertise]," and "He was so friendly; even though we are foreigners, we felt like family."

Finally, the biggest highlight: how many people travel to the United States and declare that one of its leading attractions is the Mall. They are excited to walk around and know a lot about what they want to see, but make it clear that they have carved out enough time to make the rounds. It is very heartwarming to see the affection of these international visitors for our front yard.

Leapfrog

John P. Harmon

The trail was in much better condition than when I was on it last, and the park ranger ahead of me made use of this by setting a brisk pace. He was younger and in much better shape than I was, and I took pride in being able to match his pace and keep up.

It was a sunny Saturday afternoon in the fall, but there were very few people making use of the trail. Perhaps it was because this beautiful day had been preceded by a week of torrential rains, and park visitors knew this trail would be very muddy in places. They wouldn't have been wrong either; there were places where the mud captured my boots and protested with a loud sucking noise when I pulled them free.

Yet the temperature was mild, the day bright and beautiful; and I commented to the ranger that it was a perfect day to be working on the trail. He agreed. I tugged at the straps of my daypack—laden with trail markers, nails, and a hammer—and enjoyed the view.

A few months earlier, I had a much different experience on this same trail. My youngest son and I had set out to hike the Congaree River Blue Trail at Congaree National Park in early June. I had completed the hike several years earlier and wanted to share the sights with him.

Starting from the visitor center and walking along the boardwalk, which carried us over the swamp, we marveled at the size of the cypress trees contained within the park. Their "knees" jutting above the surface of the swamp was something my son had never seen before, and he was fascinated by their purpose.

Shortly after we left the boardwalk and began trekking along the single-track dirt path, we began encountering fallen trees across the trail. We were expecting this, because we had read that the trail conditions were rough due to flooding that had occurred months earlier at the park. We are also seasoned hikers and backpackers, so encountering obstacles along the trail was something we were accustomed to running into.

However, as the miles passed and we drew closer to the river, the source of the flooding—the full impact of the damage to the trail—became apparent to us.

There simply was no trail.

The footpath had been washed away, leaving no trace of its route. Trees bearing trail markers had fallen, their roots washed away by the floodwaters. A tangled mass of tree trunks and branches lay before us.

Armed with a trail map, a GPS, orienteering skills, and fierce determination, we refused to let the damage keep us from completing the loop trail. We knew the trail was there; we just had to find it.

Using the last confirmed trail sign as a reference, one of us would stay at that point while the other scouted on for a sign of the trail ahead. The trail markers were still there, lying in the mud or still attached to a fallen tree trunk. Occasionally, we could see where trail workers had previously cleared the path and used that as a point of reference.

Our efforts were rewarded when we reached the sandbar along the Congaree River. We picnicked there and rested our weary feet in the cool waters. A great blue heron gracefully floated by, impossibly large and so beautiful.

Once we had eaten and rested, we resumed leapfrogging along the trail until we emerged from the area most damaged by the flooding. As we walked, my mind was occupied with the staggering amount of work that would be required to restore the trail to its former condition.

As I mentioned earlier, my sons and I are avid hikers and backpackers, taking full advantage of the state and national parks available to us. Sometimes, while hiking, we encounter crews working along the trail, improving them for the enjoyment of all. And we sincerely thank these workers as we meet them, taking note of how cheerfully they go about their task.

While we hiked the Congaree River Blue Trail, I wondered if Congaree National Park would use volunteer trail workers to restore the trail and, if so, how I could join them. Tired—but completely satisfied with our outing—we finished the hike and drove home.

Less than a week after our hike, an article in the news caught my eye: Congaree National Park was seeking volunteers to help repair their trails. So, at the speed of the Internet, I completed the application to become a volunteer trail worker.

That's how I found myself working alongside a park ranger on this beautiful day a few months later; we were retracing the route my son and I had taken back in early June. Since then, a contracted crew had cleared away all of the fallen trees, opening the path once more for visitors like myself.

The ranger and I leapfrogged past each other, attaching new markers along the trail, which reminded me of how my son and I had used a similar method when hiking this trail. After about four miles of marking, a hiker came by as I nailed a marker to a tree.

"Thank you for what you're doing," he said sincerely.

"It's my pleasure. Enjoy your hike," I replied, with equal sincerity.

It felt wonderful to be giving back to the park a little bit of what it had so willingly given to me.

"We are part of the universe, not lords of it. If it perishes, we do too."

—JANET HUTCHISON, LEAGUE OF WOMEN VOTERS
MEMBER, 1993

Paying It Forward

Robert Angstadt

The ad in my local newspaper jumped off the page like winning lottery-ticket numbers: "Volunteers Needed at NPS Visitor Center."

What? Volunteering for the National Park Service—really?

I immediately picked up my phone, called the number in the ad, and was greeted by voicemail. With a sigh of disappointment, I left a message for someone called a "volunteer manager." Now I had to wait.

How long before I'd get a call back? Would I get a call back? Oh the agony of waiting.

And then it happened. The call came.

I must have passed stage one, for soon after the phone conversation, I received an email with an application attached to it. The application definitely looked like a governmental form—it was organized and to the point, with lots of questions. After several rounds of proofreading, it was on its way back to the volunteer manager. Fairly soon, the application followed with an interview. And as I waited for my appointment, I couldn't help but ask myself: "What adventures am I getting myself into? Do I have what it takes to do this? What exactly will I be doing?"

At the interview, these questions and more were answered: I'd help people learn about the Santa Monica Mountains; I'd share my experiences; I'd offer support to the ranger staff; I'd help at special events—the list went on. I had hiked numerous trails in the Santa Monica Mountains, and I could easily provide recommendations to the inquiring public. I could also talk about wildlife, topography, geology, natural resources, local history, and park regulations. It almost sounded like I was about to relive every Boy Scout merit badge I ever earned. This volunteer gig could turn into quite the opportunity!

As soon as the interview was over, the torturous waiting began—again! Would I make the final cut or not? I couldn't believe all the anxiety I was

Robert Angstadt at the National Bison Range.

getting myself into, especially for a position that didn't pay a dime. I volunteered for numerous other activities in my lifetime: feeding the homeless, teaching people how to prepare a resume, collecting canned food, walking for cancer, building homes. But none of these experiences were closer to my heart than volunteering for the National Park Service. It felt like a match made in heaven. I couldn't let this opportunity slip away, but I'd have to wait it out.

As each day of waiting progressed, the thought of volunteering was one of the first things on my mind in the morning and one of the last when I fell asleep. I really hoped the selection process would not take several weeks. I had to let the process play out. As I waited, I thought about how things in life come full circle when you least expect it. I had moved out to Ventura County in 2004; and on a whim, when I saw the brown National Park Service Visitor Center sign by the freeway, I decided to stop by and see what this sign was all about.

I wasn't near a national park (or so I thought), and was curious why a national park location was in the area. To my surprise, when I entered the visitor center, I saw many exhibits and a substantial bookstore of information.

The ranger behind the counter was very helpful. It was here that I picked up numerous trail maps for each of the park's property locations and discovered what a National Recreation Area was. It was this random stop at the visitor center and those brochures that set a six-year course of hiking the trails of the Santa Monica Mountains.

The more I thought about the "circle of life" and the different paths we are exposed to during our journey, the less anxious I became. And before I knew it, I answered my phone to a hearty "Congratulations!" and "Welcome aboard!" from the volunteer manager. I had made the cut, and my next journey was about to begin—a journey that would circle back to the same location where I had picked up the trail maps several years earlier.

To say volunteering for the National Park Service has been an honor and a joy is an understatement. I've loved every task assigned to me (well, 99 percent of them), and enjoy giving back to my community and the nation through the work I do each month. And my uniform has a strong similarity to the one I wore in Boy Scouts! I've been impressed by how enjoyable the other rangers and staff are to be around, and am inspired by their gifts of knowledge. I've learned so much—but there is much, much more to learn. The Santa Monica Mountains stand for so many things, and it will take more than a lifetime to learn them all. As I pay my knowledge forward, I am always getting more knowledge back in return.

This is not just a story about my excitement in becoming a National Park Service volunteer; it is also a story with a message—one that I discovered after two years of volunteering: As my story began, I had responded to a call for volunteers from an ad in the local newspaper. But I could have also picked up a volunteer application on my own when I went in to the visitor center that very first time; all I needed to do was ask for one, fill it out, and turn it in. How much greater could our journey in life be if we asked for the things we want rather than waiting for the invitation to get them?

$\overline{6}$

Love of Place

Yellowstone National Park, 1953.
Old Faithful in winter.

Top Cottage
A Retreat Fit for a King (or a President)

Kevin Oldenburg

As a National Park Service interpretive ranger in Hyde Park, New York, I have the unique opportunity to interpret four different historic sites focusing on the Roosevelt and Vanderbilt families. Of the four sites we have, Top Cottage, which was the retreat that Franklin Roosevelt built for himself to "escape the mob," remains one of those hidden gems that, once discovered by the visitors, proves most memorable.

The cottage is very sparsely furnished and issues a challenge to the interpreter to weave the story without much in the way of artifacts to validate it. However, the most powerful artifact we have is the porch. An understated porch is just as powerful a tool as a piece of furniture or a painting; it is up to us as interpreters to paint that picture, to transform a place with words, to bring the past alive.

This porch is unlike most porches. Still tucked back in the woods, it has hosted kings, queens, presidents, first ladies, princesses, and prime ministers. The site has only been open since 2001, and I have had the honor of sitting on that porch from the beginning—and now as the lead ranger for the site.

It is a very intimate experience sitting on that porch in wicker and rocking chairs, enjoying the place really no differently than Franklin Roosevelt and his guests did (minus the martinis!). Visitors sit back and breathe in the serenity, and listen to the stories. It is far from a guided house tour; it is an experience that often leads to detailed and in-depth discussions on the man, the place, and the events that transpired there. It was where the infamous hot dog picnic occurred in 1939, when the king and queen of England came to the United States looking for support in the months leading up to World War II.

A frequent guest on the porch with me during my programs was Harry Johannesen. A former employee of Eleanor Roosevelt at Val-Kill Industries, and son of Nellie (who cooked those hot dogs!), Harry would often stop by while I was talking to a group and sit down with us. He loved to tell stories of the royal visit, and I was always happy to let him. The visitors loved hearing from someone who was actually at the picnic.

Harry used to tell the story of buying the hot dogs: "Mother sent me to town to buy the hot dogs and said, 'Harry . . . make sure you get Swift [Premium], because Swift are the best; and nothing but the best for the king and queen.'" Those visitors and I would sit transfixed as he reminisced about that day.

We lost Harry a few years ago, in his early nineties, but I always keep his stories alive when I conduct a program. The visitors continue to enjoy his stories even though he is no longer here to share them.

There is something about sitting on that porch—it's hard to describe. A feeling of place is overwhelming there. It is a retreat Roosevelt designed to not only meet his personal interests in the design elements but also his physical needs. It was designed for a man in a wheelchair to use without

Kevin Oldenburg at Top Cottage, part of the Home of Franklin D. Roosevelt National Historic Site.

assistance. It was a place where he was not afraid to show who he truly was: a man with physical limitations. Being on the porch and sharing stories with visitors about him and this home, you tend to lose track of the time and step back to a different era. With the conversations and discussions and decisions FDR was making up there, it was far from easy. From talks with the royal family about US support of the British to discussions with Winston Churchill on the development of the atomic program, the topics proved very important to world affairs.

To this day, looking out on the view, listening to the birds, or watching the leaves falling in the autumn season, you get a sense of what it must have been like for FDR. From the casual visitor to the diehard Roosevelt fanatic, people tend to connect with the history at Top Cottage. The ropes and barriers are removed, and reproduction furniture is used that visitors can sit in. It puts them in the story, sitting where history happened, not peering into it.

To sit where Roosevelt, Churchill, or Queen Elizabeth sat; to hear the stories from their visits; to walk in their footsteps there—that is what Top Cottage is all about. And I'm very lucky to be able to share all of this with those visitors who make the journey to "the top of the hill."

And We Call It . . . "Wall Magic"

Suzanne Sigona

The Vietnam Veterans Memorial may have started as one of the most controversial sites of the National Park Service. This memorial is generally referenced as "the Wall" and was dedicated in 1982.

During my first visit, I felt the emotion of the losses we endured related to the Vietnam War, and it did not subside with subsequent visits. I had a personal drive to become a volunteer.

I started working at the Wall on Sunday mornings. When I arrived at 7:00 AM, veterans would already be there. It was the nature of the experience that they did not sleep and would arrive at the Wall early in the morning. For those who could approach the Wall, I had the ability to guide them to their time frames, look up names in the directory, and research unit information for them.

We had no computers, Internet, or unit web pages; we had passionate individuals who were building a database for their own records. We had to find those people if we wanted to find anyone.

The experiences of each shift went far beyond anything that could be imagined. The pattern that repeated was what we call "Wall magic": Someone would look for a name in the sea of over 58,000 and run into the name of someone who went to boot camp with the person they were looking for. People would not realize there was an alphabetical listing as they started to look for a name on a particular panel. It was as though they were scanning faces in a crowd. As we approached to offer assistance with the directory, it was common to have the name they were randomly searching for be right on the panel in front of them. I cannot begin to count the times that someone has said, "Oh, he is right here, where I'm standing."

In the early days, it was common to have veterans who would stand in the tree line because they could not approach the Wall. Some did this for years. One told me that he took a train to DC four times, and three times

Suzanne Sigona at the Vietnam Veterans Memorial.

he got on the next train home. It is difficult for many. I have often told the corpsmen and medics, "You remember those you lost, but I get to meet the ones you saved."

One of the early volunteers served because her father was on the Wall. He was a Navy SEAL. Sons and daughters of those we lost were (and still are) always searching for more information on their fathers. There were a myriad of reasons that the silence was maintained in families; but as these young people grew older, they wanted to meet someone who knew their fathers.

Early on a Sunday morning, I was at the Wall, and at the apex was a tall man with his wife. He had his head tilted back as though the angle would keep the tears from running down his face.

While serving at the Wall, I have recognized that there is a fine line between helping and interfering. I generally approach and offer, "If I can help you locate names or time frames, please let me know." Then I move on so that they do not feel pressured to respond. Eventually, the couple approached me. The wife explained that they were on a pilgrimage that included Biloxi, Mississippi; Coronado, California; and now the Wall. I saw the trident on her husband's ball cap, and it confirmed that he was a Navy SEAL.

I left them alone a bit longer and approached to explain that one of our volunteers had a father who was killed in Vietnam, and that he was a Navy SEAL. The man asked the name and then responded, "That was my CO." Again, with concern for the intrusion, I said, "If you ever want to meet his daughter, I know she would appreciate meeting you."

As you can imagine, the thought of meeting a family member is very difficult. For the veteran, there is survivor's guilt or stories they do not wish to tell. The husband approached me again and asked for the information on contacting this daughter. They met down at the Wall that evening. Although this daughter was a volunteer at the memorial, she later told me it was the first time she really cried.

This story and so many like it come to life each day at the Vietnam Veterans Memorial in Washington, DC. We now have computer capabilities that assist with the research and the connections that need to be made. In it all, I am continually reminded of the banner at the top of a T-shirt that someone was wearing at the Wall one day. It had the map of Vietnam and read, "1959–Forever."

Going Off-Trail

Bryanna Plog

Imagine a salmon leaping, airborne, a spray of water droplets running down its sleek silver body, framed by the white churn of a waterfall. Perched on top of this falls stands a brown bear, paws gripped to the slick rock, back arched, eyes concentrated at the rush of the water below. As the salmon jumps toward the head of the bear, the animal opens its spacious jaws wide, leans forward, and snatches up the salmon in its mouth.

If you can envision this scene, or have ever seen a photo showing a grizzly bear catching a salmon in its mouth, you are familiar with Katmai National Park and Preserve. Yet, to be honest, I had really never heard of Katmai before I spent a summer there as a seasonal interpretive ranger. Turns out Katmai is located in a remote area of southwest Alaska (actually, all parts of southwest Alaska are considered remote) and is most famous for its resident brown bears (over two thousand in the park, dozens of which frequent the rushing waters of Brooks Falls each summer).

I walked the 0.6-mile trail to Brooks Falls dozens of times that summer, strolling through the forest of white spruce, greeting visitors ("Afternoon, folks. How are you?"), and backing away from bears who also walked the trails ("Hey, bear—whoa there. Yep, you go ahead . . . "). Alaskan hiking tip: if there is a bear on your trail, *get out of its way*. Back off, even if that means walking off the trail.

After years of adhering to the "stick to the trail" mentality, I would wince a bit as I heard the crunch of plants under my boots, apologizing to the lingonberries and lichens as I backed through the underbrush. But between shaking hands with a thousand-pound carnivore and stepping off the path, I realized sticking to the trail in Katmai isn't always the best option. As a ranger, I was used to figuratively getting off the beaten path, learning the ins and outs of different parks. In Katmai, I soon learned the story of Katmai was not just about bears—and that literally going off-trail was the only way to see the origins of the park, an area known as the Valley of Ten Thousand Smokes.

The valley was once a lush forest, framed by green hills and snow-covered mountains, a mere twenty-three miles away from Brooks Falls. In June 1912, superheated ash and pumice erupted from the Novarupta volcano, and the largest eruption of the twentieth century filled the valley with up to one thousand feet of deposits from Novarupta's pyroclastic flow. This was why Katmai was designated a national park in the first place, and friends and I spent a free (and finally rain-free) weekend backpacking to see Novarupta for ourselves.

A trail led us through a sparse forest of alder and willow, past patches of brilliant fireweed, across Windy Creek, and underneath the green hills of the Buttress Range. Here, at the very edge of the valley, we could see the first life returning to the volcanic floor. The trail cuts through bumpy patches of biological soil crust, where microorganisms start to create real soil. At this point of our trip, the fragile soil crust was a good reason to stay on the trail. Within the hour, however, the trail disappeared and we were simply on the vast, dry, and very flat expanse of pyroclastic flow deposits.

Bryanna Plog at Brooks Falls in Katmai National Park and Preserve.

Gray-pink pumice stones crunched under my feet. As I walked, tiny wisps of what looked like dust trailed behind: powdery ash stirred up by my boots. The valley is as flat and treeless as if someone had taken a bulldozer to the entire forty-square-mile area.

We angled toward a gray hill and Novarupta, and wandered around, trying to find a good crossing across the icy Lethe River. Blue glaciers glinted from Mount Mageik to our right, while snowy Mount Griggs towered to our left. In every direction were the volcanic deposits from the 1912 eruption.

For the trip across this entire stretch of what is best described as a moonscape, there was not a single trail to be seen. Instead, there was the expanse of volcanic matter to contemplate during the day; and when it finally got dark, an expanse of bright stars and the stretch of the Milky Way at night. Our first night in the valley, we rolled out of our tent in the chill of a late-summer Alaskan night to see the green of the aurora borealis dancing on the horizon.

The next day, we climbed up and found the source of the pumice and ash that now coated our boots, clothes, and bags: Novarupta. The small dark dome of the volcano still steams ominously; and we sat and watched it in the evening light, the pumice around us now bright oranges, yellows, and reds. Winds stirred up the abrasive ash, stinging our skin and hanging low over the whole valley as a reminder of the inevitability of ash clouds sometime again exploding out of this landscape.

The volcano was more than fourteen miles away from any established trail.

Just because we were off-trail, however, didn't mean we were the only ones in the valley that weekend. After a few hours of hiking, I peered down and saw what were unmistakably bear tracks, the imprints of the soft pads and sharp claws a reminder of what Katmai is most famous for.

We may have been a long way away from the sight of silver salmon jumping toward the waiting jaws of an Alaskan brown bear, but it was good to keep an eye out for these grizzlies anyway—on or off a trail. At least there, in the vast volcanic expanse of the Valley of Ten Thousand Smokes, if we did meet a bear, I wouldn't have to worry about crushing any plants as I scrambled off a path.

The Chattahoochee River Winds Through

Jerry Hightower

The Chattahoochee River wound through Devil's Racecourse Shoals two hundred or more feet below me. The western ridgeline across the rugged palisades was forest to its meeting with the sky. As I sat on the massive quartzite cliffs of the overlook, I pondered how this area could be preserved for the public. I was probably sixteen.

Six years later, as a young army sergeant recently returned from Vietnam, I found the river corridor under siege by developers. Fortunately, mentors within the academic and conservation community guided my involvement in a grassroots effort to gain protection for this treasure, located adjacent to

Jerry Hightower in Chattahoochee River
National Recreation Area.

the largest population center in the state. I had many opportunities to intro-duce a diverse audience to the magic of the river corridor. In classrooms and in living rooms, along trails and on the river, I slowly advanced awareness of the importance of our extraordinary resource.

After a long struggle to obtain National Park Service status through con-gressional vote, President Jimmy Carter signed the bill creating the Chat-tahoochee River National Recreation Area. Although my career goals were to teach high school biology and American history, I filled out a seasonal application for the new park. Thus began a career—a National Park Service career.

Although a career in the classroom would have been rewarding, it would also have been confining. The National Park Service legacy of legendary service and dedication to conserving America's natural and human history rescued me. For three-plus decades, I have had the privilege to serve this mission, and it has been a grand gift. The transformation of middle school students from the inner city with a three-day environmental education camp, the thousands of students and the hundreds of teachers who have attended programs, the assignments to train and be trained in many differ-ent parks, and so much more have been so enriching to me.

"The scientific worth of an unspoiled natural area . . .
is beyond description."

—LIANE RUSSELL, BIOLOGIST, 1972

Coming Home

Tracy A. Fortmann

It was a cold and, not surprisingly, wet Pacific Northwest day. I looked up at the violet-streaked sky with ribbons of pink and red as I rubbed my hands and blew into them to keep warm. The morning was electric with excitement, and many who were anxious to begin had already headed down the trail. I took a deep breath of cold air as I stood there; the air chilled my lungs and helped calm me. I could tell this was a day that I would remember for many years to come.

Stamping my feet, I looked to the east at the mammoth peak cutting its way skyward above the mountains around it. Mount Hood's white, snowy slopes contrasted sharply with the piercing blue sky. The nearby foothills were rimmed with pointed green firs and hemlocks. Ancient oaks with massive crowns grew on the plains below. A newly reestablished historical apple orchard, each tree heavily laden with pink and white blossoms, was so close the sweet scent lingered where I stood. Canada geese, with their distinctive honking, flooded the skies above where the mighty Columbia River cut through the Coast and Cascade Ranges. I waited for those who, like me, were coming to the gathering.

I smiled broadly once they finally reached me at the trailhead, and I embraced each of them awkwardly, as many were half my size and bundled up, making it difficult to get our arms around each other.

American Indian elders possess a profound aura of understanding. They bring with them knowledge of their peoples' place here over thousands of years and an instinctive ability to travel easily through time, connecting their tribes' past, present, and future together. That day, as we silently began our slow trek down the trail, words were of little import—we knew why we were there. Tribal drummers were beating a rhythm before us, and I understood then that we were bound together by this sacred place known simply as "the Village."

Tracy A. Fortmann at Fort Vancouver National Historic Site.

The Village was home to members of over thirty-five different tribes from across the continent, including Iroquois, Cree, Chinook, Multnomah, Cowlitz, and Klickitat. British, Americans, French Canadians, Orkney Islanders, Métis, and even Native Hawaiians also lived here. It was a bustling place with up to one thousand who worked for the Hudson's Bay Company. It was one of the most populated colonial areas on the West Coast—a place where people lived, raised families, feasted, worshipped, celebrated births, and mourned deaths; all while working together in spite of different languages and very different homelands.

The American military burned the Village to the ground in the 1860s, and its inhabitants were forced to move on—some to Canada, some to the new American settlements, but many to American Indian reservations. The National Park Service had been working to restore a sense of the Village, and two newly reconstructed houses now stood at the end of the trail, surrounded by ice-frosted grass. Smoke spiraled up and away from one of the rustic chimneys, creating a surreal trail to the sky. Near the houses, we gathered.

The drumming stopped. An elder burnt sage and spoke about how his tribe had never forgotten this place; it had never been lost to them. Another elder sang songs of tribute. I watched Hawaiians place fragrant, delicate *leis* at the site where their ancestors lived. An elder Hawaiian from Canada spoke of the many young Hawaiian men who came to work here and those

THE WONDER OF IT ALL

who chose to stay. Many there that day sang prayers and songs in their own languages. Some played instruments and told stories about their relatives who had lived in the Village. They spoke about the Columbia being so dense with fish that you could almost walk across the water, and how the river would freeze during the winter. Some spoke of their families who had lived here and were buried nearby—of the pain of their families burying their young and the epidemics that took so many of their people. Park rangers and members of the local community also spoke, recounting their more recent and personal connections to this special place.

The strong emotions and vivid memories surrounding the Village have not been lost. As I looked at those there with me, I wondered if they, like me, felt a sense of belonging here and a love for this place. Looking at the faces of young and old, I knew then I was not alone—their faces and words said in their own way that this place was home. Everyone was an equal that day. Everyone shared their feelings in whatever way they chose, and everyone listened respectfully. No judgments were made.

Reflecting on this momentous occasion, I believe this gathering was befitting of the Village, a place that found strength through diversity; national parks are for *all* people too. We all have our own special connections, memories, and stories to tell. In a time when there are often reasons to separate from and question those who differ from us, the Village is a place that brings us together.

The Village at Fort Vancouver serves as a symbol of tolerance, mutual respect, and wonder in our nation's diverse history. There were tears that day, but they were tears of joy for the Village, which once again had a sense of place where descendants could return to remember the old stories and visitors could become aware of its unique past.

As the circle ceremony came to a close, I watched a toddler who straddled her mother's hip suddenly reach skyward. Her tiny hands grasped wildly in the air to catch an eagle soaring slowly above us. We all watched silently as he rode the currents. As the elder next to me squeezed my hand, she told me: "This is meant to be. The eagle has come home. He is here to be with us and pay homage to the Village too."

We had all come home that day.

"There can be nothing in the world more beautiful than the Yosemite, the groves of the giant sequoias and redwoods, the Canyon of the Colorado, the Canyon of the Yellowstone, the Three Tetons; and our people should see to it that they are preserved for their children and their children's children forever, with their majestic beauty all unmarred."

—THEODORE ROOSEVELT, US PRESIDENT, 1905

Yellowstone National Park, 1927. A bugling elk.

Commuting
Winter Solstice, 2010

Melanie Armstrong

I am prepared to argue that I have the greatest commute in the world. Perhaps there is someone out there commuting between tropical islands on a sailboat, watching dolphins frolic over the hull, but I'm certain I have the continent locked up. Aside from nippy subzero temperatures (though beneath these layers, it doesn't feel *that* much colder than a sedan with the air conditioning on full blast in July), I couldn't ask for twenty miles of more scenic and lively highway to drive every day on my way to work.

I live in the Grant area of Yellowstone; and a few days a week, I snowmobile to the Fishing Bridge Warming Hut to tend the fire for a day. Today was my Monday, the first day of my workweek; and as usual, it took more time than I'd planned to put on all my layers and gather my gear for the ride.

After checking over my snowmobile and fueling it up, I pulled out onto smooth roads. The groomer had neatly packed down yesterday's snowstorm, and my first stop of the day would be to do some grooming by snowshoe on the boardwalks at the West Thumb Geyser Basin. A fog bank swirled around the thermal area, cooler temperatures trapping the steam from the geysers close to the ground. Though the sun was trying to peek through, the air temperature hovered around freezing. The West Thumb of the lake is almost completely frozen now, and the stillness of the ice teamed up with the eeriness of the fog to chill the spine inside and out. It seems right that the lake is freezing, though, and snowmobiling near open water these past few weeks has been unsettling. A friend reminded me today that we could still go kayaking on the lake. *Brr.*

Driving north from West Thumb, the sun finally broke the fog ten miles up the road at Pumice Point. I was the only commuter, but I still pulled my sled to the side of the road to look at the view. At this promontory where the Thumb meets the main part of the lake, the ice gave way to open water, and the nearby shores were stacked with blocks of ice pushed up by the waves below. As I was admiring the power that pushed up icy ridges, two dark shapes slipped from water onto ice. The river otters had discovered the boundary of their habitat too and, like me, were dabbling in both ice and sunshine.

No commute is complete without a little traffic jam. Three groups of bison stood today on the road to Fishing Bridge. The first group seemed startled by the day's first snowmobile and quickly trotted to the side of the road. Three miles north, I encountered three cows and their calves. I pulled close to the animals and waited for them to move to the side of the road, but they hardly noticed—or cared—that I was there on my choking snow machine. It looked like breakfast time; and for ten minutes, I watched these three mamas nurse their calves.

My thoughts on this public display? First, *ouch!* I know breastfeeding can be painful, but it looks so much worse when it's three degrees outside. Still, watching these cows stand squarely in the road, feeding their offspring when there was absolutely nothing around for them to eat themselves, I was impressed by the sacrifice of their own calories on behalf of the next generation.

Ever the impatient commuter, at one point, I boldly tried to slip between the trio, only to come far too close to the flailing limbs of an awkward dance between a cow bison and a calf clinging to her teats with its mouth. I pulled back (hoping the loud beep of the reverse signal wouldn't further aggravate the animals) and waited. Eventually, snack time ended and the group started walking, allowing me to zip around them by hugging the edge of the road. The third group of bison were walking head to heel, just like they describe in the textbooks, and I was halfway around the group before I realized we were side by side on the bridge over Bridge Bay. I punched the gas and prayed the bison wouldn't have the same compulsion my brothers do to throw random objects into any body of water, just to watch it splash and sink.

On the return trip, I now faced the bison head-on; and this time, the lead animal was the meanest looking bull I have ever seen. Not particularly large in size, he had the look of the class bully about to set the locker room on fire. His horns were literally askew, the left one curving gracefully upward while the right horn pointed directly out from the skull, bending ninety degrees at the very tip and at the eye level of a five-foot-seven-inch human straddling a snowmobile. Perhaps because of the skull injury, the animal's fur grew forward on the right side, dropping into his eyes and giving him a one-eyed, crooked-horn look. It was as neutral as any bison stare, but his look registered in my mind as "I want to beat my head against something . . . right now!" I drove a little faster, just in case.

I am a tremendous fan of the winter solstice because it marks the moment when the days start turning longer. Commuting on the shortest day of the year, however, means the sun begins to set just about the time I head south.

On this winter solstice, the mountains were glowing pink and doubling their reflection in the lake. I watched a coyote testing the new ice floes, taking a shortcut across the neck of the lake. A fox scampered down the road a few feet before bounding easily over a four-foot snow bank. I pulled up to the garage just before night set in, the nearly full moon just starting to rise.

7

Looking Back, Moving Forward

Yellowstone National Park, circa 1930. Seated around the campfire, second from left is John White, superintendent, Sequoia National Park, and seated fourth from left is Horace M. Albright, director, National Park Service.

The Pilgrimage

Shelton Johnson

Anyone who has ever stood at the edge of the world (which, in Yosemite National Park, is called Glacier Point) has felt the current of a thunderbolt. The heart stops, you breathe deep, or you don't breathe at all. But that first immersion into this space rarely marks the end of life; rather, it's a birth—an awakening into the cosmos itself. You realize that you're not standing still at all but are adrift with cloud and sky, caught in the tow of the sun, unstuck from Earth like a seed in the wind.

Nothing before you as far as the eye can discern is motionless. The granite slowly rises beneath your feet; the fir trees gently rock back and forth; and plants move as one, like sea grass caught in a tide. The distant thunder of Vernal Fall and Nevada Fall to your right is pitched high at the edge of our hearing compared to the deep bass of Half Dome humming like a struck bell, and all of Creation is flowing along in the grip of waves seen and unseen.

These are my thoughts as I stand gripping the metal railing, peering down at Curry Village thousands of feet below, holding fast to the Earth. I don't want to be swept away into the abyss below, but a part of me is already gone, lost to the light and shadow, with only the frailty of fingertips to keep what's left of me in this world.

There are worse fates than to become one with the planet, but it's a risk you're taking if you ever visit Yosemite Valley with an open heart. This is why cameras come equipped with shutters in order to damp out a fierce light; or why there are limits to human sight, hearing, and touch. It's all literally too much to take in, but how our bodies struggle with the challenge!

For over twenty years, I've worked as a park ranger in Yosemite Valley, which means that I've been tasked with not only trying to see, hear, and feel Yosemite but with communicating that grand vision to all of its visitors. To some degree, these pilgrims who come from all over the globe have already glimpsed or caught the whisper of this wonder, but some arrive unprepared—as if you can prepare yourself to be in the presence of the "Range of Light" John Muir described. All anyone can do is simply jump in, tread the waves, and try to keep the senses clear from a universe eager to overwhelm them.

Water is at the root of it! Everywhere, there's water swirling around, churning under, foaming on the top, or hissing through every sort of space until the world itself becomes liquid; shooting, splashing, roaring, booming, dripping, leaping, and coldly reflecting upon itself.

In our collective attempt to tell the story of Yosemite, our immersion and union with this place turns our words into autobiography. We become Yosemite telling its own story! Exaggeration, you might ask? Can a mule deer be considered separate from the meadow where it grazes, or the musty hollow of a fallen tree separate from the bear that makes it its den in winter? Can you have a meaningful conversation with a peregrine falcon and never bring up what blue sky feels like over wings?

Everyone who visits Yosemite (and we're all visitors to Yosemite) has the potential to become a lasting part of it by simply being present when we are in its presence. The longer we stay, the greater the likelihood that Yosemite will stay with us. We breathe it all in, and our sweat is wicked into the air or falls to the ground. Particles of quartz and potassium get under our nails, and the dust of all that granite gets into our lungs and slowly drifts into our bones. With enough visits, protecting Yosemite becomes as natural as self-preservation.

Shelton Johnson in Yosemite National Park.

The world did not begin on June 30, 1864, but it's as good a date to mark the awakening of human consciousness as any other birthday. That was the day President Lincoln signed the Yosemite

Grant Act, which preserved Yosemite Valley and the Mariposa Grove of Giant Sequoias for all time, the day when some of us realized where we really were and the value of that realization, the day we gave ourselves a compass and instructions on how to use it, and the day we realized that we're not alone in the universe and that we have plenty of company right here on this Earth. Yosemite Valley is not just the cradle of the National Park idea, it's something much more profound. I don't know what that is—that's not my job. It's not yours either. It's the responsibility of all our descendants to figure that one out.

Because Yosemite is a national park, because it was set aside "for the benefit and enjoyment of the people," just like Yellowstone was when the Organic Act of 1872 created the world's first national park, and because that status was made "inalienable for all time," those words from the Yosemite Grant Act give us the time to figure out the "usefulness" of a gift that is beyond human comprehension.

After all, Abraham Lincoln didn't just set aside a valley and some big trees in 1864, nor did Benjamin Harrison simply set aside a few mountains in 1890 when he signed the legislation that created Yosemite National Park. Both of these presidents had the power to set aside the Earth itself for all of us and for our children, down through the ages. As long as we have national parks—have sacred places like Yosemite, Yellowstone, Grand Canyon, Zion, Arches, Denali, Great Smoky Mountains, Glacier, Wrangell-St. Elias; Serengeti, Banff, Royal, Huangshan, Fuji-Hakone-Izu, Berchtesgaden, Kruger, Gran Paradiso—there's hope for all of us.

The American writer Thomas Wolfe erred slightly—at least in regard to our national parks—when he titled his novel *You Can't Go Home Again*. He was thinking about a return to some provincial town; a backwater existence after a life in a metropolis. Returning to the mountains is entirely different. As John Muir put it, "Going to the mountains is going home."

Not just Yosemite or Yellowstone, but every national park in the world is a doorway facilitating a homecoming for our species; so after that pilgrimage, we'll walk back through that door and have a much better idea as to where we're going, not just as individuals but as one tribe.

"Indeed, a journey through this park and the Sierra Forest
Reserve to the Mount Whitney country will convince even
the least thoughtful man of the needfulness of preserving
these mountains just as they are, with their clothing of trees,
shrubs, rocks, and vines."

—COLONEL CHARLES YOUNG, BUFFALO SOLDIER AND
SEQUOIA NATIONAL PARK SUPERINTENDENT, 1903

Yosemite National Park, 1956. Jeffrey pine on Sentinel Dome.

Budding Young Environmentalists

David Kronk

In January of 1990, I was managing the Hidden Lake Environmental Education Center in Everglades National Park, a residential learning center where middle school children from South Florida come with their teachers to study the park for three days. Superintendent Mike Finley called me into his office one day and told me to get ready to prepare some students for a special program later that month: a walk in the park with President George Herbert Walker Bush!

On the morning of the presidential visit, I was quite nervous preparing what I would say to the president during our one-hour tour, and telling a group of a dozen students to relax and have fun during their visit with him. These students had just finished a three-day camp experience in the park led by one of my staff—Ranger Warren Griffith—and I was confident that Ranger Warren had taught these students well. It was my intent to let the students tell the president about the many things they had just learned.

The president was very friendly and gracious, and obviously loved children. The students did a great job pointing out different birds and plants, and explaining alligator behavior, among other things. It was a beautiful morning in the Everglades, and everyone was having a fun time!

Then the president asked me to step aside with him, away from the news media and students. He asked me what Everglades National Park needed from him. And as instructed, I told him what Superintendent Finley had asked me to relate: the park needed funds to buy nearby farmland to use as a buffer zone to protect the park wildlife; and even more important, it would be most helpful if the president could direct the US Army Corps of Engineers to redesign the canal system north of the park to direct water into the center of the peninsula and eventually into the park, rather than out to the Atlantic Ocean.

As our tour neared an end, I made a quick decision to abandon my program conclusion and let the students tell the president in their own words why he needed to protect Everglades National Park. Then I crossed my fingers and hoped for some good comments!

One curly-haired fifth-grade boy raised his hand and told the president that he had lived in Miami all his life but was amazed by all the beautiful stars he saw in the sky his first night camping in the park. He went on to explain how everyone got up one morning before dawn and witnessed the sunrise too. He was so impressed with the sunrise experience that he had written a poem, which he then shared with the president.

A girl raised her hand and went on to carefully explain how the water supply is very limited in South Florida because the aquifer is just below the surface; and that we need to conserve and share all the water so that there is enough for the animals and plants in the park, besides the farmers and city residents.

Everglades National Park, undated. Visitors on an elevated, wooden walkway.

With time for one more comment, I called on a young boy who I later learned was from Pakistan. In a clear, calm, and eloquent voice, this boy told President Bush: "This beautiful park is part of our heritage and you need to protect it, so my children and grandchildren can enjoy it someday too."

Wow! What awesome comments from these students! I looked at the president and he looked back at me, nonverbally suggesting that I had told the children what to tell him. I quickly replied, "Mr. President, no one prompted these kids to say any of these things, I swear to you. They just completed three days of exploring the park with their teacher and rangers."

He smiled and nodded as we all said good-bye.

This was indeed the highlight of my career with the National Park Service. That day, I was never prouder of my job, my agency, my staff, and the children who had learned about the park and shared it with our president.

Later in the month, I listened to the State of the Union speech by President George Herbert Walker Bush and was very moved by his statement about "recently meeting some budding young environmentalists in Everglades National Park." It was one more example of how education programs in national parks can indeed make an impact and a difference!

Memories of My Father
Bob Flame, Rocky Mountain Ranger

Gail Stephens

Today, I am a veteran volunteer of seventeen years at Monocacy National Battlefield, and I love it. I also come naturally to this; my father John S. McLaughlin ("Johnny Mac") spent forty-five years in the National Park Service. What follows is the story of only one man, but there were hundreds like him—men and women whose love of nature, dedication to the national park idea, and sheer hard work helped create today's National Park Service.

My father joined the National Park Service in 1928 as one of the first rangers in Yellowstone National Park who was also a college graduate. He loved his career and ultimately served as the superintendent of five national parks: Grand Canyon, Grand Teton, Mesa Verde, Sequoia and Kings Canyon, and Yellowstone.

His career began in June, when he reported to Yellowstone with what was then required gear: a .22 rifle and a saddle. The superintendent of Yellowstone was a bit concerned about the ability of his college hires to handle hard labor in the wilderness, so he sent them out to acquire wilderness skills. My father described his first boss, a former army scout, as a "real, real man," who taught him valuable wilderness skills, like how to build a snow cave for shelter when out on ski patrol in the brutal Yellowstone winter.

In 1930, my father moved to Rocky Mountain National Park to serve as chief ranger. There, he renewed his friendship with park naturalist Dorr Yeager, whom he had known in Yellowstone. Yeager was keen to write a book for young adults about the life of the ranger and decided to use my father as his model; and *Bob Flame: Rocky Mountain Ranger* was born (followed by *Bob Flame: Ranger* and *Bob Flame in Death Valley*). After father's death, Dorr Yeager wrote, "Johnny Mac fit perfectly—a young ranger [who was] conscientious [and] likeable, with a great sense of humor and [dedication] to the parks."

While the Bob Flame series promoted a very positive image of the National Park Service, not everyone appreciated national parks, leading to some difficult and dangerous times for NPS personnel. My father's 1946 assignment as superintendent of Grand Teton National Park put him in the middle of just such a situation.

Powerful forces were at war in Jackson Hole, the valley presided over by the Teton Range. On one side: American tourists, on the road after the Great Depression and World War II, joined by John D. Rockefeller Jr., who was willing to use his enormous fortune to buy land in Jackson Hole for the national park. On the other side were area ranchers and Western hunters, who wanted to use the land for hunting elk and raising cattle. They were backed by the power of their representatives in Congress. The National Park Service and my father were in the middle.

Dad understood his position. He was in public life, and expected controversy; but he always tried to keep the discussion as friendly as possible. Controversy, he said, was "democracy in action, and if a thing is right it's going to turn out to be okay in the long run." Sometimes things were definitely not friendly. I was born on July fourth; and Father went into the town of Jackson, in uniform, to buy cigars to pass out to friends. Unfortunately, he passed a group of cowboys, who decided it was time to teach the ranger a lesson. My father only escaped a beating by running and slipping into a store owned by a park sympathizer, who let him out the back door. In 1950, the park idea won out, and a large part of Jackson Hole was incorporated in Grand Teton National Park.

My father could laugh about bad times. While he was superintendent of Yellowstone, controversy erupted when the National Park Service used rangers to shoot elk in the northern part of the park in order to prevent mass starvation, because the herd was too large for the available food sources. In the middle of the erupting media storm, my father received a letter from "Canis Lupus" (the scientific name for the gray wolf), who was clearly an unidentified friend of the National Park Service. "Canis" sympathized with the Yellowstone rangers accused of "savage slaughter," adding "you would think they were talking about me," and offered his help in the elk reduction. Father replied that he appreciated the sympathy: "When you are in a box, there is nothing so good as to receive encouraging words from somebody in a similar fix." My father, the lover of wildlife, told his friend the wolf, "You may be sure that we would like to see some of your family around," and counseled, "Be of good patience—your time will come"; and so it has.

He could change. Throughout his NPS career, the cardinal rule had been complete fire suppression; but in the late 1960s, as superintendent of Sequoia and Kings Canyon National Parks, he approved a program of "let burn" for naturally ignited fires in about 70 percent of the park. He agreed with the emerging science that fire had a place in a natural ecosystem.

Above all, my father believed in the national parks and the National Park Service. In an interview after one of his many park-planning trips overseas, he commented that the United States was respected everywhere for "the national park concept. . . . We can't overexport it." In answer to another question about park expansion into urban areas and seashores, he said, "There is no one better prepared than this National Park Service; no one has a clearer mandate than this National Park Service—to look after and consider the preservation of the land, the preservation of the resource itself. No bureau of the US government is better prepared to undertake these things, to do the planning on them, and see that they are properly preserved, not only for today but for the future. The future is the important thing."

So, how could I not be a proud National Park Service volunteer?

Why Wilderness?

Mike Reynolds

It was September 2005, and we had been hiking for eleven days straight. Carrying everything we needed on our backs, we trekked through the wildest country Yellowstone National Park had to offer.

After spending some time in the Thorofare region (arguably the spot farthest from roads in the Lower 48) and seeing the headwaters of the great Snake River, we were approaching the end. I had grown up a Boy Scout, and played in the woods and fields of Kentucky as a child, and I had spent all of my free time working and living in national parks and on its trails; but almost all of those experiences didn't last long. Though they might have been long in miles, I was always out in a day—day hiker extraordinaire. It was on the last day of our eleven-day backpacking trip in Yellowstone that I realized this; we had just lived the wilderness experience. We had gone eleven days without seeing a car, without hearing civilization. The only human imprint we saw for eleven days was the trail and our own gear. I had spent my whole life without realizing it. Only when I had truly experienced a landscape untrammeled by humans did I realize I had never in my life gone a day without seeing a car.

I was hooked—but that's not to say that I didn't appreciate wilderness previously. I wanted it to be there; I knew its value. I enjoyed it within the span of a single day. But I had never truly *experienced* it. I had never lived it.

Why wilderness? Because we can visit and experience and transcend ourselves. We do not need wilderness just for wilderness' sake; we need it to better understand who we are. It comes full circle: wilderness helps us understand ourselves, and by experiencing it, we better understand the value of wilderness.

Wilderness is academic. Designated wilderness has certain specific qualities, outlined by the US Congress, that make it truly wilderness. But it is also experiential; wilderness is intangible. It is made up of feelings and emotions. The humbling feeling of not being in control. The fear of not knowing what is around the next bend. The loneliness and solitude. The euphoria of the freedom to explore. The unfathomable size. The pride of testing yourself in difficult conditions and tough terrain. Day-to-day life as we know it is different here—this is what wilderness is all about. This is why wilderness should exist. So, we, as humans, can put ourselves in perspective; so we can see ourselves in the scope of the world.

As a national park ranger, I have come to accept the premise on which the National Park Service was built. We don't just designate a national park and protect the resources therein; we designate a national park and invite the world to experience it. It is our belief that without visitors, we would have no constituents. Without visitors, no one would care about the great and important resources we are protecting. We need to have visitors or we do not have parks. I believe this is also true with wilderness. I know it is not possible for many to truly experience wilderness—it is costly, physically taxing, difficult to understand; and life sometimes gets in the way. But some people must visit wilderness to truly understand it. Without understanding, we might lose it forever.

Though physically smaller than the wilderness that got me hooked back in Yellowstone National Park, the wilderness at Lava Beds National Monument, where I now live and work, is every bit as experiential. Though the landscape is different, the emotions and feelings are the same. I love the feeling of looking up through the branches of a juniper tree into the deepest, darkest night sky; the smell of the sage in the slight moisture of the morning; the silence of the heat of the afternoon; the unknown of the terrain; the wonderment of the small adaptations of life. There is a lot to explore in the high-desert vegetation and the rugged lava flows. It is a tangible place with intangible values.

Why wilderness? Because the feelings it delivers are a renewable resource.

Walking through History

Holly Bundock

Nixon's helicopter lifted off from the South Lawn of the White House for the last time as some of us from the National Capital Regional Office watched. Its eggbeater wings *wap-wapped* overhead for what seemed to be a long time, passing the Washington Monument and Jefferson Memorial before going out of view. All these years later, the world events surrounding the president's resignation seem amazingly approachable, touchable, haunting for us National Park Service employees who work behind the scenes, often managing special events.

Time after time, these opportunities to walk through current American history afforded NPS stewards a rare glimpse of our collective story of citizenship. We welcomed, for example, Queen Elizabeth II and Prince Philip to the balcony of Boston National Historical Park's Old State House for the Bicentennial Celebration Parade in 1976; Jazz genius Eubie Blake to the one hundredth anniversary of the phonograph at Thomas Edison National Historical Park; reporters from around the world for the liftoff of Gertie, the oldest reticulated dinosaur as of the 1980s, from the canyon floor at Petrified Forest National Park; the celebrations—and lamentations of the tribes—of the Lewis and Clark Bicentennial; Hollywood and Ken Burns; presidents, senators, members of congress, governors, world leaders, and the many families visiting national park areas.

But it is the World War II commemorations that stand out in my mind for the poignancy and even bitterness of American history stories occurring before our eyes. Before the fiftieth commemoration of Pearl Harbor, State Department officials counseled too often not to apologize for Hiroshima, commenting on talking points for dignitaries, and urging rangers not to address the issues involving the conclusion of the war. Employees at the USS *Arizona* Memorial (now called World War II Valor in the Pacific National

Monument) managed with aplomb a weeklong commemoration of history conferences, special tours, events involving the Pearl Harbor survivors, and countless media interviews, all within the parameters of the State Department dictates.

On December 7, President George H. W. Bush addressed the thousands gathered quayside. All had just had their hearts wrenched, again, with the Hawaii Air National Guard's missing man formation, which flew out across the moorings and ships anchored in Pearl Harbor. Some distance behind the crowd, three Japanese monks huddled over a white cloth. Two held corners and stretched it taut over the seawall just beyond the visitor center, while the other monk slowly poured something from a pottery bottle over the cloth. They bowed at length to the white memorial just a few hundred yards across the water. Trees swayed in the wind. Mynah birds hopped, squawked, and fluttered about. The smell of the dew on the grass was rapidly disappearing, and the day was heating up. All this is still in sharp focus to me. The monks turned and saw me watching them from perhaps twenty feet away. They bowed slowly again and, in halting English, said, "We are sorry."

Rangers with American Memorial Park invited veterans to the sixtieth commemoration of the Battle of Saipan in the Northern Mariana Islands— not an easy place to get to in the war or in 2004. Yet many returned for the commemoration, including General Paul W. Tibbets, Jr., who flew the B-29 *Enola Gay* from North Field on Tinian (the island just south of Saipan, about 1300 miles from Japan), dropping "Little Boy," the atomic bomb, on Hiroshima. The area around the atom bomb pit (from which Little Boy was loaded onto the plane) had been cleared of the invasive tangantangan (castor-oil plant); but so dense is this tall bush that, even with the clearing done, one still had the feeling of walking in a maze. Interpretive signage was installed, and a media event with the general was one of the weeklong events. Tangantangan shrouded the edges of the main North Field runway; only the ocean at each end of the runway provided perspective. The afternoon the frail, eighty-nine-year-old general returned, not a cloud was in the sky. It was hot—the sun was piercing.

The general sat by one of the historical plaques he would unveil, under the shade of an E-Z UP shelter, while the press and VIPs scoped out the bomb pit and the runway beyond, through the weeds. For some time, he was alone. When I close my eyes and think of this day, it is the general I see, hunched in his chair. The man who changed the world forever.

These national park areas are etched in our national psyche, their stories told by the superb rangers of the National Park Service today. They paint historical perspective for visitors and scholars, offering a picture through a lens that so few people have a chance to see. It is a rare privilege to have worked alongside the greats—the parks and their people—and to see history happening before our eyes.

I'm Proud of What We Did

Ed Rizzotto

In 1988, I left the Mid-Atlantic Regional Office of the National Park Service for a job in Gateway National Recreation Area. My next seven years in Gateway helped me recognize the unique role that urban parks play in people's everyday lives.

During an interview conducted by historian Alison Steiner for the Association of National Park Rangers Oral History Project, I reflected on the decisions I made while working as a center director (for the residential NPS school within the park), management assistant (to the General Superintendent), and superintendent of the Staten Island sub-unit. The following is an edited version of that interview and provides some highlights.

The last night I was in the regional office, I boxed twenty-eight crates of references and books that I'd accumulated for shipment to New York. It was ten o'clock at night when this protection ranger came through to ask what I was doing.

"I'm packing for my next job," I said.

"Where are you going?"

"I'm going to Gateway," I told him—where, coincidentally, he used to work.

We talked about it a little bit, and then he said to me, "You know . . . there's a right way, there's a wrong way, and there's the Gateway."

I asked what he meant, to which he replied, "You'll find out."

Working at Gateway National Recreation Area was indeed a unique experience. It was trying to do park service stuff for people in a big urban area who were never going to see a national-park unit any other way. There are people in New York who never leave the city. Never drive.

At some point in that experience, I was at lunch with Bob Barbee. (He was superintendent at Yellowstone National Park at the time, and we were schmoozing.) I had worked as a young ranger at Yellowstone and ended up telling him things like, "You have a great job—what a terrific job! I would love to have your job."

"You know, you're really doing a more important job in some ways," he said, "because the average visitor to Yellowstone travels more than eight hundred miles to get there, which means lots and lots of people never get there. It is too far and too expensive. So they aren't going to see the mother park or the premier sites that we all know about."

His point was that they had to see the green and gray in New York City. Because then, when their congressman comes home for a town-hall meeting and asks, "Do we need more jails? Do we need more highways? Do we need to build a sewer plant?" someone might put up his hand and say, "The National Park Service has taught my eighth grader environmental science. The only time we camped out was at Gateway National Recreation Area." They would, in a small way, see the park service there.

Jacob Riis Park is a big ocean beach in Queens that the National Park Service runs. When it was very hot, a lot of people came down to the park from what we would call tenements—housing that typically didn't have any air conditioning. They were living in little boxes, not necessarily even with airshafts, and they'd come down to the park for the day, which nor-

mally closed at sunset. But we let them stay; we put a few extra rangers on. The visitors would bring their blankets and their picnic gear, and they'd kind of roll up in those blankets. We'd let them sleep on the beach because it was so much better than forcing them back up into what you'd probably call slums.

At Gateway, when I was superintendent of the Staten Island unit, we went through a big development program. We renovated the marina, and built new bathhouses and new

Ed Rizzotto at South Cape Beach State Park.

concessions. We did a lot of fun concerts and environmental activities, and we hopefully exposed people to the park service in the process.

There is a Gateway, but it's not a bad way.

I believe very strongly that urban parks are critical not only to the populations that use them but also to the National Park Service in accomplishing its mission. It doesn't mean that the urban parks are more important; they're a little bit different—and may even be less important. But they are part of creating a national picture for our citizenry.

We need to educate as many people as we can about the lessons the National Park Service holds—I think it is a vital role. And I think the urban parks are included in that because they're going to reach lots and lots of people who are never going to get to the wilderness places.

When you look at how the balance is in Congress, we need people valuing us, understanding us, supporting us from everyplace. They can't be just rich white kids who went to prep school and had the summer to travel out west. It's got to be kids from the city, kids from poor families. Most of the urban parks don't have entry fees. If you're having a hard time buying food and an annual park pass costs twenty dollars, you wouldn't go. But you can go to Gateway and remember that the rangers took you in on nights when it was too hot and uncomfortable to go home.

People died in those tenements—typically older people who were under stress. No air conditioning, and maybe nobody watching them. It was merely shelter. But some of those people got to come to the parks, got to have the comforting experiences.

It's a hot day—but don't worry. The parks are open. Everything will be fine. Rangers are here to watch you.

I'm proud of what we did.

"Look, Daddy, a Castle!"

Janis M. Buckreus

Spruce Tree House at Mesa Verde National Park may not be a castle by medieval European standards, but in the eyes of a child, imagination is timeless.

Spruce Tree House was, and still is, one of Mesa Verde's few cliff dwellings that you can get up close and personal with on your own time, while rangers are stationed nearby to keep a watchful eye and answer questions. One of our rangers likes to tell the story of a moment that he experienced while working at Spruce Tree House in 1979.

This ranger was tending his post one day when he saw a young girl of six or seven approach the dwelling with her father. Her eyes were wide, and

Mesa Verde National Park, 1955. Spruce Tree House was built between 1211 and 1278 CE by the ancestors of the Puebloan peoples of the Southwest.

she was pulling her father forward by the hand as she excitedly exclaimed, "Look, Daddy, a castle!" The ranger was so struck by this comment that he made it a part of his tours to illustrate how special these places are, and how one only needs a little imagination to picture how spectacular and lively they must have been eight hundred years ago.

I always thought that this was a charming story coming from the other ranger, and I didn't think much more of it until about a month ago. I was talking to a gentleman while stationed down at Spruce Tree House, and out of the cor-

Janis M. Buckreus at Mesa Verde National Park.

ner of my eye, I noticed a young girl dressed in a princess costume. Kids wear all kinds of outfits these days, and Halloween had occurred recently; so I wasn't too surprised. As the young girl moved closer, though, I couldn't help but compliment her on her glittery attire.

As it turned out, the gentleman with whom I'd been talking was the girl's father. After my compliment, he casually replied, "Oh, she thought this place looked like a castle and asked if she could wear her princess dress, so we brought it along."

Yes, Daddy, whether it's 1979, 2014, or 2114, these castles will hopefully remain timeless far into the future for other imaginative children.

Fa'asamoa
The Samoan Way

J. Douglas Cuillard

It's not often in the career of a park ranger that you get an opportunity to establish a new national park. It was my good fortune to be able to help establish our nation's fiftieth, the National Park of American Samoa.

Most of us living on the US mainland know little, if anything, about this remote US possession, our only territory south of the equator. It's probably best known by World War II veterans who trained in the capital city, Pago Pago, while on their way to the Pacific theater.

In 1990, after a long, five-hour flight from Hawaii, I remember disembarking at the Tutuila island airport and asking myself, "What am I doing here without an office, a place to live, a staff, a social network, and a defined job?" I had come to convince the Samoans that a national park was in their best interest despite the fact that most Samoans had no idea what a national park was. Luckily, I had a very understanding boss whose parting (joking) words to me were: "If you ever tell me you know what you're doing in Samoa, I'll fire you!" (After three years working there, I never once worried about my job security.)

What complicated the establishment of this new park was that it was to be leased, not purchased. Even though American Samoa is a US territory, only 1 percent of the land is free hold, which is land that can be purchased outright by US citizens. The rest is held in common by the Samoans themselves, and passed on only to other native Samoans through an ancient and complex hierarchy of titles. US Congress, respecting this traditional land-tenure system, authorized the park to be established but only upon the signing of a fifty-year lease agreement between the affected villages, the Samoan government, and the United States. It was my job to negotiate the lease and get it signed.

My first major hurdle was that I knew very little about this three-thousand-year-old Samoan culture (the oldest in Polynesia) and language. As a former Peace Corps volunteer, I sought out a Peace Corps Samoan language instructor, and took several weeks of intensive language and culture instruction. Then, with very rudimentary skills, I began the long process of convincing the chiefs of seven villages, who were spread out over three remote islands, that they would benefit by leasing about ten thousand acres of traditional lands and waters to the US government for fifty years.

To help me in negotiations with the village chiefs, many of whom spoke little to no English, I was assigned a "Talking Chief," a titled Samoan working for the governor of the territory. The Talking Chief was my cultural intermediary and translator during meetings with the traditional village councils. Sitting uncomfortably cross-legged in open-air thatched meeting houses, I recall the many times I felt nervous when my Talking Chief got into lengthy discussions (in Samoan) with the village chiefs about this national park idea, as I had no idea what they were saying.

Because few Samoans travel to the US mainland, I was met with blank looks when I mentioned places like Yellowstone or Grand Canyon National Parks. Many thought that a national park was a place to plant gardens in order to help beautify the islands. Several friends of the park and I decided that the only way to bridge this knowledge gap was to somehow fly the highest-titled village chiefs to Hawaii so they could experience firsthand several operating national parks. Through very generous donations from a private family and others, we were able to take the chiefs from the proposed parklands along with other officials on a two-week tour of Hawaiian parks. One of the memorable highlights of this trip was when the Samoan chiefs met their native Hawaiian counterparts at a traditional 'ava ceremony. Native Hawaiians are the cultural progeny of the seafaring Samoans of one thousand years ago.

After this very successful orientation trip, there was an additional hurdle to overcome: setting a dollar lease value on the land and reefs that spanned the three islands. Traditional Samoan lands have never been bought or sold, and authority over the land and its use has been passed down from titled chief to titled chief for millennia. However, after much trial and error, we arrived at a settlement of value and an agreement on the distribution of lease funds to each of the seven villages. The fifty-year lease was signed by all parties in 1993 and our fiftieth national park became a reality.

This green gem in the South Pacific is unique in so many ways. Unlike the tropical parks in the Caribbean, Everglades, or Virgin Islands, the biodiversity of Samoa originated in Southeast Asia—hence, it is Paleotropical. Although relatively small in size, the park protects an amazing diversity of terrestrial and aquatic fauna and flora not found anywhere else in our National Park System. Moreover, it recognizes the traditional use rights of the Samoans themselves; allowing, for example, the gathering of plants for ceremonial or medicinal purposes.

I recall walking one day through the same village on Ta'ū island where Margaret Mead did her research for the book *Coming of Age in Samoa*. Another day, I was snorkeling on the coral reef on Ofu island, trying to identify some of the hundreds of species of fish and coral. And on another day, I slogged through dense jungle, trying to catch site of the giant Samoa fruit bat and rare tropical bird species.

What a privilege it was to be the first superintendent of this new park, and what pride I felt with the successful establishment of the National Park of American Samoa, knowing that we did it *fa'asamoa*—the Samoan way.

"I think having land and not ruining it is the most beautiful art that anybody could ever want to own."

—ANDY WARHOL, ARTIST, 1975

The National Park Service
First Agency to Protect Its LGBT Employees from Discrimination

Rebecca Mills

It all began with an unlikely superstar—Don Henry. Another superstar, Stanley Albright, carried it forward, took a stand for National Park Service employees, and won. That's how the park service became the first federal agency to adopt a policy against discrimination based on sexual orientation. And it all started in the Western Regional Office, now called the Pacific West Regional Office.

No one would have called Don a star. He was quiet and competent, nice looking and warm hearted, with brown eyes and wavy hair to match; he had a law degree and a rarely revealed silly streak. After I was hired in 1982 as equal opportunity manager for the western region, Don approached me with an interest in the vacant lead equal-employment-opportunity counselor position. Already at the grade, he could be transferred directly into the job if he qualified. He did. His understanding of law and legal argument, his writing skills, and his caring manner made him an excellent candidate.

Before I hired him, Don let me know that, as a white man, he nevertheless was acquainted with discrimination because he was gay. This was not a secret, but it was a closeted piece of information.

Don served well in the job. He had a devoted group of park counselors that he advised as they walked through their always-complex, emotionally fraught discrimination-complaint-counseling work. What we didn't know was that, as part of this work, he was becoming the point man for counseling on issues experienced by gay and lesbian employees in the western-region parks and beyond.

In those days, the term "sex discrimination" covered only discrimination based on gender. Judges parsing Title VII of the Civil Rights Act of 1964 found that discrimination based on sexual orientation was legal. Also, in those days, the gay pride movement was developing in San Francisco. Only a year or so before Don and I worked together, Mayor George Moscone and openly gay Supervisor Harvey Milk were shot and killed by former Supervisor Dan White in San Francisco City Hall, which was visible from my office window in the San Francisco Federal Building. The AIDS epidemic was spreading with seemingly no hope of recovery, and several of our fellow employees died from AIDS.

Still soft spoken, Don became a passionate advocate. One day, he came to me with an idea: could he write a proposal to Regional Director Stanley Albright arguing that the National Park Service should adopt a policy against discrimination based on sexual orientation? Yes, he knew this would be beyond legal requirements, but it was the right thing to do. I thought it a great idea (although pie in the sky and doomed to fail), but I was proud to sign and send it up.

Don's brief was simple and masterfully written. He argued that LGBT (lesbian, gay, bisexual, transgender) employees deserved protection and the same opportunities as others. He described examples of the kinds of trouble they experienced—some day in and day out; others just once in a while, but nasty and outrageous all the same.

Stanley Albright listened and heard. I was surprised but shouldn't have been. I learned then how much Stan knew and cared about his employees. Stan organized a meeting of the regional directorate and asked our office to make a presentation. Don followed up by inviting employees from throughout the region and job classes (e.g., a motor-vehicle operator, a secretary, a seasonal law-enforcement officer, an interpreter) to make the presentation themselves, and be videotaped. This courageous group convinced Stan and the rest of the regional directorate.

Stan took the proposed policy Don had drafted to the National Leadership Council (regional directors and national directorate) and proposed a national policy. He didn't win this first round, as the Equal Opportunity Office in WASO (Washington Support Office) vigorously opposed it. There was no legal basis for it, they said. But Stan came home and signed that policy for all western-region employees. And he didn't give up.

Rebecca Mills in Great Basin National Park.

Sometime in all of this rapidly exploding history, Don and his friend, the editor of the NPS in-service newsletter, the *Courier*, cooked up content on the topic of discrimination and the new policy proposals. The day the issue went to press was the editor's last day in the National Park Service before she assumed a job with the Fish and Wildlife Service. She had not shared with her boss the scope and content of the issue. Don had his mischievous ways, and he enjoyed the moment when that issue hit our desks.

Eventually, the National Park Service adopted the western-region policy. By then, the idea that the western region could go it alone appeared ridiculous and unjust to employees. (Was it because it was located in that hotbed of San Francisco?) After the director signed, it was not long before Secretary of the Interior Bruce Babbitt and President Clinton issued similar policies.

Don's final surprise act in his campaign for LGBT employees came after he planned an in-service association for them. He asked two of the earlier presenters, one from Sequoia and Kings Canyon National Parks and the other from Golden Gate National Recreation Area, to help him build the organization.

Don's recruits showed up at his house to meet with him, but he wasn't there; his serious heart disease had carried him off the night before. One of them said, "If that isn't delegation, I don't know what is." They went on to found and build the organization. Don's memorial at Golden Gate National Recreation Area was attended by people who loved and admired him within the National Park Service but also by people from his diverse paths—his living-with-heart-disease group, his gay-pride friends, his neighbors, his family, even a local TV news reporter.

Stan is remembered for many wonderful contributions to the National Park Service in his multiple roles, including associate director for operations and western regional director. His uncanny understanding of and support for employees shines through his work. That's why Stan Albright led the park service to adopt the first policy against discrimination based on sexual orientation in the federal government.

Horse Patrol in Yosemite
Bridging the Gap for the Last One Hundred Years

Debbie and Fred Koegler

In the spring of 1891, the Fifth Cavalry rode in formation out of the Presidio of San Francisco, over Pacheco Pass, across the Central Valley, and into the newly formed Yosemite National Park in the Sierra Nevada mountains. Setting up base camp in the south end of the park, troopers rode out in patrols, which took them into almost every part of Yosemite.

For twenty-three years, the US Army continued their mounted patrols, ousting outlaw cattlemen and sheepherders who were overusing meadows as pasturelands. The cavalry had the sole jurisdiction given to them by the US government of blazing trails, charting unmapped territory, planting high-elevation lakes and streams with trout, and generally acting as the law enforcers. Today, many "T" markers blazed into trees by the cavalry along Yosemite trails are visible signs still guiding the park visitors. Descendants of planted fish are still living in high-elevation lakes.

The cavalry was succeeded by a group of civilian rangers, who were tough, hard-riding, and uncompromising. These guardians were, in turn, replaced by park rangers in 1916, at the inception of the National Park Service. It was here that a strong tradition of protecting resources and providing for the enjoyment of the park by the visitor had its beginnings, and has continued uninterrupted to this day. Although many changes have taken place in Yosemite National Park's history, one thing remains constant: the ranger and his horse.

Tragically, park budget woes have reduced the great horse-patrol program in Yosemite to a shadow of what it once was. During the 1970s, Yosemite Valley had ten full-time horse-patrol seasonal rangers; today, in the park, the number of full-time horse-patrol rangers changes from season to season, and there may be several rangers on horseback at any given time.

Horse-patrol duties include patrolling the valued watershed and wilderness; resource protection; public relations; ceremonial activities; interpretation; education; proactive, positive law enforcement; and the daily care and feeding of the stock.

There are dangers as well as controversy in regard to the job description, but it is served with a sense of privilege. One needs only to follow a mounted ranger for a few minutes to realize why a horse and mule in Yosemite is a valuable tool.

A ranger can't ride more than one hundred yards through a campground or public area without attracting a crowd of visitors snapping their cameras and needing answers to questions. A horse and mule are like a magnet symbolizing a traditional way of life from the Old West—a symbol leading back to National Park Service beginnings, when most rangers could ride a horse.

Visitors from all parts of the world and country gather around ranger and horse, asking many questions about what a mounted ranger does. They are interested in the horse's name and age, and ask if it is okay to touch

Fred Koegler in Yosemite National Park.

and pet the animal. At the same time, the ranger has the golden opportunity to promote a positive image, provide information, and educate the general public on the national parks.

From the outside, dealing with the horses and mules looks like an easy job, but riding in public areas is serious business. Ideally, there is a bonding process that happens between the ranger and horse; and training the rider along with the animal is intensive, in order to have the trust and reliability needed. Horses and mules have an innate

Debbie Koegler in Yosemite National Park.

ability to sense danger and read the terrain, but the rider also needs to know the capabilities of the animal and how to read its body language. Intensive training between horse and rider is needed for these dynamics to exist.

The cadre of park service horses and mules are specifically trained for the rigors of horse patrol. They are used for medical evacuations from the wilderness, which involve a ranger on horseback leading another horse or mule to provide a carryout for injured people. They are effective as first responders to provide aid for people lost or injured when it is not deemed necessary for a helicopter evacuation. Days can be long in such circumstances, and riding seven to twenty miles a day is commonplace.

Consider the thrill as a park visitor steps off a tour bus or rounds the corner of a wilderness trail and sees a mounted ranger available to greet them and to address any concerns they might have. Stepping back in time, it is a bridge from the inception of the cavalry in Yosemite National Park to the present day, preserving the original park idea of oversight and protection.

My Role Was to Listen

Dick Martin

In 1985, I became the second superintendent of Wrangell-St. Elias National Park and Preserve. My five years in Wrangell taught me to work with local communities in the face of controversy. During an interview conducted by historian Alison Steiner for the Association of National Park Rangers Oral History Project, I reflected on these lessons learned while living and working in rural Alaska.

The regional office told me to report to Wrangell-St. Elias National Park and Preserve in January, the coldest month of the year in Alaska. I got up there, and it was 60 below. I couldn't rent or buy a place in town because they wouldn't rent to the Park Service. We were the least-loved people in this small, rural town. You'd go into the grocery store, and people gave you dirty looks. The clerks were surly. You'd buy gas and hear snide comments from the back of the station: "There's a goddamn parkie out there." We were pretty much socially ostracized from polite society.

I finally found a place to rent a little ways out of town. A one-room cabin with a loft for sleeping. No running water. Outhouse and a woodstove. I lived there for five years.

The place was one of the most controversial parks in the system at the time, and we weren't the only park in Alaska that was having that problem. There were several new or expanded parks then as a result of the Alaska National Interest Lands Conservation Act of 1980. If we'd been the one new park with thirteen old ones, we would have been fine; because the regional office and the other parks could've supported us. But there were ten new national park areas established, and three older parks expanded all in one swoop in 1980. To manage these vast areas, the National Park Service set up seven completely new management units. Wrangell was just one of those.

The work requirements were just plain overwhelming because of all the demands and needs of the park, as well as our limited staff to perform them. Every day, we had to do about a hundred things, and we could only do about ten of them. It was a great exercise in setting priorities—a real lesson learned in dealing with the big rocks, not the little rocks.

Wrangell was, of course, the largest park in the system then, by far. Thirteen million acres. It was essentially the size of the state of West Virginia. And there were a lot of ongoing uses that had been allowed prior to the establishment of the park that made it very controversial. One of the big ones was sport hunting. There was also mining under BLM (Bureau of Land Management) jurisdiction; and folks who lived in the park, sometimes under permit but more often not.

I felt, in my particular case, I was poorly prepared (to put it mildly) for the level of controversy, acrimony, and downright hostility toward National Park Service management. Having been a ranger for twenty-three years at that time, I'd dealt with a lot of unhappy people in field situations such as searches and rescues, fatalities, or law enforcement, and in dangerous situations of wildfires or weather extremes. However, dealing with a room full of unhappy local people was something I was poorly prepared for.

It became obvious to me that there were few people I could go to in the National Park Service to provide me with advice on how to deal with this issue productively—productively being how to move the park forward; how to establish NPS principles in management; and how to do this in a way that does not result in a mushroom-shaped cloud of acrimony, hostility, and political repercussions.

The approach that finally evolved in my mind: listening. My role was to be sympathetic and understanding—to assure folks that I understood what their concerns were and was considering them; to explain what the National Park Service was actually doing and proposing to do; to explain that it was a national park—that the national park program would, in fact, be established and followed—and that we would mitigate that to the extent we could when folks had a legitimate concern.

I decided, for lack of a good alternative, to hold regular meetings, to talk to anybody that would talk, to listen to anybody that had anything to say, to get back to folks who had questions, to promise that we would always be available to hear their concerns and would respond with what we knew to be correct.

The first year I was there, we had thirty-nine public meetings, all over that part of Alaska. I never turned down an invitation to go to a meeting, even if it was in a bar. I went and listened; responded as best I could. And I kept my promise to got back to people regarding their concerns, thoughts, and worries.

Over the course of a year, I believe that the park staff gained credibility with people because we were speaking facts, not fantasy. We weren't making promises we couldn't keep, and we weren't saying things that weren't true. We were responding sympathetically, understandingly.

The second year I was there, we had fewer meetings; and by the third year, some amazing things began to happen. Many of the concerns that had previously been expressed began to relax a little bit. Totally? No. But I began to feel like I was more welcome when I went to the grocery store and the gas station in the towns around Wrangell.

I found it a tremendously rewarding experience and a lot of fun—very inspiring. I learned a *tremendous* amount about dealing with controversy. This helped me so much in my later career in Washington, DC, and particularly at Death Valley National Park. At Wrangell, I also found that I grew as an individual: I grew as a parent, I grew as a family member, and I grew as a leader.

I thank the National Park Service for giving me that experience. If it hadn't been there to trust me to succeed, I wouldn't have been able to learn and grow.

My Journey over the Mountains and to the Water's Edge

Forrest "Ed" Harvey

As a boy growing up in the southeastern and midwestern United States, I visited numerous national parks, monuments, and battlefields with my family. And while my love for parks was no doubt kindled there, as a boy, these visits were simply fun romps in neat places that delivered no true understanding of the importance of parks, or any hint of how they would come to later change my life. Such realizations would not come until the summer following my sixteenth birthday. That summer, I took my first real journey apart from my parents to attend a church youth retreat at the YMCA camp just outside of Rocky Mountain National Park. That visit would forever change my life. That visit would, for me, be truly transformative.

I hiked the many trails, climbed to the continental divide, drank from glacial springs, splashed in the icy streams, and watched crimson sunsets behind rocky peaks. I fell in love with the mountains, nature, wilderness, wildness, Colorado, the park, and the very idea of national parks. I was both fascinated with and moved by the concept that this park and all the other national parks belonged to me—parks that were set aside so I could discover wilderness; parks that protected scenery I had only seen in books or on television; parks in which I could search for life's meaning and discover who I was, what I valued, and what I was destined to be and do. I couldn't believe I was actually there. I was humbled. I was in awe. I was moved.

My visit that summer inspired me to want to know how mountains formed, why glaciers moved, why rivers flooded, how nature worked, and how the Earth I was growing to love and cherish came into being. That visit inspired me to ask questions, to seek to satisfy my curiosity, to study science. I would return that fall to my hometown and focus my high school studies on the physical sciences. Later, in college and graduate school, I

Rocky Mountain National Park, 1938. Lakeside view of Hallet Peak.

THE WONDER OF IT ALL

would major in geology and water resources, going on to take my first job as a professor of hydrogeology.

That one visit to Rocky Mountain National Park launched me on a life-long journey that would lead me annually to visit our national parks—to map their rock formations, to study their fossils and minerals, to learn their Earth history, to measure their hydrology and water quality, and to hone my skills as a geologist and hydrologist; and also, to immerse myself in the beauty and serenity they offered, to heal my weary mind and body, and to pacify my soul. While I have come to love many of the parks over the years—Yosemite, Glacier, Bryce Canyon, Great Smoky Mountain, Yellowstone, Olympic, Denali, etc.—Rocky Mountain National Park will always be my favorite. I found myself there, as a young man. There, atop those majestic peaks and within those tranquil valleys, I began to shape my worldview, and discover my own spirituality and belief in things greater than myself. And there, I would also fall in love.

The fall after I first met my wife, Carol, we journeyed to the park for a long weekend where we hiked together, explored, shared our life stories, and kindled our love for each other. As our relationship grew, we visited annually to reconnect with the wild, to rediscover serenity, to refresh our spirits, and ultimately, to fall deeply in love with each other and our shared mountain sanctuary. We would eventually be joined in marriage within Rocky Mountain National Park—beside Dream Lake; in the shadow of a snow-capped Hallett Peak; on a crisp, sunny, late-May morning. For the past nineteen years, we have returned there as often as possible, and we long to rest there for eternity one day.

But my park story does not end there; it also lives on in my professional life. A few years ago, after seventeen years serving as a faculty member at the University of Nebraska-Lincoln, I began to feel a strong pull toward the National Park Service. I was no longer content to just be a visitor to parks; I wanted to connect more formally to the NPS mission. I wanted to offer my service to my nation as a way to give back for all the joy and inspiration the parks had given me, and for the lasting impact parks had made on my life. I wanted to ensure that the gift I had been given could and would also be passed on to others.

So, when a rare opportunity became available, after a great deal of reflective thought and soul searching, I made the decision to leave my tenured, full-professor position at the university to embark on a new career as chief of the National Park Service water resources division—a Washington field office based in Fort Collins, Colorado, that provides service-wide program management; and specialized advice and assistance to parks for the protection, restoration, and management of water resources. This was an afforded opportunity that I truly believe was destiny.

I love serving in my new role within the division. I love working alongside my highly talented and dedicated leadership team and staff. I love serving parks. And I love being an active part of the National Park Service and its mission. I feel so lucky, so blessed, and so grateful to have a career that is so satisfying, so purposeful, and so meaningful. Now I don't just explore and enjoy the parks as a visitor, I have the privilege to help preserve and protect them through my work.

Upon learning that I work for the National Park Service, people often ask me, "So, what park do you work in?" to which I smile and respond proudly, "All of them."

The Hydrothermal Research Program

Jim Milestone

Between 1987 to 1989, Crater Lake National Park was the location of one of the National Park Service's premier research programs. Around 1984, Crater Lake's staff became aware that a geothermal company from San Francisco was seeking permits to drill wells along the park boundary in the Fremont-Winema National Forest to tap into Mount Mazama's volcanic heat. Mount Mazama had erupted in one of North America's largest volcanic explosions 7,700 years ago, leaving behind the deepest lake in the United States and the seventh deepest lake in the world. Furthermore, the lake and its surrounding environment was one of the cleanest places on Earth; and the lake's water quality was so pristine that scientists could not find clearer water. The deep lake was also surrounded by forest that scrubbed the air from the Pacific Coast over the crest of the Cascades, giving Crater Lake National Park unprecedented air quality.

In the fall of 1986, I replaced Jon Jarvis as the biologist managing the park's resources management program. Jon had worked hard with the Seattle Regional Office scientists and scientists from Oregon State University in Corvallis to propose a three-year Hydrothermal Research Program. Local Senator Hatfield was very protective of Oregon's only national park, and he and other Senators pushed for a congressionally authorized research program to determine whether or not Crater Lake had active hydrothermal vents on the lake bottom.

Scientists Jack Dymond and Bob Collier from Oregon State University, both renowned oceanographers, had determined through deep-depth water samples that hydrothermal water existed on the lake bottom. But the geothermal company eager to tap into Mount Mazama's geothermal resources dismissed that the lake had any active hydrothermal vents, or that what the company was seeking was connected to the resources they wanted to exploit.

Some twenty or more drill sites were permitted to be explored on US Forest Service land, a stone's throw from Crater Lake National Park's boundary.

As the drilling rigs removed cores from Mount Mazama's hillside, the National Park Service and Oregon State University's Dr. Gary Larson, Dr. Jack Dymond, and Dr. Bob Collier; and NPS Biologist Mark Buktenica and I planned how we were going to find the hydrothermal vents 1,945 feet below the lake's surface.

Dymond and Collier proposed using a Canadian company's submersible—a one-person submarine that could dive to the deep bottom of Crater Lake. In order to accomplish this task, the park would have to convert the remote Wizard Island into a research base camp. The proposed submersible weighed some seven thousand pounds and the caldera's rim was around seven thousand feet above sea level.

The National Park Service would need one of the world's most powerful high-altitude helicopters to fly such a heavy machine into Crater Lake's Wizard Island. The park headquarters' water lab would also need to be converted to a university-level chemistry lab that could run deep-lake water and gas samples twenty-four hours a day. Fuel, food, and supplies would have to be transported daily up and down the steep cliff-side trail, from the caldera's rim down to the dock on the edge of Crater Lake.

In 1987, the first summer of research, a small robot submersible tied to a long cable was deployed from the park's pontoon research boat. Through the month of August, the robot submersible explored various areas of the lake bottom that had elevated levels of hydrothermal chemicals and radon gas. One afternoon, the robot found a small hole in the lake bottom that appeared to have water flowing out of it. The video feed was poor quality due to an electrical power issue, and it was very inconclusive. The discovery, though, did provide hope that the following summer's research season would generate some documentation of active hydrothermal activity.

In 1988, an Erickson Air-Crane helicopter arrived and lifted the submersible over the rim of the caldera and placed it softly into the cold water of Crater Lake. The Canadian submersible technicians from CAN-DIVE Construction went to work and added all the necessary gear to make the submersible operational. This was the first of two field seasons in which the submersible was used to conduct deep dives to the bottom of the lake. Dr. Dymond, Dr. Collier, and Mark Buktenica were the primary pilots of the submersible; and NPS rangers who were trained as high-elevation scuba divers assisted the submersible in each daily deployment.

Big discoveries were made in 1989 when the submersible "Deep Rover" revealed large shallow blue pools on the bottom of Crater Lake that were filled with heavy, dissolved mineral salts. Jet-black mud in the pools contained off-the-chart levels of radon gas; and three-foot-high bacteria mats around the pools were very fragile and easily disturbed. It is believed these ancient mats were being fed by the hydrothermal chemicals coming up through Mount Mazama's volcanic core. Crater Lake's water column has an ambient temperature of some 37 degrees Fahrenheit, and the temperatures in the blue pools reached over 64 degrees Fahrenheit. These and other discoveries stopped the commercial geothermal exploration along the park boundary in the Winema National Forest, protecting the park's pristine air quality and unique hydrothermal resources from commercial exploitation.

It was an incredibly exciting time to be part of the park staff during this exceptional research program. The park was not prepared for the overwhelming media interests in this exploration. Reporters from all over the world were on hand to see "Deep Rover" arrive and begin its historic dives.

Visiting Crater Lake today, the only traces that remain of this exciting research program are a few wayside exhibits. But lake research continues, further exploring the mysteries of Crater Lake's depths.

Hard Work Will Pay Off

Dwan Wilcox

My experience working at Badlands National Park has taught me that it is a wonderful environment. I began working at Badlands National Park as a high school intern with my good friend and my math teacher. I have loved meeting new people, from my supervisor to different coworkers from all over the world, and getting a chance to be a role model for the younger generation. My experience here inspired me to make a change for my community, teach more kids about the Badlands, and show them there is more in life to appreciate. I enjoyed teaching elementary students at my tribal school about the park so the next generation can be part of the park service as well. My twelve-year-old sister wants to be a ranger like me, so that shows me that I must be a role model!

On the Pine Ridge Reservation, where I am from, it is a hard life for many American Indians due to the struggle with unemployment. There are not many jobs in the community, so we have to go off the reservation— leave home—to find a stable job. Now that I am a young American Indian woman who is employed at Badlands National Park, I would like to help more American Indian youth get the opportunity to be employed here. For many years, the Lakota people passed down the traditions, and kept and preserved their lands for the children; my goal is to see more youth involved, to build their communication skills, and to help them in the real world.

Becoming a leader was not easy, and I worked hard for it. I changed my ways, brought my grades up, and had good school attendance. Last January, I was an ambassador for Badlands National Park in New York City— it was a once-in-a-lifetime experience. My math teacher at Crazy Horse School in Wanblee, South Dakota, picked me because of my personality, the respect and love I shared with my fellow students, and for never giving up on hard work.

I also became interested in a career in wildlife and biology through my work at Badlands National Park. I plan to pursue a career as a wildlife biologist because I care for wild animals, and I would like to travel around the world and study different habitats; I love to learn about different species. The park showed me that you can be anything as long as you love what you do. You can teach people what you learned so that, years from now, the next generation appreciates it as much as you do. I am attending Black Hills State University to get a four-year degree in environmental studies or biology, and I will still be curious to learn more about wildlife after I graduate.

In the end, I do know that "the hard work you do will pay off"—it is the philosophy I live by every day. I am thankful to be part of the staff at Badlands National Park; and I will continue to work for a better future, more youth involvement in the Badlands, and more improvement in the community.

Dwan Wilcox at Badlands National Park.

Presence

Jason Ransom

Park biologists see amazing things. We also see a lot of paperwork and computer screens.

Having just accepted the wildlife biologist position in North Cascades National Park, I now sit squarely between those two phenomena and find myself staring at the park topo map a lot. So many places to see and learn. So many difficult places to reach. So much wilderness. So much . . . presence. I'm eager to learn my proverbial neighborhood as I've done in other parks—who nests where, who uses this trail or that, where each stream begins and who lives there. I'm eager to watch the hunting cougar, find the ever-elusive pygmy owl, or gaze at the impossible night skies—experiences that will

Jason Ransom in North Cascades National Park.

THE WONDER OF IT ALL

surely come in the years ahead. I'm also eager to practice my science, rigorously collecting data, fitting ecological processes into equations that may tell me what is happening and what management we should be doing. But every day, my eyes get pulled back to the grizzly bear photo snapped by a camera trap near the park a couple years ago; it is on the corkboard at my desk. The bear looks so matter of fact—as if it doesn't realize how small the world is out there. Right next to it is a photo of my six-year-old son, also matter of fact, not realizing how big the world is out there.

I took my son to Yellowstone National Park when he was ten months old, and he saw his first grizzly bear. He doesn't remember it aside from the photo I show him, but he was there; he had the privilege of standing on the same Earth, breathing the same air, and sharing the same moment with the great bear. It defines wildness for me. It is the reason that upon finishing field work in Africa and returning to the United States, I headed directly west into the interior of Alaska. I needed to feel the Earth live, and that means knowing that things eat each other. It means true wildness, a requiem for human-dominated perspectives. It means facing yourself on equal ground with nature and discovering yourself over and over again. Countless hours alone in Denali National Park brought me countless hours among grizzly bears. Giving my son even the tiniest sense of that feeling is one of my parental aspirations.

If I had taken him to North Cascades, where I work now, we wouldn't have seen a grizzly bear. As far as we know, they're all but gone. A few were here in the 1990s, but then sightings dissipated, and the bears quietly vanished. Grizzlies were killed in large numbers long before North Cascades became part of the park system, and the bears never could recover. The park, in all its foresight, has continued managing for grizzlies. It is an empty nest, so to speak, but it is still a nest. Fortunately, miles and miles of roadless wilderness have been carefully preserved for a day like today. Wildlife issues here are now largely in my hands . . . and it is a daunting challenge.

As I sit here writing this, we are just beginning the long process of figuring out how to recover grizzly bears in the Cascades. No matter how we do it, it will take much longer than my career. It may be fifty or one hundred years before a viable population once again persists here—if it does at all.

And it may be the most uncomfortable process in my career, with many people opposing any recovery efforts. For various reasons, all of which are important, people are uncomfortable with the idea of bringing back a very large predator. And I get it. All of the years living with grizzly bears came before I was a parent or before I owned livestock. The world is different now.

The problem is this: the world does not exist for my son or me or anyone else specifically. It is an impossibly complex wonder of biodiversity and relationships and processes among countless living and nonliving things. It happens. It breathes. It changes. We are privileged to be a part of it.

Spring is coming soon; and the busy visitor season will bring families and students, school groups and adventurers, rock climbers, hikers, birders, poets, photographers, bikers, and all kinds of people from around the world who want to be close to nature. Most will be delighted to experience the park and won't notice the absence of grizzly bears. Interpreters and rangers will help educate visitors about why the bears are gone, but the mountains and glaciers, big trees, great trails, black bears and deer are quite enough for anyone to process. That is exactly the point—to notice the presence of things. It is to become a child again when we experience nature: to notice the detail, the beautiful things, the scary things, the awesome things. It is to feel inspired and humbled and whole. It is to notice the very things that gave rise to our national parks.

I look forward to the visitors coming, in hopes that the small everyday things we do in resource management go completely unnoticed. If we mitigate wildlife issues well and we do a good job every time human activities risk impacting wildlife, then you won't see our work. If we understand how large and small processes are changing and we communicate it well, you won't see our work. If we have to temporarily close trails for a nesting bird or a sensitive animal den, you might shift your plans, but you won't see our work. The truth is, as long as you notice the presence of wildlife being wild, then park biologists are succeeding.

One day, long after my retirement, I hope to sit with my son on a mountainside in North Cascades National Park and show him a grizzly bear foraging across the valley. He won't have known the absence of the bears, but he'll notice the presence of true wildness. Then I'll know I've done my job.

Land Protection Is Job One

Sheridan Steele

As instructed, I stood under the Legal Sea Foods sign in Boston's Logan Airport, waiting for the right stranger to approach me to begin our long-anticipated meeting. I wondered: What would he look like? How good was his English? And how would we identify each other and begin a conversation that I long thought would never happen?

I had spent several years trying to learn more about the reclusive family from Milan, Italy, that owned 3,200 acres of land adjacent to Acadia National Park. Their property included more than a mile of spectacular granite shoreline, two pristine islands, important wildlife corridors, and high vantage points with sweeping views of Frenchman Bay and the picturesque mountains beyond. The owners seemed to be hiding under layers of protection, resisting all attempts to talk to people like me who might oppose their plans to develop the property.

As a career National Park Service manager, the prospect of seeing this land developed caused me great concern since protecting land is the best way to conserve nationally significant natural, cultural, and scenic resources—the very resources that millions of Americans come to enjoy. Sitting on the northern boundary of one of the most scenic and wild peninsulas in the park, the Schoodic District of Acadia National Park was now threatened with a massive development: eight hundred villas, three resorts, an air strip, and a golf course—plus the lights, traffic, and sounds that would come with it, forever altering the nature and character that attracted visitors from all over the country and the world to this part of Maine.

I had contacted the US embassy in Rome and friends in Italy, and had spent hours on the Internet to learn more about the owners, without success. Even after they had begun to harvest timber and made public their plans for a huge development, their identity and motivations were protected by consultants and secrecy. The family name was Modena, but I could find little else—until one day in 2011, when I received a surprise phone call from their project manager in Florida.

"I understand you have been trying to contact Mr. Modena," she said. "He will meet with you if you can be in New York City or Boston next week." I was scheduled to be in Washington, DC, but immediately changed my plans. And here I was.

The meeting lasted an hour and a half. Fortunately, Mr. Modena spoke fluent English.

I told him of my three goals for our meeting: (1) to establish and maintain contact with him as the landowner of a property; (2) to inform him that if the family wanted to sell the property, I believed conservation interests in Maine would purchase it; and (3) to encourage him to meet with a conservation-minded developer, The Lyme Timber Company, who had a solid record of developing properties near conserved lands in ways that were compatible with the values of those areas.

Mr. Modena replied that they were not interested in selling the land, but if they were, it was worth "probably $250 million." After the initial shock, I said we could never raise that amount. He then qualified his estimate: "If all of our plans were approved and ready to go. But in its present, undeveloped state, it is probably worth $50 million."

I asked him if they would divide the land into two parcels, thinking that the south half was the most ecologically and scenically important, containing the key coastal land and islands. He said he would think about that and get back to me. We departed with each other's email addresses and phone numbers, and (on my side) new hope for the property.

About the same time, the world economy was in serious trouble. Many building projects in the United States had stopped or slowed. And as the financial gains from developing properties declined, the prospects for purchasing lands for conservation seemed to be improving.

Meanwhile, with our conservation partners, we continued the campaign to raise public awareness of this major threat to Acadia National Park, building support for preserving at least the southern half of the property. The next time I heard from Mr. Modena, he provided prices on different parts of the property, which added up to $29 million (the south half alone was

Acadia National Park, 1996. Visitors enjoying the view on Cadillac Mountain.

valued at $21 million because of the ocean frontage, the islands, existing road access, and the recreational opportunities of the adjacent national park). The Modenas also contacted The Lyme Timber Company, whose representatives developed a concept whereby they would purchase the entire property and hold it until conservation partners could raise money to buy it for around $17 million.

While the price continued to go in the right direction, I knew that it would still be difficult to raise that much money.

Soon after, in August, an individual mentioned to me at a cocktail party that they were looking for worthy conservation projects that would also benefit local communities. I mentioned this 3,200 acres as one possibility, and they asked how much the property would cost. I said we had an old appraisal under $10 million, providing a low estimate, hoping not to scare them off. To my surprise, they replied, "Oh, we could do that"; and the next day, I delivered maps, and a brief on the property and its importance to Acadia National Park and the American people.

Within three months they had an agreement to purchase the property for $12 million, with a closing date set for December. I was astonished at the speed and nimbleness with which private individuals could act. In the philanthropic tradition that originally created Acadia National Park, these anonymous donors acted swiftly and decisively to protect the park from significant impacts, and to make this property a spectacular gift to all Americans.

Reflecting on that early-morning meeting in Boston reminds me that we never know what can evolve from a clear set of priorities, some tenacity, increased public awareness, good partnerships, communication with your opponents, and being in the right place at the right time. Acadia National Park, cherished by millions, remains an extraordinary place thanks to the actions and generosity of many individuals, volunteers, and donors acting in the best interests of present and future generations.

Sheridan Steele in Acadia National Park.

Black Canyon
A Wild Landscape of Hope

Paul Zaenger

The morning air is cool and silent. Not even the wisp of a breeze flutters the oak leaves. Twilight lightens the sky as the sun approaches the horizon. The stillness is marked by the aroma of big sagebrush. Standing in a small clump of sage, I can almost taste its pungent odor as it permeates the blue air before daybreak. It seems all the world is quiet, all is at rest before the dawn.

Out past the draw is a wall of pinnacles and spires—some of them rounded, some squared at the top. I'm here to witness the first rays of day bathe the pink, maroon, ochre, and chocolate of these columns. Arrayed like a pipe organ, the rows descend, rank upon rank below Pulpit Rock Overlook. They vary in size—large for lower principles or base instruments, narrow for the higher pitches—and they appear grouped, as if they were placed in a great cathedral. I want to feel the hope of a new dawn as the first soft rays of light bring out a symphony of color in this rock—in Black Canyon of the Gunnison National Park.

As we mark the centennial of the establishment of the National Park Service, many commentators around the country will make the point that we are different people now than we were one hundred years ago. Some will point to changes in society—our lost vigor or desire to experience the land on its own terms. Some will highlight our fractured political dynamics, pointing to our inability to respect diverse opinions as we approach the land from different perspectives. Maybe it would be helpful for us to refocus on the land.

It's easy to let a wave of nostalgia flow over us, especially when we have the chance to behold a wild sunrise. It's fun to picture in our mind's eye how a scene might have appeared to the first people who happened upon this overwhelming landscape. How might this mountain vista have appeared to people in the 1950s or the 1850s, for instance? Did they hear the music?

Old photographs contribute more feelings. How did the land fuel these people's dreams decades ago? Did their hearts ache to experience wild territory the same as ours do today? Did they have patience for knowing the land, for seeing changes on the land, for being a part of nature?

Nostalgia can be a tricky emotion. It can ground us in our values, transferred from generations before, but it can also cloud our thinking about the land that remains today. To be sure, proponents for national parks generations ago very much wanted our lives to reflect a relationship with the land, as generations decades before them had wanted.

A few years ago, a visitor at Black Canyon brought this point home. We were standing at an overlook, gazing upon a terrific scene and talking about what's really important in life. He said that he worked in a multistoried skyscraper for a time, many floors above street level, in a large city. He told me he knew a colleague whose sole ambition in his career—perhaps his life—was to move from his office with one window to a corner of the building, where he would have two windows.

The visitor turned to me, holding back tears, and said that he left that job; life seemed much more valuable to him than a window. He wanted to be in touch with wild landscapes. He could hear the refrains from the past but was searching for hope in the future.

National parks preserve landscapes all across our land: Denali, Saguaro, Acadia, Grand Canyon, Isle Royale. Some of these are easy to reach, some not so much. Regardless of the approach, noted author Wallace Stegner commented about experiencing wild land when he wrote, "We simply need that wild country available to us, even if we never do more than drive to its edge and look in. For it can be a means of reassuring ourselves of our sanity as creatures, a part of the geography of hope." (Excerpted from *The Sound of Mountain Water: The Changing American West* by Wallace Stegner, 1997.)

After one hundred years, can we still gain a relationship with our wild land heritage? Do national parks, monuments, lakeshores, seashores and recreation areas fire our imaginations and fuel our dreams? Let's say yes—for the national parks give us hope to have courage, optimism, and faith that our culture is the culture of the future. That promise of the future comes from people a century ago who believed that wild lands are our most cherished resource to fully engage in the symphony of life.

Back in the draw near Pulpit Rock, the sun's rays beam across 93 million miles of space and spill over the horizon. The colors in the columns take on a new, more vibrant hue. The pinks become richer, the chocolates more luxuriant, the ochers more plush. What I like most about this rocky pipe organ before me is that I can wonder about the detailed erosion that occurred here: I can wonder about the variegated colors in the rock; I can wonder about how the way we measure time is irrelevant; I can stand in the silence, feel the music from this masterpiece of rock, and wonder about how previous generations watched for the sun to rise.

Then I feel that same sense of hope welling up from within that comes from open wild land that we find in our national parks.

"Most of the people who visit the parks, whether they realize it or not or whether they put it into words, are impelled to visit them because of the quest for a supreme experience."

—NEWTON B. DRURY, FOURTH DIRECTOR OF
THE NATIONAL PARK SERVICE, 1941

The Park Service Saved My Life

Wayne Rogers

I am a three-time Iraq veteran. And as we come upon Memorial Day weekend, we are to remember and honor those who paid the ultimate sacrifice in our country's defense. I would also like us to remember those who came home but were not whole—those who may have needed help and were ignored, or had nowhere to turn and took their own lives. I want us to remember this because there was a point in my life when I was heading down that same path.

For me, it started almost immediately after my first tour to Iraq; but the trouble really began on Memorial Day of 2007, outside of Fallujah, when a suicide bomber driving a dump truck loaded with what we approximated to be about 1500 pounds of explosives forever changed my life. Today, I am a park guide at Independence National Historical Park; and I recently wrote the following:

Wayne Rogers at Valley Forge National Historical Park.

Three times I went to war
Experiences most only see in movies
Endured stresses no person should ever endure
The Park Service saved my life.

Three times I came home from war
Experiences most only read about
Endured stresses no person should ever endure
The Park Service saved my life.

A daily struggle to get out of bed
Forcing myself to go back to the suck
The Park Service saved my life.

Proudly serving
Too proud to ask for help
The Park Service saved my life.

My wife trying to be strong for the both of us
More than she ever bargained or planned for
The Park Service saved my life.

A family outing, a chance meeting
Volunteers needed!
The Park Service saved my life.

The crowds closing in
The roar of the cannon makes me want to run
Regret slowly sinking in
The Park Service saved my life.

Weeks go by, the crowds seem thinner
The thought of making that cannon roar gets me through the week
The Park Service saved my life.

My beautiful wife sees a new spark, she fans it into a flame
I swallow my pride, I kiss my wife
I seek help
The Park Service saved my life.

It is a Friday, I step away from the role of defending my country
It is now Monday, I step into the role of preserving my country
The Park Service saved my life.

My marriage is strong, my kids are my life, my life has a path
A family outing, a chance meeting
The Park Service changed my life.

If you cannot tell, I am no poet, but my words are what matter. First and foremost, I thank my beautiful wife, Michelle, for having the strength to not leave me when I was at my worst, believing in my dream. I thank every person I ever worked with as a volunteer and a seasonal at Fort Pulaski National Monument; without them, this might be a whole different story. I thank everyone at Valley Forge National Historical Park for bringing me home to Philadelphia; and, of course, everyone at Independence National Historical Park for giving me the chance to prove myself as one of the newest permanent park guides.

I promise not to let any of you down.

INDEX OF FEATURED
NATIONAL PARK SERVICE UNITS

Chickamauga and Chattanooga
    National Military Park, 170
Fort Pulaski National Monument,
    286

HAWAI'I
Hawai'i Volcanoes National Park,
    158, 186
World War II Valor in the Pacific
    National Monument, 246

IDAHO
Craters of the Moon National
    Monument and Preserve, 27
Minidoka National Historic Site, 134
Yellowstone National Park, 8, 58, 86,
    153, 183, 229, 241, 244

MAINE
Acadia National Park, 179

MARIANAS ISLANDS
American Memorial Park, 246

MARYLAND
Appalachian National Scenic Trail,
    202
Assateague Island National Seashore,
    73
Harpers Ferry National Historical
    Park, 88
Oxon Cove Park and Oxon Hill Farm
    (of National Capital Parks-East),
    160

MASSACHUSSETTS
Appalachian National Scenic Trail,
    202
Cape Cod National Seashore, 11, 104

MICHIGAN
Isle Royale National Park, 6

MISSOURI
Jefferson National Expansion
    Memorial, 22

MONTANA
Big Hole National Battlefield
Yellowstone National Park, 8, 58, 86,
    153, 183, 229, 241, 244

NEVADA
Death Valley National Park, 46
Great Basin National Park, 26, 64

NEW HAMPSHIRE
Appalachian National Scenic Trail,
    202

NEW JERSEY
Appalachian National Scenic Trail,
    202
Gateway National Recreation Area,
    249

NEW MEXICO
Gila Cliff Dwellings National
    Monument, 115

NEW YORK
Appalachian National Scenic Trail,
    202
Gateway National Recreation Area,
    249
Governors Island National
    Monument, 30
Home of Franklin D. Roosevelt
    National Historic Site, 214
Statue of Liberty National
    Monument, 131
Upper Delaware Scenic and
    Recreational River, 129
Vanderbilt Mansion National
    Historic Site, 27

NORTH CAROLINA
Appalachian National Scenic Trail,
    202
Cape Hatteras National Seashore, 11
Great Smoky Mountains National
    Park, 75, 94, 147

"Never be discouraged! . . . If your cause is right, if it is economically and environmentally sound and for public benefit, you can win!"

—JUDITH COLT JOHNSON, ACTIVIST, 1976

INDEX OF AUTHORS AND TITLES

QUOTATION SOURCES

PREFACE

Stephen Mather, quoted in Elizabeth H. Coiner, ed., *Quotes: National Park Service 50th Anniversary, 1916–1966*. (Washington, DC: United States Department of the Interior, 1966), 10.

ACKNOWLEDGMENTS

Robert Hass, quoted in Sarah Pollock, "Robert Hass," *Mother Jones* (March/April, 1997): 22.

CHAPTER 1: GETTING STARTED

John Muir, *Our National Parks*, (New York: Houghton, Mifflin, and Company, 1901), 1.

Ken Burns, as quoted in "Ken Burns's Documentary *The National Parks: America's Best Idea* Talks on Yellowstone," YouTube video, 0:25, posted by the Wyoming Office of Tourism on February 26, 2009, https://www.youtube.com/watch?v=HQwn2txq8Js&feature=youtu.be.

Horace Albright, quoted in Paul Schullery, *Searching for Yellowstone: Ecology and Wonder in the Last Wilderness* (Ann Arbor: Edwards Brothers, 2004), 139.

CHAPTER 2: LIFE-CHANGING MOMENTS

Marguerite Lindsley, quoted in Polly Welts Kaufman, *National Parks and the Woman's Voice: A History* (Albuquerque: University of New Mexico Press, 2006), 79.

Lorraine Mintzmyer, quoted in Kaufman, *National Parks and the Woman's Voice*, 176.

Adolph Murie, quoted in Eugene Joseph Palka, *Valued Landscapes of the Far North: A Geographical Journey Through Denali National Park* (Lanham, MD: Rowman & Littlefield, 2000), 107.

Chiura Obata, quoted in Susan Shumaker, *Untold Stories from America's National Parks* (Arlington, VA: Public Broadcasting Service, 2009), 196.

CHAPTER 3: PEOPLE TO REMEMBER

Genevieve Gillette, quoted in Polly Welts Kaufman, *National Parks and the Woman's Voice: A History* (Albuquerque: University of New Mexico Press, 2006), 196.

Fran P. Mainella, quoted in Charles R. "Butch" Farabee, Jr., *National Park Ranger: An American Icon* (Lanham: Roberts Rinehart Publishers, 2003), v.

CHAPTER 4: STORIES FROM THE FIELD

Betty Reid Soskin, quoted in Cameron Keady, "America's Oldest Park Ranger, 93, Is a Fierce Advocate for Young Women of Color Everywhere," *Huffington Post*, May 19, 2015, http://www.huffingtonpost.com/2015/05/19/americas-oldest-park-ranger_n_7314424.html.

Stewart Udall, *The Quiet Crisis* (New York: Holt, Rinehart, and Winston, 1963), 124.

Henry David Thoreau, *Walden, Civil Disobedience, and Other Writings*, ed. William Rossi (New York: W. W. Norton and Company, 2008), 213.

Franklin D. Roosevelt, quoted in Elizabeth H. Coiner, ed., *Quotes: National Park Service 50th Anniversary, 1916–1966.* (Washington, DC: United States Department of the Interior, 1966), 13.

CHAPTER 5: VOLUNTEER ADVENTURES

Vim Crane Wright, quoted in Polly Welts Kaufman, *National Parks and the Woman's Voice: A History* (Albuquerque: University of New Mexico Press, 2006), 194.

Emma "Grandma" Gatewood, quoted in Ben Montgomery, *Grandma Gatewood's Walk: The Inspiring Story of the Woman Who Saved the Appalachian Trail* (Chicago: Chicago Review Press, 2014), 160.

Janet Hutchison, quoted in Kaufman, *National Parks and the Woman's Voice*, 200.

CHAPTER 6: LOVE OF PLACE

Liane Russell, quoted in Polly Welts Kaufman, *National Parks and the Woman's Voice: A History* (Albuquerque: University of New Mexico Press, 2006), 196.

Theodore Roosevelt, *Outdoor Pastimes of an American Hunter* (New York: Charles Scribner's Sons, 1905), 353.

CHAPTER 7: LOOKING BACK, MOVING FORWARD

Colonel Charles Young, quoted in Brian G. Shellum, *Black Officer in a Buffalo Soldier Regiment: The Military Career of Charles Young* (Lincoln: University of Nebraska Press, 2010), 150.

Andy Warhol, *The Philosophy of Andy Warhol: From A to B and Back Again* (Orlando: Harcourt, 1975), 71.

Newton B. Drury, quoted in *The Regional Review,* vol. VII, nos. 1 and 2 (July/ August 1941), 1.

INDEX OF AUTHORS AND TITLES

Judith Colt Johnson, quoted in Polly Welts Kaufman, *National Parks and the Woman's Voice: A History* (Albuquerque: University of New Mexico Press, 2006), 189.

PHOTOGRAPH CREDITS

Murdock

l Park Service

bin

J. Pingree

otte Plog

Roger Christophersen

d: Arlene Ash

s, Clair A.: Elizabeth Appling Roberts

ogers, Wayne: Wayne Rogers

Sammartino, Jenna B.: David Shapiro

Schreier, Cheryl A.: National Park Service

Shafer, Jonathan: David Shafer

Siebers, Eleanor Hodak: Scott Howell/National Park Service

Sigona, Suzanne: Dan Arant

Steele, Sheridan: Barb Steele

Tabern, Kandace and Robert: Kandace and Robert Tabern

Tardona, Daniel R.: Steve Kemp

Wilcox, Dwan: NPS/Dakota McCoy

Wilhelm, Jef: Jef Wilhelm

Williams, Daniel: Christine White Loberg

Winkler, Daniel: M. Osgood

Winslow, Don: Marion Winslow

HISTORIC PHOTOGRAPHS

All historic photographs are courtesy of the National Park Service (NPS) Historic Photograph Collection.

2: Stephen T. Mather in motorcycle sidecar, NPS photograph by Frautz

5: Badlands evening campfire talk, NPS photograph by Jack E. Boucher

23: Jefferson National Expansion Memorial, NPS photograph by Cecil W. Stoughton

32: Battery Park/Castle Clinton, NPS photograph by Jack E. Boucher

36: Ranger Susan Gail Estes with snake, NPS photograph by Abbie Rowe

42: Lassen Peak/Manzanita Lake, color-applied lantern slide from NPS Lantern Slide Collection, no photographer identified

53: Lincoln Memorial, NPS photograph by Thomas C. Gray

63: Yenta Glacier, Alaska, NPS photograph by Norman Herkenham

79: Hikers resting in Olympic National Park, NPS photograph by Gunnar O. Fagerlund

85: Visitors at Mount Rushmore, NPS photograph, photographer not identified

98: Carl Sharsmith making monkey flower move, NPS photograph, no photographer identified

120: Vietnam Veterans Memorial, NPS photograph by Thomas C. Gray

132: Statue of Liberty, NPS photograph by M. Woodbridge "Woody" Williams

140: Sonja Johnson on horseback, NPS photograph by Clare C. Ralston

143: Double O Arch, NPS photograph, no photographer identified

157: Sea lions on beach, Channel Islands, no photographer identified

190: Winter in Shenandoah National Park, NPS photograph by Richard Frear

192: Dr. Harold C. Bryant conducting nature walk, original image obtained from Wayne Bryant for NPS 75th Anniversary. Duplicate image made and original returned to Mr. Bryant.

198: Stone house ruins, NPS photograph by Thomas C. Gray

212: Old Faithful geyser, NPS photograph, no photographer identified

228: Bugling elk, NPS photograph by Samuel T. Woodring

232: Campfire scene with John White and Horace M. Albright, NPS photograph, no photographer identified

237: Jeffrey pine, NPS photograph by Jean Speiser

239: Visitors at Everglades National Park, NPS photograph by Bob Hauger

252: Spruce Tree House, NPS photograph by Don Watson

268: Lakeside view of Hallet Peak, NPS photograph by George A. Grant

281: Visitors atop Cadillac Mountain, NPS photograph by Thomas C. Gray

305: Personal equipment display, NPS photograph by J.E. Armstrong

Sequoia and Kings Canyon National Parks, 1941. The personal equipment used by
J. E. Armstrong while making a grazing study of the Roaring River district in Kings Canyon.

YOSEMITE
CONSERVANCY.

Providing For Yosemite's Future

Through the support of donors, Yosemite Conservancy provides grants and support to Yosemite National Park to help preserve and protect Yosemite today and for future generations. Work funded by the Conservancy is visible throughout the park, in trail rehabilitation, wildlife protection and habitat restoration. The Conservancy is also dedicated to enhancing the visitor experience and providing a deeper connection to the park through outdoor programs, volunteering, wilderness services and its bookstores. Thanks to dedicated supporters, the Conservancy has provided $92 million in grants to Yosemite National Park.

yosemiteconservancy.org